List of tables and figures

Tables

Figures

Foreword: The European Union's evolving social policy and national models – seeking a new balance

Nikolaus G. van der Pas, Director-General Employment, Social Affairs and Equal Opportunities, European Commission, and Kari Välimäki, Permanent Secretary, Ministry of Social Affairs and Health, Finland

This publication comes out of a conference organised by the EU Finnish presidency in November 2006. The objective of the conference was to analyse the future of European social protection systems and of the European social model (ESM) against the challenges of increasing internationalisation, global competition and an ageing population.

Member States remain largely responsible for social policy. EU competence is limited by the principles of subsidiarity and proportionality. However, social policy at national level is increasingly influenced by the European Union (EU), in fact more so than was anticipated 10 years ago. As a consequence of demographic ageing, Member States all face the challenge of modernising their social protection systems.

We are accustomed to examining social and health policy issues from the perspective of individual Member States. Social and health policies are closely linked to national socio–political systems. However, the EU has created a new environment for Member States' social and health systems. The establishment of the internal market represents both a challenge and an opportunity for Member States' social and health policies. Furthermore, a number of Community policies, and notably social cohesion, competition, employment and economic policies, have an impact on social outcomes. How can we reconcile the autonomy of national social systems and the growing influence of Community policies on them?

Participants in the conference generally felt that the social dimension of Europe should be strengthened and identified two possible ways to achieve this. On the one hand, the values of the ESM, such as social cohesion and solidarity, should be better taken into account in competition, single market and economic policies at Community level. On the other hand, participants rightly emphasised the need to enhance cooperation between Member States and with the Commission in order

Contents

THE EUROPEANISATION OF SOCIAL PROTECTION

Edited by Jon Kvist and Juho Saari

European Commission

First published in Great Britain in 2007 by

Policy Press
University of Bristol
6th Floor
Howard House
Queen's Avenue
Clifton
Bristol BS8 1SD
UK
Tel +44 (0)117 331 5020
Fax +44 (0)117 331 5367
e-mail tpp-info@bristol.ac.uk
www.policypress.co.uk

North American office:
Policy Press
c/o The University of Chicago Press
1427 East 60th Street
Chicago, IL 60637, USA
t: +1 773 702 7700
f: +1 773-702-9756
e:sales@press.uchicago.edu
www.press.uchicago.edu

Transferred to Digital Print 2014

British Library Cataloguing in Publication Data
A catalogue record for this book is available from the British Library

Library of Congress Cataloging-in-Publication Data
A catalog record for this book has been requested

ISBN 978 1 84742 019 0 paperback
ISBN 978 1 84742 020 6 hardcover

Cover design by Qube Design Associates, Bristol
Front cover photograph by Anatoli Styf
Printed and bound in Great Britain by Marston Book Services, Oxford

to make the social dimension more visible, including in the context of the open method of coordination (OMC).

On 25 March 2007, Heads of State and Government renewed their commitment to preserve 'our ideal of European society in future for the good of all European Union citizens' in the Berlin Declaration on the occasion of the 50th anniversary of the signature of the Treaties of Rome. The ESM needs to be dynamic and responsive to change. It needs to take account of the expectations of many citizens for a more social Europe: a Europe that protects, a Europe that combines economic success with social responsibility.

The Berlin Declaration also recalls that 'there are many goals which we cannot achieve on our own, but only in concert'. This is certainly true of social and health policies. The conference provided useful insights as to how to strengthen the social dimension of the EU. Both the Commission and the Member States are committed to this joint endeavour.

Acknowledgements

We are grateful for the funding provided by the European Commission and the Finnish European Union Presidency in 2006. We would like to thank Natalie Reid for language editing. Finally, we would also like to thank the civil servants who provided comments and suggestions on earlier drafts of the case studies.

Juho Saari, Helsinki
Jon Kvist, Copenhagen
1 April 2007

List of abbreviations

BEPGs	Broad Economic Policy Guidelines
ECJ	European Court of Justice
EEA	European Economic Area
EEP	European Employment Pact
EES	European Employment Strategy
EMCO	Employment Policy Committee
EMU	Economic and Monetary Union
EPC	Economic Policy Committee
ESA	European System of National and Regional Accounts
ESF	European Social Fund
ESM	European social model
EU	European Union
Eurostat	The Statistical Office of the European Commission
EU15	European Union Member States from 1995 to 2004
EU25	European Union Member States from 2004 to 2007
EU27	European Union Member States after 2007
GDP	gross domestic product
IMF	International Monetary Fund
JAP	Joint Assessment of Employment Priorities
JIM	Joint Inclusion Memorandum
NGO	non-governmental organisation
OECD	Organisation for Economic Co-operation and Development
OMC	open method of coordination
PROGRESS	Community Programme for Employment and Social Solidarity
R&D	research and development
SGEI	services of general economic interest
SGI	services of general interest
SGP	Stability and Growth Pact
SPC	Social Protection Committee
UN	United Nations

List of contributors

Milena Büchs, Lecturer, School of Social Sciences, University of Southampton, UK
Email: m.buechs@soton.ac.uk

Maciej Grabowski, Vice Director, Polish Lisbon Strategy Forum, Gdansk Institute for Market Economics, Poland
Email: Maciej.Grabowski@ibngr.edu.pl

Ana Guillén, Professor, University of Oviedo, Spain
Email: aguillen@uniovi.es

Anton Hemerijck, Professor, Erasmus University Rotterdam, and Director Scientific Council for Government Policy (WRR), The Hague, Netherlands
Email: hemerijck@wrr.nl

Karl Hinrichs, Professor, Centre for Social Policy Research, University of Bremen, Germany
Email: hinrichs@zes.uni–bremen.de

Olli Kangas, Professor, The Danish National Institute for Social Research, Denmark
Email: olk@sfi.dk

Jon Kvist, Senior Researcher, The Danish National Institute for Social Research, Denmark
Email: jk@sfi.dk

Julian Le Grand, Professor, London School of Economics and Political Science, UK
Email: j.legrand@lse.ac.uk

Morgan Long, Senior Consultant, Fleishman Hillard, UK
Email: morganlong@fleishmaneurope.com

Elias Mossialos, Professor, London School of Economics and Political Science, UK
Email: e.a.mossialos@lse.ac.uk

Bruno Palier, CNRS (National Centre for Scientific Research) Researcher, Center for Political Research, Sciences Po, Paris, France
Email: bruno.palier@sciences-po.fr

Luana Petrescu, Research Assistant, Institut d'études politiques de Paris, France
Email: lpetrescu@kpmg.com

Martin Potůček, Director, Centre for Social and Economic Strategies, Prague, Czech Republic
Email: potucek@fsv.cuni.cz

Juho Saari, Ministerial Adviser, Ministry of Social Affairs and Health, and Professor, University of Kuopio, Finland
Email: juho.saari@stm.fi

Stefano Sacchi, Professor, University of Milan and URGE, Collegio Carlo Alberto, Turin, Italy
Email: stefano.sacchi@urge.it

Theodoros Sakellaropoulos, Professor, Panteion University, Athens, Greece
Email: thesak@panteion.gr

Peter Sleegers, Researcher, PhD student, Amsterdam School for Social Science Research (ASSR), University of Amsterdam, Netherlands
Email: sleegers@uva.nl

Kari Välimäki, Director-General, Ministry of Social Affairs and Health, Finland
Email: kari.valimaki@stm.fi

Irena Wóycicka, Head of the Social Research Area, The Gdansk Institute for Market Economics, Poland
Email: woycicka@ibngr.edu.pl

ONE

European Union developments and national social protection

Juho Saari and Jon Kvist

Social protection in the European Union (EU) is primarily a national preserve. The EU has little competence in social protection: regulative powers are limited and resources scarce. The EU cannot stipulate specific social protection policies, for example, the harmonisation of Member States' social protection systems, nor can it carry out its own social protection policies. Member States are left to decide what type and level of social protection they want and are able to afford. While 10 years ago this was a fairly accurate picture of social protection in the EU, since then developments at both national and EU levels have had direct and indirect effects on social protection in Europe. In particular these developments have led to national and EU levels becoming more interwoven, a process we describe as the *Europeanisation* of social protection.

In order to understand the ongoing Europeanisation of social protection, four sets of developments at EU level are of particular importance: new policy processes and areas taken up at the EU level; the increased application of internal market rules to the (new) area of social protection; the European Economic and Monetary Union (EMU); and the recent enlargement of the EU (nearly doubling the number of Member States).

During the 1990s an increasing belief in the European Commission and among Member States was that social protection should be seen as a productive factor (see, for example, European Commission, 1993a; Ministerie van Sociale Zaken en Werkgelegenheid, 1997). This belief led first to the inclusion of employment objectives in the 1997 Amsterdam Treaty, with Member States' cooperation based on the open method of coordination (OMC). In 2000 the Heads of State and Government agreed to put social objectives at the same level as economic objectives in the Lisbon Strategy, and extended the use of the OMC to the field of social protection. Before 2000 positive integration in the sense of creating common EU social protection policies was at a virtual halt because the Community method in social policy required unanimity among Member States before anything could be taken forward, and because the principle of subsidiarity and proportionality applied to social policy, that is, that the EU should intervene only if the Member States could not deal with the problem themselves. The new modes of governance were a jump-start to EU social policy.

Free competition and the freedom of movement for labour, capital, goods and services are at the heart of the EU. Historically, these principles have played a small, albeit important, role for national social protection in two respects. First, gender equality has been greatly promoted, originally to prevent the distortion of free competition, both through case law by the European Court of Justice (ECJ) and by the European Council adopting a series of directives reflecting a still broader understanding of discrimination. As a result, Member States must not discriminate in social protection and many other areas on the basis of gender and nationality, or, increasingly, on grounds of age, disability, ethnicity, sexual orientation or religious beliefs. Second, the coordination of migrant workers' social rights is meant to secure freedom of movement for labour. Extensive ECJ case law has, over the years, vastly widened the material and personal scope of application (see, for example, Martinsen, 2004; de Búrca, 2005).

Besides these two old and well-known developments in EU social policy there was a division between, on the one hand, functional competence relating to the internal market with competition law and free movement and, on the other, sectoral competence in, for example, social protection. The former is of legitimate concern to the EU and the latter to the Member States. But this balance is shifting. Following the 1998 ECJ rulings in the *Kohll* and *Decker* cases there has been a gradual move towards applying internal market and competition law in the social protection field. Perhaps most visible has been the national and European debates on the Services Directive that highlighted as a political minefield the extension of the internal market to social protection areas.

The development of the European Economic and Monetary Union (EMU) is the third EU-level development that may impact on national social protection. In short, from 1997 the Stability and Growth Pact (SGP) introduced stricter budgetary disciplines, making, for example, financing social protection systems by running budget deficits more difficult. In addition, the EMU has limited the number of policy tools; as monetary and currency policies are no longer available to governments, structural reforms of labour markets through reforming social protection appear higher on the agenda.

While new policy processes or modes of governance, internal markets, the EMU and enlargement all have a potential impact on Member States' social protection systems, they are only part of the story of the Europeanisation of social protection. Other contributing factors include the reform of the coordination regulation; mutual recognition of professional qualifications; the right of EU citizens and their family members to move and reside freely; economic and social cohesion (including the European Social Fund, ESF); social dialogue; discrimination and gender equality; and recent ECJ judgments.[1] Given the space limitations of this book, however, we devote the remainder to dealing with new policy processes, the internal market, the EMU and enlargement.

The main purpose of this book is to analyse how Member States react to these four sets of developments. What has been the impact of recent EU developments on national social protection systems? What are the Member States' governments' responses to the EU developments? We consider the first question by investigating whether recent national welfare reform in Member States has been informed by EU-level developments and has led towards a European social model (ESM). For the second question, we examine Member States' governments' responses to a series of EU initiatives under the four sets of developments. The bulk of the book therefore consists of country studies that reflect the diversity of EU Member States, namely the Czech Republic, Denmark, Finland, France, Germany, Greece, Italy, the Netherlands, Poland, Spain and the United Kingdom.

All the contributors were interested in one dimension of the Europeanisation of social protection: the domestic impact and national government responses. They analyse how Member States' responses to different proposals, recommendations and policies submitted (or 'downloaded') by the Commission *reflect* their institutional structures of social protection, recent and current trends in reform making, and certain visions of the future of the ESM. In particular, they investigate Member States' responses to certain Commission communications and proposals, thus analysing their basic attitudes and understandings, whether Member States support ('pace setting') or resist ('foot dragging') different proposals, or whether they do not have any opinion for or against ('sitting on the fence') (see Chapter Eleven, this volume) (Börzel, 2002). By systematically and comparatively investigating such responses, it is possible to build a stronger platform for future debate on European social protection policies and to gain a better understanding of the processes of Europeanisation.

The authors of the national case studies investigate policy responses to areas that are relevant for social protection and in which Member States' responses and European policies could be considered mutually reinforcing. The four areas investigated comprise a number of underlying EU initiatives:

- *Policy processes:* the Lisbon Strategy, Social Policy Agenda 2000-05 and 2005-10, OMC and demographic change.
- *The interplay between internal markets and social policy:* Services Directive and the services of general interest (SGI).
- *The EMU:* including the 1997 and 2005 SGP and its socio-political implications.
- *Enlargement* of the EU in 2004 and 2007, and its socio-political implications.

In other words, to build an information base and a framework for the European debate on the future of the ESM, this book investigates four complementary areas of potential importance for the Europeanisation of social protection.

As both the impact of EU developments and government responses to them are likely to differ not only across areas but also countries, the following 11 chapters (Chapters Two to Twelve) present a variety of countries of different sizes, with different welfare regimes, years of EU membership, political legacy and competitiveness.

Because the case studies follow the same thematic framework, in Chapter Thirteen their findings provide the empirical basis for a comparative analysis of the Europeanisation of social protection. In the final chapter, Chapter Fourteen, Juho Saari and Kari Välimäki set out different views on whether the current process of the Europeanisation of social protection has the right balance between economic policies and objectives and social policies and objectives. First, however, this chapter sets out EU developments in more detail, thereby substantiating the ways in which the relationship between the EU level and national social protection has become more interwoven and thus entered a new phase – the Europeanisation of social protection.

Evolving perspectives on European policies in social protection

From a legal and historical perspective, up until recently the EU had little competence in social protection. The Treaty of Amsterdam (signed in 1997 but coming into force in 1999) expanded the EU's competencies in employment, discrimination and gender policies, public health and some elements of social policy. It also incorporated the Social Protocol. Not much happened with the Treaty of Nice (signed in 2001 but in force from 2003), with the exception of Article 144 on the Social Protection Committee (SPC), sister committee of the Employment Policy Committee (EMCO) and Economic Policy Committee (EPC), and some minor extensions and revisions to the Articles on discrimination and public health. Furthermore, the Charter of Fundamental Rights of the Union was accepted as a political declaration (to be incorporated with the Constitution). The Constitution, yet to be ratified by the Member States, includes a set of major revisions in the field of social protection, aimed mainly at allowing some time for adjustment (known as emergency brakes in the coordination of social security and external/global trade policy), at mainstreaming social protection and social inclusion into all policies, and at clarifying the competencies of the Member States and the EU in the organisation and production of health services.

Although we now see a move towards more EU competence and a focus on social protection, the overall impression is that such changes are incremental and that, compared to most other policy areas, the EU has little to do in social protection.

Part of the reason why there has been incremental change in EU social policy competence is because Member States have different welfare regimes and values, making it difficult to reach the required unanimity to adopt policies. But that difficulty does not mean that Member States are unwilling to discuss social policy, nor that they do not cooperate. Indeed, a closer look at the recent history of cooperation in the field of social protection reveals a deepening and broadening of the understanding of social protection in Europe.

In 1997, social protection was introduced by the Dutch presidency as a productive factor (Ministerie van Sociale Zaken en Werkgelegenheid, 1997). The key message was that the institutional design of social protection systems and the incentives they create for organisations, households and individuals were more important factors in explaining differences in economic and employment performance than the absolute levels of social expenditure or replacement rates of certain benefits, a point that has been repeated on a number of occasions (see, for example, Fouarge, 2003).

Portugal's presidency in the first half of 2000 became the scene for the Lisbon Strategy. Heads of State and Government decided that the EU set itself the ambitious goal of becoming 'the most competitive and dynamic knowledge-based economy in the world, capable of sustainable economic growth with more and better jobs and greater social cohesion by 2010'. 'Greater social cohesion' appeared at the same level as 'competitive economy'. The aim was to modernise the ESM by investing in human resources and combating social exclusion. At the subsequent Nice Summit in December 2000 the annex to the presidency conclusions characterised the ESM 'in particular by systems of high level of social protection, by the importance of social dialogue and by SGI covering activities vital for social cohesion, ... [the ESM] is today based, beyond the diversity of the Member States' social systems, on a coherent core of values'.

In 2001, the Belgian presidency did some path-breaking work in designing what it called 'new welfare state architecture'. More precisely, it commissioned scholarly work that, for the future of the European welfare state, emphasised the importance of family policy and the politics of equal opportunity in terms of gender and socio-economic groups (Esping-Andersen, 2002). This theme has steadily increased in weight in European debates. The Belgian presidency spearheaded the development towards setting up a number of social indicators to monitor the situation and development in the Member States, followed up by the 2005 Luxembourg presidency (see, respectively, Atkinson et al, 2002, 2006).

In the second half of 2005 the UK presidency worked together with the Policy Network to design a policy-relevant approach to the debate on the ESM (Diamond et al, 2006). Finally, in the first half of 2006 the Austrian presidency investigated the ESM from a number of perspectives, and among other things located it in a global context by comparing the EU and the United States (see also Alber, 2006).

Although presidencies over the past 10 years have reflected a broader and deeper understanding of social protection and its contribution to the ESM, their starting point was that social protection is a national preserve. Despite the limited competence of the EU in social protection and despite the general understanding that social protection is a national concern, we argue that a series of policy processes at the EU level directly address certain issues of social protection: namely the new policy processes, the internal market, the EMU and enlargement. The following sections outline recent developments in each of these areas, demonstrating that together they constitute a new phase in the relationship between the EU and social protection.

The new relationship between the European Union and social protection

Table 1.1 illustrates the new relational phase by indicating some of the key changes in the interplay between the policies of the EU and those of the Member States around 2000, in 2003-04, and during 2005-07. The table covers four EU areas of relevance for social protection: policy processes, the internal market, the EMU and enlargement. The remainder of this chapter sets out developments in each area. The 11 country chapters use this structure as a background for investigating the domestic impact of and government responses to developments within these four areas. In other words, Table 1.1 both points to important EU developments of potential significance for Member States' social protection and provides a common analytical framework for the whole book.

All areas, events and policies in Table 1.1 reflect the EU level's (mostly the Commission of European Communities' and the ECJ's) initiatives, proposals and rulings. Therefore, the table excludes those initiatives made by individuals or Member States during different EU presidencies, the convent on the future of the EU, or constitutional negotiations. Furthermore, Table 1.1 focuses attention on the Commission's communications and proposals rather than on the Council's conclusions and decisions. This approach underlines the crucial roles of the Commission (and the ECJ) in designing European policies. By introducing these communications, rulings and other documents, the table illustrates the dense network of proposals that became more concrete and more directly linked to Member States' social protection systems during the period under investigation.

Policy processes and social protection

The invention of the Lisbon Strategy is a well-known turning point in the history of European integration and its social dimension. The famous paragraphs of the Lisbon Summit (23-24 March 2000) conclusions reflect a quite hopeful and future-oriented approach: 'The EU', so the Heads of the Member States concluded, 'is confronted with a quantum shift resulting from globalisation and the challenges of a new knowledge-driven economy'. The way forward was a new strategic goal for the next decade: to become the most competitive and dynamic knowledge-based economy in the world capable of sustainable economic growth with more and better jobs and greater social cohesion. To reach this objective, the EU agreed 'a challenging programme' aimed at 'building knowledge infrastructures, enhancing

Table 1.1: The European Union and social protection: themes, events, concepts and policies (2000-07)

Areas	c 2000	c 2003-04	c 2005-07
Treaties	Amsterdam Treaty (May 1999)	Nice Treaty (February 2003)	Constitution, to be ratified (2006-)
Policy processes and social protection			
Lisbon Strategy (policy framework)	Lisbon Strategy Mutually reinforcing social and economic policies	Spring 2003 European Council	Reform of Lisbon Strategy (2005), focus on growth and employment
Employment and economic policy	Separate European Employment Strategy (EES) and Broad Economic Policy Guidelines (BEPGs)	The coordination of employment and economic policy cycles	Integrated guidelines (EES and BEPGs + microeconomic guidelines)
Social Policy Agenda	Social Policy Agenda 2000-05, a new strategic thinking	Mid-term review of Social Policy Agenda	Social Policy Agenda 2005-10, adjusting with the new Lisbon Strategy
Open method of coordination (OMC)	Modernising social protection – four strands of the OMC	Streamlining social protection – towards streamlining	Streamlined national reports on strategies on social protection and social inclusion
Demographic change	Ageing as a common economic and social challenge	Green Paper on demographic change – a life-cycle approach	Communication on demographic change

Table 1.1: contd

Areas	c 2000	c 2003-04	c 2005-07
Internal markets and social protection			
Services of general interest (SGI)	Re-evaluation of the concept of SGI	Opening the debate on non-economic SGI	The criteria and the role of the markets in the social SGI
The free movement of social and health services	The free movement of services in certain cases (professions, some services)	Proposal on the Services Directive, also covering health care and the principle of origin	Towards a Services Directive, reform of coordination regulation, and consultation on health services
Monetary policy and social protection			
Economic and Monetary Union (EMU)	Lowering transaction costs and maintaining stability	Challenges of SGP, resulting problems for some public economies	Reform of SGP, allowing more space for structural reforms
Enlargement and social protection			
Enlargement	Rules of the enlargement	Agreement on enlargement – fears of social dumping and social tourism	Adjustment into enlargement (EU27): transition periods for free movement of labour

innovation and economic reform, and modernising social welfare and education systems'.

Five years later it was time to assess the achievements of the 'challenging programme'. In Brussels in March 2005 the European Summit concluded:

> Five years after the launch of the Lisbon Strategy, the results are mixed. Alongside undeniable progress, there are shortcomings and obvious delays. Given the challenges to be met, there is a high price to pay for delayed or incomplete reforms, as is borne out by the gulf between Europe's growth potential and that of its economic partners. Urgent action is therefore called for.

The political message was clear:

> To that end, it is essential to relaunch the Lisbon Strategy without delay and re-focus priorities on growth and employment. Europe must renew the basis of its competitiveness, increase its growth potential and its productivity and strengthen social cohesion, placing the main emphasis on knowledge, innovation and the optimisation of human capital.

In other words, the 2005 focus was quite different, reflecting the partial failure of the Lisbon Strategy: sometimes some Member States were better at producing documents and declarations than implementing agreed policies and guidelines.

Economic and employment policies. Social protection is not an isolated policy area. Traditionally, the most important conclusions on social protection are drawn in Broad Economic Policy Guidelines (BEPGs) and the guidelines of the European Employment Strategy (EES). The BEPGs approached social protection expenditure and institutions from the points of view of public expenditure and the 1997 SGP. Here the focus was traditionally on the long-term sustainability of public financing. More recently, however, as the BEPGs have paid more attention to medium-term issues, some attention has also gone to the structural characteristics of social protection systems (broadly understood), including those of pensions and health care/services. Besides the BEPGs, the EES has analysed and made recommendations on social protection, devoting much systematic attention to the reconciliation of work and family life, unemployment and early retirement (European Commission, 1998).

The EES was renewed in 2003 by the establishment of a new pillar structure and the creation of a more stable set of guidelines (European Commission, 2003a). Simultaneously, there was more attention on the implementation of guidelines in different levels of governance (European Commission, 2004a). In addition, the interplay between employment and social protection issues was highlighted, underlining a need to find policy synergies and institutional complementarities between the two fields (European Commission, 2001a). A crucial part of the reform of the new mode of governance was the streamlining of the policy cycles of the BEPGs and the EES (European Commission, 2002a). Finally, in 2005, the BEPGs and the EES were merged into the integrated guidelines of the revised Lisbon Strategy (sometimes also called the Growth and Jobs Strategy); at the Member State level of governance, National Reform Programmes replaced previous reporting duties.

Social Policy Agenda. An ambitious Social Policy Agenda, aimed at supporting the modernisation of social protection systems and European social policy (European Commission, 2000a), supported the Lisbon Strategy of 2000. The document reflected, perhaps better than anything else, the new approach to social protection adopted by the Commission and the Member States at the Lisbon Summit. This document paid much attention to a new strategic thinking and commitment for balanced socio-economic growth and development, where policies were mutually reinforcing (European Commission, 2000b). That such an approach in such a delicate field of policy making resulted in the risk of lip service is quite clear; that is, more emphasis should have been paid to policy implementation. Some observers also claimed that the Lisbon Strategy – especially the Social Policy Agenda – lacked a clear core, as it consisted of a significant number of objectives and targets with different competencies in the Treaty and different levels of commitments (sometimes not mutually supportive).

In 2003, a mid-term review partly reflected these challenges (European Commission, 2003b, 2003c). A year later, the role of social protection at the European level was further reflected by the High Level Group (2004a), aimed at giving some input – together with two other working groups chaired by Wim Kok – on the reform of the Lisbon Strategy as part of the 2005 review. Some of the Group's ideas were taken into account in the reform, which focused on growth and jobs, thereby sidelining social protection. Closely following new strategic guidelines, the Commission delivered a new Social Policy Agenda in 2005 (European Commission, 2005a). Besides the four areas introduced earlier, the new Agenda underlined the need for strengthening solidarity between generations.

During the 1990s the key challenge of European cooperation in the field of social protection was the lack of suitable policy tools acceptable both to the Member States (systematically underlining the need to respect the principles of subsidiarity and proportionality) and the Commission (placing much emphasis on modernising social protection systems). Consequently, in the early and mid-1990s, cooperation in the field of social protection remained a rather marginal element of the social dimension of the EU. Cooperation mainly focused on employment, some parts of labour law, and social dialogue, regardless of the enthusiasm of the Commission (European Commission, 1994, 1995). Indeed, at the beginning of the 1990s, Jacques Delors, when president of the Commission, tried to establish a social dimension to the internal market, but without much success in the field of social protection. The lack of EU cooperation in social protection reflected the then-dominant interpretation of the concepts of subsidiarity and proportionality, which allowed only a limited role for cooperation at the European level.

However, in the late 1990s the situation slightly changed. There was an important communication on modernising social protection in 1997 (European Commission, 1997), soon supplemented in 1999 by another communication on implementation (European Commission, 1999a). On the basis of the 1999 communication, later adopted by the Council, the Lisbon European Council in March 2000 established a new method, appropriately called the open method of coordination (OMC). This method combined previous experiences with the EES with recent experiences on the dialogue in the field of social protection. The OMC, or, more generally, new modes of governance in the EU, has been subject to an exponentially growing body of literature, also in the field of social protection (see, for example, de la Porte and Pochet, 2002; Zeitlin and Pochet, 2005). (The OMC was also applied to some other policies, for example, education and Research and Development, R&D.) For social protection, the OMC was first applied to poverty and social exclusion, then to pensions, and later, more lightly, to health services and long-term care (European Commission, 2000c, 2001b, 2001c, 2003d).

As the Member States considered separate processes to be quite heavy and time consuming, given their rather modest results, in spring 2003 the Commission launched a streamlining process, aimed at more effective reporting practices (European Commission, 2003e). In 2005, the Commission (2005b) delivered another communication on the topic, with a new set of common objectives. This document relied on, among other things, recent evaluation reports submitted by the Member States in 2005. The new streamlined framework was first applied in spring 2006 and will be applied again in national reports on strategies for social protection and social inclusion (European Commission, 2006a).

Demographic change is not a new topic in European discourse. To the contrary, for some years the Commission has investigated different aspects of ageing and family policy in different forums and debates. For instance, around the turn of the last century, much attention was devoted to ageing workers (European Commission, 1999b). Another point of reference was the European Council in Stockholm (March 2001), which gave a clear message on the importance of the subject, and resulted in a thorough investigation of this multidimensional phenomenon (European Commission, 2002b). Another aspect of ageing has been the sustainability of pension systems, of common interest to all relevant policy committees (for example, European Commission, 2000d). Clearly, the long-term sustainability of pension schemes (especially those of the first pillar) is a question of some importance for EU citizens.

More broadly, a 2005 Green Paper analysed the consequences of demographic change for European societies and economies. It pointed out the crucial role of reconciliation of family/private life and work in promoting higher fertility and longer working careers (European Commission, 2005c). The follow-up communication on demographic change was delivered during the Finnish EU presidency in October 2006. Here the Commission made several proposals aimed at improving the long-term sustainability of public finances, the employment rate, and the competitiveness and productivity of the EU (European Commission, 2006b). More recently, in June 2006, the Commission delivered a communication on the rights of children (European Commission, 2006c).

The internal market and social protection

The interplay between the internal market, competition laws and national social protection systems has recently resulted in much debate in the Member States, the European Parliament and the Commission. The debate has not least been sparked by recent ECJ rulings and, in particular, the Commission's proposals in the fields of social and health services. Historically, there was a balance between sectoral (social and health areas and public policy) and functional (internal markets and competition law) competencies: Member States generally had sectoral competencies, and the EU had functional competencies. According to this balance, Member States had the competency over social protection, with EU competency limited to issues involving securing the four freedoms and free competition. In social protection this EU mandate implied securing the free movement of labour through the coordination regulation 1408/71, and the principle of free competition resulted in equal treatment legislation. But the balance between sectoral and functional competencies is rapidly changing in the field of social protection. In other words, social protection systems in the Member States have increasingly been assessed from the point of view of the internal market and competition law.

The ECJ has played a crucial role in redesigning the balance between the four freedoms and the social and health policies of the Member States. Some rulings have indicated a shift in balance. As is commonly known, in the late 1970s the rulings of the ECJ on the coordination regulation 1408/71 resulted in some successful revisions of the Treaty aimed at restoring the previous balance. Among recent judgments, the path-breaking ones were *Decker* (C-120/95) and *Kohll* (C-158/96), both made in April 1998. Since then, a steady stream of rulings has further clarified the fragile balance. The implications of these rulings are subject to a growing number of scholarly studies (see, for example, Mossialos and McKee, 2002a; de Búrca, 2005; Martinsen, 2005a, 2005b; Prosser, 2005).

More recently, the Commission has made some effort towards expanding free movement to services, with possible consequences for health and social policies. In 2004 the Commission (2004b) launched the proposal for a Services Directive (commonly known as the Bolkenstein Directive). It has been debated thoroughly, partly as a result of misunderstandings in which unrelated issues in this sensitive area were connected to each other. In essence, we are witnessing another shift in the history of integration, where the internal markets and people (EU citizens) meet directly as consumers and producers (service providers), resulting in certain fears and uncertainties. For social and health services, the situation is slightly different, given previous phases in which the socio-politically relevant free movement of services focused mainly on certain professions and patients. Furthermore, the proposal on the Services Directive intermingled in certain cases with the spheres of solidarity, social cohesion, labour market practices and social protection, all of which are highly valued by the citizens of individual Member States.

After some months of debate, the Commission delivered a new proposal. It deleted Article 23 and the provisions dealing with the reimbursement of health care received in another Member State, and replaced the much-debated country-of-origin principle with a provision on the freedom to provide services (European Commission, 2006d). Next, the Commission decided to make a separate initiative on health services (although some borderline cases would need further investigation). As for social services, the new Services Directive proposal stated that:

> This Directive does not cover those social services in the area of housing, child care and support to families and persons in need provided by the State or by providers mandated by the State – at national, regional or local level – with the objective of ensuring support to those who are in a particular state of need because of their insufficient family income, total or partial lack of independence or to those who risk to become marginalised. These services are essential to guarantee the fundamental right to human dignity and integrity and are a manifestation of the principles of social cohesion and solidarity and should not be affected by this Directive.

This statement indicated that the Directive would cover some social services other than those mentioned in the text. However, the political agreement of 29 May 2006 further clarified this issue by underlining that 'this Directive does not affect the principle of universal service in Member States' social services'. Nevertheless, some further investigations appear necessary for defining the precise scope of the Directive in this field of services, including the definition of the concept 'social services', which seems to have different meanings in different contexts (European Commission, 2006e).

The discussion of the concept of social services actually pre-dates the Services Directive. In 2000 the common point of departure for analysis and debate was the communication by the Commission (2000e) on SGI, and the consequent report for the Laeken European Council. The report started to redefine the SGI concept to include social and health services, however defined (but often including social insurance and social housing). Since then, the concept of SGI has been important in defining and designing the boundaries between the economic and non-economic (or social), as well as between markets and solidarity in the field of social protection. As the Member States have different traditions and institutional structures in this respect, clarifying these issues seems to be a common interest.

Consequently, in spring 2003, the Commission delivered a Green Paper on SGI. This document included certain crucial analyses on social and health services, again including social insurance and social housing (European Commission, 2003f). The Green Paper generated considerable interest among stakeholders in the area of social and health services, who expressed a need for greater predictability and clarity to ensure the smooth development of these services.

A White Paper was submitted in 2004 (European Commission, 2004c). In it the Commission declared its support for the view that developing a systematic approach is useful 'in order to identify and recognise the specific characteristics of social and health services of general interest and to clarify the framework in which they operate and can be modernised'. The White Paper said that the communication on the social SGI, including health services, would be adopted in 2005. However, policy and preparatory works in this very complex area were overshadowed by the proposal on the Services Directive, where the SGI were often considered as a borderline case, resulting in some delay. Finally, as the proposal on the Services Directive was redesigned in a way that further clarified the role of health and social services in service markets, the Commission submitted a new communication on social SGI in April 2006 (European Commission, 2006f).

Economic and Monetary Union and social protection

Twelve of the EU's 27 Member States currently form part of the euro area. Denmark and the UK have a special opt-out status. Sweden decided not to join after 56% of its voters said 'No' in a 2003 referendum. The remaining countries, 'Member States with a derogation', expected to adopt the euro once they fulfil the necessary conditions (European Commission, 2005d). There was much debate in the 1990s on the possible socio-political consequences of the convergence criteria of the EMU. While focusing on interest rates, deficits and the stability of currency, they lacked – as critics have regularly pointed out – any employment- or poverty-related criteria. In the public debate of the mid-1990s, positive economic effects legitimised the EMU. These included lower transaction costs and interest rates, and higher economic growth rates.

In 1997 the establishment of the SGP set permanent external limits for the public deficit as defined in the ESA95 (European System of Accounts 1995) classification. This phase was followed by an intense debate over the consequences of such a pact for social policy as a part of the public economy during downturns and structural deficits. Some scholars pointed out that such a 'constitutional' structure as the EMU may seriously limit the Member States' political space to manoeuvre in the field of social protection (Pochet and Vanhercke, 1998). They also noted possible conflicts between the democratic decision making of the Member States and an independent European central bank in defining policy objectives. Other scholars paid more attention to the unwanted consequences of lowering transaction costs, and claimed that the EMU might increase pressures to redesign social protection systems in ways that would promote the competitiveness of export industries, thereby resulting in some cuts in social expenditure or employers' social security contributions. Finally, for some the EMU was something positive: an opportunity to speed up economic growth, and, in the long run, to also generate additional public incomes considered vital for guaranteeing the long-term financing of social expenditure.

More recently, the EMU has been legitimised by arguments linked to the stability of public economies. The SGP criteria have direct consequences for social expenditures, as the Member States in the EMU have to allocate their resources in ways that are considered productive (for example, education, innovation and R&D), possibly leading to some crowding out of social expenditures, especially in Member States with significant public debts. Difficulties that some Member States had in coping with this rather stringent pact led to it being reformed in 2005, allowing some space for structural adjustment in pensions while taking a stronger approach towards any attempts at temporary measures for maintaining the balance in public economies (see Council Regulation [EC] 1056/2005).

Enlargement and social protection

A final area that may have a certain impact on social protection in the EU is the *recent enlargement* from the EU15 to the EU25. The enlargement of the EU12 to the EU15 in 1995 did not result in any socio-political worries, as the institutional structure of the social protection systems of the applicant countries (Austria, Finland, Sweden, which joined the EU in 1995, and Norway, which rejected membership in a referendum) were well embedded in the Member State social structures and provided, comparatively speaking, quite high levels of security. A common expectation was that the new Member States would help to consolidate the ESM and induce some positive changes in European social policies. The results have not necessarily met these expectations, with the partial exception of the active labour market policy measures.

The enlargement from the EU15 to the EU25 was a different story for social policy. The enlargement of 2004 concluded a long process that started during the 1993 Danish presidency, which decided that to join the EU a new Member State must meet three accession criteria (commonly called the 'Copenhagen criteria'):

- *political:* the stability of institutions guaranteeing democracy, the rule of law, human rights and respect for and protection of minority groups;
- *economic:* the existence of a functioning market economy and the capacity to cope with competitive pressure and market forces within the Union;
- *acceptance of the Community acquis (often called the acquis communautaire):* the ability to take on the obligations of membership, including adherence to the aims of political, economic and monetary union.

Negotiations ended nine years later in 2002, also in Copenhagen, with 10 new Member States (the EU10) entering the EU in May 2004 and Bulgaria and Romania in January 2007. Socio-politically, the enlargement resulted in a certain political stress within some old Member States, which discussed risks of social dumping, welfare tourism and welfare raiding (that is, short-term visits to the EU15 to access certain social and health services and transfers) (for a more general exposé of the 'new spatial policies of social protection', see Ferrera, 2005).

Such worries increased because the social protection dimension of the enlargement negotiations was 'overwhelmed by the liberal approach'. Indeed the EU was not seeking to promote the ESM in the Central and Eastern European region immediately following the collapse of socialist regimes, thereby giving political space for other international actors (for example, the World Bank and the International Monetary Fund, IMF) to impose their ideas and strategies in favour of the privatisation of pensions and health care, means testing (when applicable) and financial stability. Because of the path dependence, the later attempts (if any) by the Commission and other EU bodies to promote its social model were not fully successful. Policy openings remained broad statements in favour of social cohesion and strong social protection that were backed up by actions. 'This policy – or lack of policy – reflects in great part what Member States currently allow (or in this case do not allow) the European Commission (and European institutions in general) to do in the field of social protection' (Vaughan-Whitehead, 2003, p 156). Consequently, the fears of social dumping rapidly multiplied.

The enlargement was also the subject for many studies on the potential of migration from new to old Member States (perhaps most authoritatively by Boeri and Brücker, 2003). Research that sought to assess the foundations of fears and expectations concluded that the *direct* social costs involved with the enlargement would be marginal and dramatic retrenchments highly unlikely (Kvist, 2004). Recent follow-up studies imply that these analyses have been correct. Some evidence even shows that migration flows have had positive effects on economies, indicating that EU10 nationals 'positively contribute to the overall labour market performance, to sustained economic growth and to better public finances' (European Commission, 2006g).

However, around 2002-03 *indirect* pressures on the labour markets of the EU15 from the inflow of labour and immigration in general were considered quite significant by some of them. Consequently, to protect their workers, labour markets, industries and social protection systems, many Member States agreed on transitional mechanisms and arrangements that would buffer or prevent outright the unwanted consequences of population flows. With the exception of Sweden and, to a large extent, the UK, Ireland, Denmark and the Netherlands, transitional arrangements were implemented in the EU15 (see Kvist, 2004). Understandably, the EU8 (Cyprus and Malta were exempted from transitional schemes), which faced these barriers, were not happy. Poland, Slovenia and Hungary applied reciprocal restrictions to the nationals from the EU15. In 2006, most Member States in the EU15 reconsidered their previous positions, opening up their labour markets either partly or completely for workers from the EU8. But as some of them also introduced transitional schemes for workers from the newest members, Bulgaria and Romania, at the moment the picture is very complex. In any case, transitional schemes can last only for seven years, ending in 2011 for the EU8 and in 2014 for Bulgaria and Romania.

To conclude, we find strong evidence at the EU level pointing towards the Europeanisation of social protection. In short, not only the Council but also the Commission have been increasingly active in social protection issues, sharing information, proposing guidelines and, in some cases, using the Community method. Information flow has been significant, resulting in an increasingly dense web of communications on a growing number of issues related to social protection, and thereby allowing or forcing Member States to develop and design more solid and systematic policy positions and responses to meet the requirements of the new phase in the relationship between the EU and social protection. Evidently, as the following case study chapters show, for institutional and historic reasons not all Member States are equally well prepared for such position building. However, as European integration to an increasing extent becomes interwoven with the fine institutional structures of the Member States, political pressure and the need for such an activity will increase.

Note
[1] The EU's external or global relations could be added to the list since more attention has recently been devoted to the socio-economic aspects of globalisation. For example, social and sustainable development, international labour standards and poverty reduction have emerged as key concepts since the United Nations' (UN) Copenhagen Summit on social development in 1995 and the Millennium Development Goals.

TWO

Germany: moving towards Europe but putting national autonomy first

Milena Büchs and Karl Hinrichs

An analysis of the German government's response to European Union (EU) social policy initiatives may be a more difficult task than for several other Member States for three interrelated reasons. First, Germany is a federal state. It gives the single states (Länder), as well as the municipalities, certain jurisdictions in the area of social policy, and the Länder have constantly opposed EU interference in their competencies. Moreover, the Länder have power via the Bundesrat, the second chamber, and may take social policy positions that contrast with that of the federal government or the Bundestag, independent of proposed or legislated responses to EU initiatives. Second, federal elections in September 2005 produced a change of government. The Christian Democrats (CDU/CSU), the major opposition party from 1998-2005, now lead a coalition government with the former government's major party, the Social Democrats (SPD), which previously formed a coalition with the Green Party. Thus, the conflicting interests and cross-party positions of the two political parties now forming the federal government still persist. Third, the two parties of the 'Grand Coalition' have agreed to tackle a number of social policy reforms during this parliamentary term (2005-09). Therefore, social policy is in such a state of flux that this chapter is unable to foresee all imminent changes.

We first explore the relationship between the 'European' and the German model of social policy and analyse the direction of social policy reform in Germany since the early 1990s. We then examine official responses to various EU initiatives. Our study shows a considerable difference between the European 'third way' social model as promoted by scholars such as Giddens (1999) and Esping-Andersen (2002) and the German approach to a social market economy. However, Germany generally welcomes an EU role in social policy and has already moved to some degree to the EU's 'third way' model. Despite this, however, politicians in Germany are not prepared to carry out a complete shift and are reluctant to further extend EU competencies in social policy.

The European social model versus the German model

Analysing the relationship between Germany's social model and what the EU envisages as a model for European social policy requires a discussion of two questions. First, what do domestic politicians think about EU competencies in social policy more generally, and do they accept EU competencies in this area and, if so, why, and to what degree? Second, how can Germany's social model be characterised, and how much does it differ from what one might call a European social model (ESM)? Extensive academic discussion has centred on the question of whether or not an ESM is identifiable in the sense of common 'European' characteristics of the Member States' social models (Baldwin, 1996; Kaelble, 2000; Scharpf, 2002). While no consensus has emerged in the literature as to whether such European commonalities exist, we use the term here in a different sense.

By 'ESM' we mean the 'third way'-oriented concept that the European Commission has promoted as a model for both EU and Member State social policies since the early 1990s (for example, European Commission, 1993a, 1994). This model aims to reconcile economic efficiency with social justice (Giddens, 1999). Social justice is mainly framed as inclusion in the labour market. Therefore, the ESM aims at reforms of national social security systems in a way that they 'make work pay' and simultaneously foster flexible labour markets and high-level social protection. Does the German concept of a social market economy differ from this 'third way' model, and how has the German model changed during recent years?

The development of the German social model (Sozialstaat) has been closely related to the social market economy. That concept of economic and social order reconciles the central value positions of Christian conservatism (subsidiarity), Social Democracy (equality) and Liberalism (freedom). While the Sozialstaat concept leaves room for interpretation about concrete implementation, basically it includes a certain arrangement of industrial relations (workers' participation at firm and enterprise level; free collective bargaining) and of social security based on the standard employment relationship and the male breadwinner model. Thus, the German postwar Sozialstaat expanded as a 'social insurance state' that contained the features attributed to a corporatist-conservative welfare state in an almost ideal-typical fashion (Esping-

Andersen, 1990). In short, until recently (see the next section), it was a wage earner-centred welfare state that provided status maintenance for covered employees and their dependent relatives for old age, disability, sickness and (short-term) unemployment. Since the model rewards individual achievement, redistribution within the social insurance schemes has always been limited. Insurance against typical social risks of wage earners was complemented by highly codified industrial relations, quite strict labour market regulation and comprehensive coverage of collective bargaining. The family was perceived as the primary provider of social services and, thus, de-familialisation policies are comparatively underdeveloped. Instead, due to the focus on income replacement and universal cash benefits for families with children, the German Sozialstaat is transfer-heavy (apart from medical care), but with little importance attached to means-tested benefits. This *social* market economy came under stress when full employment disappeared, when new social risks emerged, when the economy arrived at a post-industrial stage, and so on. Therefore, modernisation of the established arrangement ranks high on the political agenda.

If there were ideas about the design of social policy in Member States, the definite position of any German government has been that all Member States are or should become social market economies or variants thereof. Therefore, the term 'ESM' is hardly used in official documents in Germany, except vaguely as part of the Lisbon Strategy. For example, Chancellor Schröder, in his speech at the Bundestag on 14 March 2003 when he presented the Agenda 2010 as a central reform programme of the Red-Green government, referred to the ESM as universal participation in prosperity and precautions against unfettered market forces (Deutscher Bundestag, 2003a, p 2480). And in the coalition agreement of the current government reference was made to the necessity to improve 'flexicurity' (CDU et al, 2005, p 40).[1]

Both major political parties (and others) have constantly insisted on retaining the principle of *subsidiarity*, which is a central dogma of the social market economy concept. According to the CDU, in developing the frame of a European order, this principle has to be given 'first priority'; therefore, the party was very sceptical about the European Employment Pact (EEP) (CDU, 2001, p 108). Again, the coalition agreement emphasised that the government will 'take efforts to induce the European Union utilising its competencies in a responsible manner for not hollowing out the jurisdictions of the Member States' (CDU et al, 2005, p 149).[2] While the competencies of the EU with regard to issues of the internal market and freedom of movement are not called into question – indeed, they are fully supported as long as basic security benefits are exempted from export and social security (social insurance) schemes are not subject to common competition and cartel law – any further extension is firmly rejected. All new EU initiatives need examining as to whether they deliver 'European added value' or should completely remain in Member State jurisdiction (Federal Ministry of Labour and Social Affairs, nd). In that regard, the government values the open method of coordination (OMC) process as an instrument for enhancing the exchange of experiences and transnational learning. However, the Ministry of Social Affairs emphasises that the process must not mutate into a vehicle for 'system comparison', and rejects an 'inflation' of guidelines and indicators (Federal Ministry of Labour and Social Affairs, nd).

Likewise, the former government supported the (reformed) Lisbon Strategy as does the present one (CDU et al, 2005, pp 26, 149). Although the new government holds fast to its objectives, it also stresses the independent role of the 'social dimension' within the Lisbon Strategy: one-sided attempts by the Ecofin Council and corresponding bodies to subordinate social issues to fiscal sustainability need countering because of the economic value of social policy as a productivity factor (Federal Ministry of Labour and Social Affairs, nd). The actual influence of this major EU project on the decision of the Red-Green government to adopt its Agenda 2010 remains unclear. However, the Agenda was regarded as a strategy to *modernise* the social market economy by means of reconstructing the Sozialstaat. In the parliamentary debate Angela Merkel, then leader of the opposition, demanded a more rigorous move towards the Lisbon Agenda by a *new* social market economy, a concept the CDU had already developed in 2001 (CDU, 2001).

Before 2003, the tension between the understanding of the ESM (as promoted by the European Commission) and the Sozialstaat model institutionalised in Germany was somewhat larger. Germany's traditional social insurance-oriented welfare state is now more in line with the European version conceptualised by the EU as a third way approach, reconciling efficiency and competitiveness with social solidarity, high social standards and a focus on employability and activation, after Agenda 2010 was made the core of the former government's reconstruction policy. Although the new government has abolished the term 'Agenda 2010' (for example, it is not mentioned at all in the coalition agreement), the information on the website of the Ministry of Social Affairs (led by the Social Democratic Vice-Chancellor) in March 2006 still said that it would ensure that EU institutions acknowledge the 'paradigm change' in Germany, and it emphasised strengthening self-responsibility and activation of individual potential as an expression of a (re)definition of social justice at the *national* level where it rightly has to happen.

In sum, before 2003 (at the latest), there were considerable differences between the German social insurance model and the European third way approach, and Germany made several attempts to influence the Social Policy Agenda at the EU level, for example, by the insertion of 'social market economy' into the list of the Community's objectives. Through various reform processes in Germany these two social models have moved somewhat closer together. Nevertheless, the German government opposes any further shift of competencies away from the national level – the level at which reform decisions must occur according to national values and priorities. However, the government endorses social policy cooperation at the EU level and more concern for social issues among all EU bodies in general.

Main principles in national reforms

In 1990 Germany experienced a most singular event: the unification of two states. The consequences of this event, particularly the dramatic decline of employment in East Germany, contributed greatly to the mounting problems of the welfare state arrangement and enduring deficits in the state budget, consequently leading to a still increasing public debt. However, not before 1996 did social policy reform enter a new stage and a re-conceptualisation of the social market economy begin. Previous reform efforts – of which the 1992 pension reform (passed by Parliament the day the Berlin Wall came down, 11 November 1989) was a prime example – were a smooth consolidation of the German welfare state. In 1994, a new social insurance scheme providing comprehensive long-term care benefits was enacted. Until 1996, *status maintenance*, the main principle of the transfer-heavy German social insurance state, was not called into question. Retrenchments were mainly but not always adopted in agreement between the two main parties in Parliament as an informal Grand Coalition, with the social partners involved in a corporatist style of policy making.

Around 1995, in view of rising unemployment, an exploding inflow of older workers into early retirement schemes and intensified attention towards topics like economic globalisation, demographic ageing or generational equity made the need to reform the German welfare state increasingly urgent. A series of recurrent reforms covering all major schemes started in 1996. This process was interrupted only during the first year of the Red-Green government's incumbency, when it undid a number of changes legislated by its predecessor. Several trends implying a break with previously valid principles and concepts are clearly discernible.

First, the *financing* of the German social insurance state shifted towards increased tax funding. The share of contribution-financed spending dropped from exactly two thirds in 1991 to 60% in 2003 (Bundesministerium für Gesundheit und Soziale Sicherung, 2005, p 202). The drop was compensated for through the infusion of more tax revenues (raised out of higher indirect taxation – VAT and ecology tax), mainly into social insurance schemes to attain stable or even lower contribution rates. A further attempt to keep employers' non-wage labour costs under control was to shift the burden of social security to employees and private households. This shift happened in several ways. Employers and employees no longer pay an equal share of contributions to the statutory health care scheme, and patients face increased co-payments and other out-of-pocket expenses. The contribution rate to the public pension scheme (rising to 19.9% in 2007) must not exceed a ceiling of 22% until 2030, meaning a maximum burden of 11% for employers. Consequently, employees are expected to carry the burden of voluntary and supplementary private pensions to make up for a lower and no longer status-maintaining replacement rate.[3]

The departure from *status maintenance* and, correspondingly, the trend towards basic security through social insurance schemes accompanied innovative changes to means-tested schemes: since 2003 pensioners with too-low income are referred to a separate scheme outside social assistance, and in 2005 the merger of both means-tested and earnings-related unemployment assistance and the social assistance schemes became effective. The introduction of this means-tested benefit for people of working age with no or insufficient unemployment insurance benefits or too-low earnings was accompanied by a 'modernisation' of active labour market policy, predominantly by various means of *activating* unemployed people.

A lower degree of *inclusion in social insurance* schemes is a further trend. While the total number of gainfully employed people remained largely unchanged between 1991 and 2005, the share of those liable for social insurance contributions has decreased, from almost 78% to 67%. Although mainly caused by employers' strategies, to some extent this decline also results from reform activities that strengthened incentives for finding jobs outside the format of the standard employment relationship (for example, marginal part-time work, self-employment). The decline in covered employment means less social protection for the workers affected, as well as fewer revenues for the social insurance schemes.

Finally, beside numerous and, quite often, substantial retrenchment and cost-containment measures in other social policy areas, there is a new *emphasis on family policy*. So far, family policy has been very transfer-biased (with child allowances quite generous by international standards), whereas the focus is now on expanding childcare services (for children below the age of three and after morning school); however, the federal government has hardly any jurisdiction in this area. These recent reforms are motivated mainly by the low fertility rate in Germany and meant to ease the combination of parenthood and labour market participation and to shorten employment interruption after childbirth. To that end, the federal government reformed the parental leave allowance scheme. Since 2007 benefits are earnings related (two thirds of former net earnings up to a maximum of 1,800 euros) and paid for no more than 12 months or 14 months if the other parent leaves the job for at least two months.

The pension reform of 2004, the modernisation of active and passive labour market policy, the health care reform of 2003 (still to be supplemented by a compromise on refinancing) and measures deregulating the labour market were parts of Agenda 2010, launched by the Red-Green government in 2003. The contents of these reforms were presented in the recent National Strategy Reports, National Action Plans and further reports to the EU, arguing that Germany is on its way to meeting EU objectives and guidelines. Reforming welfare state schemes and programmes one by one – often more than once and in a number of areas still unfinished (like the long-term care insurance scheme) – demonstrates that efforts were not based on a well-integrated concept. The established institutional setting and the national discourse largely determined which reform levers could be pulled for coping with perceived present and future problems. Thus we cannot regard these single, incremental reform steps as attempts to realise a certain model of social policy developed by the EU, the World Bank (although Germany has embraced the 'multi-pillar' approach in pensions) or any other international organisation. However, certain reform features were inspired by Scandinavian arrangements and achievements, for example, more employment-friendly tax financing of social expenditure (the main direction of reform efforts), comprehensive inclusion of mothers in paid work through better care services, and fewer long-term unemployed people through stricter activation and a focus on employability (drawing on Dutch and British experiences).

National responses to the EU initiatives

Lisbon Strategy and the reformed Lisbon Strategy 2005

The federal Red–Green government welcomed the launch of the Lisbon Strategy in 2000 and presented it as a contribution to transforming an industrial society into a 'knowledge economy' (Deutscher Bundestag, 2000a, 2000b). It promoted the underlying 'third way' approach of the Lisbon Strategy to combine economic efficiency, the consolidation of public finances and social justice. Therefore, it approved the different aims of the strategy: on the one hand, social objectives related to 'lifelong learning', improving gender equality, and increasing employment rates, and on the other hand, economic objectives of a further liberalisation of the gas, electricity, postal services and transport sectors, and an overall cut of state deficits (Deutscher Bundestag, 2000a).

From the beginning, however, the federal government addressed potential concerns of the Länder governments that the Lisbon Strategy could interfere with their jurisdiction in education and social policy. Due to the ensuing demands of the German government, the European Council made clear that the Member States should only pursue the Lisbon objectives according to their constitutional prerequisites (Deutscher Bundestag, 2000a, p 9084).

The position of the federal government did not change substantially during the following three years. It only added new domestic objectives for implementing the Lisbon Agenda, for example the adjustment of social security systems to demographic change in 2001, environmental issues in 2002, and the competitiveness of industries in 2003 (see, respectively, Bundesrat, 2001, 2002, 2003a). At the 2004 European Summit the government presented its new and partially unpopular Agenda 2010 as a response to the Lisbon Strategy (Bundesrat, 2003b; Deutscher Bundestag, 2003b).

The mid-term review of the Lisbon Strategy issued by the Kok-led High Level Group was discussed in the Bundesrat in early 2005 (Bundesrat, 2005). At that time, the Red–Green government was confronted with a majority of conservative-led Länder governments in the Bundesrat. The Länder repeatedly accused the government of being responsible for failing the Lisbon goals and urged it to pursue a strictly growth-oriented fiscal policy agenda (while the government blamed the deterioration of economic conditions for the failure of the Lisbon targets) (Bundesrat, 2004, p 2). This discussion shows that the opposition strategically used the Lisbon Strategy to press for structural changes in social and economic policy (Deuscher Bundestag, 2004a; Bundesrat, 2005).[4]

The federal government endorsed the conclusions of the Kok report, particularly the refocusing of the Lisbon Strategy on economic growth and employment (Bundesrat, 2004; Deutscher Bundestag, 2004a). While the Lisbon Strategy had a comparably strong social policy component when launched in 2000, it now prioritises economic growth and more and better jobs. The philosophy of the new Lisbon Strategy is that economic growth will 'secure our unique social model' (European Commission, 2005e). In its direct comments on the reformed Lisbon Strategy, the government did not express concerns that the focus on growth and employment might come at the expense of the social policy objectives. The main reason seems to be that the government faced widespread criticism at home for its reform strategies. To this extent the Lisbon Strategy and the related peer pressure to pursue structural reforms were a welcome external support for the government's position. Despite this general approval, however, the factions of the Social Democrats and the Greens in the Bundestag emphasised that the EU Commission should not take the role of a 'moral instance' exerting reform pressure by 'naming, shaming and blaming'. Instead, it preferred that the Commission build a real partnership with the Member States but without defining in more detail how such a partnership should be designed (Deutscher Bundestag, 2005a, pp 6-7). The position of the new Grand Coalition government on the Lisbon Strategy is very similar to that of the former government (Bundesregierung, 2005a).

Social Policy Agenda 2005-10

Overall, the federal government endorsed the Social Policy Agenda 2005-10. The government stressed that the Agenda should strengthen the trust of European citizens in the integration process and that the social dimension of the Lisbon Strategy should remain in place (Bundesregierung, 2005a, pp 1-2). The government also critically commented on several points. While it welcomed partnership and consultation between the government, the social partners and other civil society actors, it questioned establishing a national forum for evaluating the implementation of the Social Policy Agenda since various other consultation forums already existed (Bundesregierung, 2005a, p 2). The government also expressed strong scepticism towards introducing a voluntary framework for transnational collective bargaining because of the differences of national bargaining systems in the EU and the constitutional right to free collective bargaining in Germany. In particular, the government disliked the proposal for further labour law initiatives and a comparison of minimum income schemes in the EU. It stressed that the EU should play only a supporting and complementary role in these areas because the main competencies still remain with the Member States.

Open method of coordination

While the overall attitude of the Red–Green federal government to the OMC was positive, in response to the Commission's questionnaire, the government also mentioned some critical points related to the OMC instruments and the EU's competencies. According to the government, participating actors perceive the procedures of drafting the National Action Plans for various OMCs as time consuming and criticise the existence of several overlaps between individual OMC processes. Therefore, the government welcomed the streamlining of the OMC in pension and social inclusion, while emphasising that such actions should not undermine the social dimension of the Lisbon Strategy (Bundesregierung, 2005c, pp 5, 10).

A further issue relates to the use of quantitative indicators. While generally endorsing the use of quantitative indicators in the OMC, the government stressed that the process of developing indicators needed careful handling. It insisted, for instance, that Member States' governments' influence on indicator building should be guaranteed and that indicators should not be overused. The government also emphasised that political conclusions should not be drawn from the results of indicator-related benchmarking without a careful interpretation of the respective national context. While the government generally endorses the further development of quantitative indicators in the areas of pensions and health care, currently on the way in the Social Protection Committee (SPC) of the EU, it rejects a systematic ranking of Member States resulting from this benchmarking process (Bundesregierung, 2005b, 2005c, p 11).

Another critical point relates to the question of the impact the OMC has had to date on domestic policy making and political processes. In its response to the questionnaire, the government stressed that the OMC did not change consultation procedures in Germany because consulting social partners, the Länder governments, and other civil society actors had widely practised them already (Bundesregierung, 2005c, pp 6-7). It also denied that the OMC had a traceable impact on national social policy development in Germany (Bundesregierung, 2005c, p 3).

The real picture, however, is a bit more complicated. The OMC is special in that it primarily issues relatively unspecific policy objectives. Therefore, the contents of the OMC are interpreted differently by different actors, whose references to the OMC in policy-making discussions back up various political positions and demands. For example, in 1998/99 the new Red-Green government interpreted the contents of the European Employment Strategy (EES) in a way that fitted with a traditional social democratic understanding of labour market policy (active labour market policy, social security, tripartism at the EU level). From 2001 onward (at the latest), the labour market policy orientation of the Red-Green government changed, emphasising activation, employability and flexicurity. Since then, the government used references to the OMC to support and justify these changes (for example, in the draft laws of the 'Hartz IV' Act by which the social assistance and unemployment assistance schemes were integrated and the pressure on unemployed people to accept job offers was intensified) (Deutscher Bundestag, 2003c, p 44). Another example illustrating the use of references to the OMC to back up domestic policy reforms is part of a statement by the factions of Social Democrats and Greens in the Bundestag in 2005: 'the benchmarking process that is related to the open method of co-ordination may be beneficial for implementing reforms since it can increase the reform pressure on national governments' (Deutscher Bundestag, 2005a, p 6).

The opposition also played a part in this game of 'naming, shaming and blaming'. For example, the Bundesrat, with its majority of state governments led by Christian Democrats, welcomed the OMC as an instrument for intensifying pressure for reforms aiming at growth and competitiveness. The Bundesrat even asked for a more rigorous benchmarking and ranking of Member States: 'debates about policy reforms will progress too slowly in the Member States if they are not backed up with arguments by the EU Commission.... The Bundesrat regrets that the Commission's proposal to integrate a comparative evaluation and ranking of Member States according to their performance into the National Action Plans has not been realized' (Bundesrat, 2005, paras 16, 21).

However, apart from this shaming and blaming game, the government was very clear that the subsidiarity principle should remain intact, respecting Member State jurisdiction in the area of social policy.[5] Therefore, the EU bodies should limit their role in these policy areas to setting non-binding targets, disseminating information, presenting best practice, 'raising awareness' of reform pressures and supporting national strategies through structural funds (Bundesregierung, 2005c, p 10).

Thus the overall position of the government towards the OMC is ambivalent. While regarding the OMC as a useful instrument for exchanging experiences and backing up national plans for policy change, the government worries about a 'creeping' expansion of EU competencies in the area of social policy via the OMC process. Concretely, on the OMC in pension policy, the Ministry of Social Affairs considers the present scope of cooperation as sufficient, with no need for extending or deepening it. Furthermore, the Ministry is concerned about the 'threat that European institutions, above all the European Commission, may be partly successful when they, without legal foundation, attempt to restrict the scope of national sovereignty to their advantage' (Federal Ministry of Labour and Social Affairs, nd).

Demographic change

In the national response to the Green Paper's questionnaire, Renate Schmidt, then Minister for Family Affairs in the Red-Green government, welcomed this Green Paper (Bundesregierung, 2005d, p 1). In the minister's view, this initiative could make a valuable contribution to the ongoing debate on demographic change through raising awareness about the processes involved and making them more transparent. She agreed that demographic change was a problem that not only affected single nations but also had European and global dimensions. Furthermore, since demographic change affected almost all policy areas, she supported a 'demography check' for policies in other areas.

Similar to other EU initiatives, the minister's main concern was that the principle of subsidiarity remained untouched and that no additional bureaucratic burdens followed from this strategy. The minister urged that the Member States should tackle the problems resulting from demographic change 'at home' and that the Green Paper should not aim at developing an independent EU policy in this area because of the topic's overall complexity and the considerably different situations in the Member States. In addition, the minister regarded an extra coordination strategy for the pension OMC as unnecessary and emphasised that no double structures should be introduced in addition to the processes conducted by the United Nations (UN) and the Council of Europe.

The Ministry for Family Affairs responded in detail to all the Green Paper's questions addressing the potential contribution of various policy areas in coping with demographic change. For example, the Ministry emphasised the importance of support for reconciling work and family life through childcare, suitable parental leave, part-time work arrangements and financial support for families (Bundesregierung, 2005d, pp 2-5). The Ministry was not in favour of a reduced VAT rate for childcare and care for the elderly services to improve the supply of these services, since most of these services are already exempted from purchase taxes by EU law. Instead, the Ministry mentioned several German initiatives that aim at better integrating young people into the labour market and enhancing solidarity between the generations. Furthermore, the Ministry expressed support for active ageing, a life-cycle employment approach and a phasing out of early retirement schemes, and stressed that in Germany the social partners have the authority to come to agreements in some of these areas. It also regarded a statutory retirement age as necessary due to the provisions that regulate the German pension system's funding, but endorsed the proposal to discuss more flexible forms of transition between working life and retirement. Finally, the Ministry was sceptical as to what degree further immigration might contribute to solving the demographic problem, although it did not deny that immigration could be part of the solution (Bundesregierung, 2005d, pp 6-7).

Services of general interest

The federal government's response to the Green Paper on services of general interest (SGI) was rather cautious and sceptical (Bundesregierung, 2003). While the government valued the Green Paper as a contribution to a mutual understanding between the EU Commission and the Member States about the nature of these services, it strictly rejected any EU competencies regarding the 'definition, design, organisation, and financing' of SGI by developing European standards or a framework directive (Bundesregierung, 2003, p 1).

The government stressed that in Germany the local authorities, charities and churches provided the bulk of social services, and that their role needed protection. It complained that the EU law on state aids had been arbitrarily applied and consequently negatively influenced investment and personnel planning in the area of social services in Germany. Therefore, the government demanded that the EU and the Member States develop a clearer definition of 'typical non-profit-oriented activities' that should be excluded from EU state aid and competition law.

The reason for this sceptical position is that EU competition and state aid law has already had a restricting influence on the provision of social services in Germany. The government's position is to protect the interests and authorities of a variety of stakeholders in this field and, moreover, to remain able to steer and support the provision of these services through civil society actors.

Proposal on the Services Directive

Overall, the discussion about the Services Directive in Germany shows that the government, on the one hand, supports the opening up of markets but, on the other hand, is quite concerned about market liberalisation possibly threatening national social standards. The former Red-Green government (together with France's President Chirac) openly criticised the country-of-origin principle, arguing that it could lead to social dumping in those Member States with higher social standards and high wage levels (Deutscher Bundestag, 2005a, p 5; 2005b, p 15493; 2005c). Both the German government and the French President claimed that the country-of-origin principle – which would have set all 25 Member States into direct competition over working conditions, wages and social standards – is not justified through the treaties or cases before the European Court of Justice (ECJ) and would even violate international private law. They further demanded the restriction of the Services Directive to commercial services and those outside national regulation, with SGI exempted in any case (Deutscher Bundestag, 2005a).

The new government welcomed the EU Parliament's 16 February 2006 decision on the Services Directive to remove the country-of-origin principle and to exempt several branches from the Directive, for example, those in the social and health sector. Like its predecessor, the new government stressed that the establishment of a common market for services must go hand in hand with the protection of the ESM. National employment policy, wage-setting procedures and social and labour law must not be restricted through the Services Directive, and the Directive should not aim to privatise or liberalise the SGI sector. The new government also criticised plans to change the Posting of Workers Directive because it sought to retain full control over the application of national social regulations to posted workers (Bundesregierung, 2006a).

European Economic and Monetary Union

The Red-Green government has taken an ambivalent stance towards monetary union and the Stability and Growth Pact (SGP) in particular. During the first year of its incumbency, when Oskar Lafontaine was still Minister of Finance, the Red-Green government supported a demand-side approach at both the national and European levels, opposing a strict supply-side-oriented approach. After Lafontaine's resignation, the federal government clearly pursued a supply-side strategy and stressed the importance of consolidating state finances. However, this proved difficult in view of still transferring large amounts of public funds from West to East Germany.[6]

Since 2002 Germany could not fulfil the budget deficit target for several years in a row (and also violated constitutional requirements). The Council suspended the 2002 and 2003 deficit procedures against Germany, which the ECJ declared as unlawful in July 2004. Afterwards, the Commission itself suspended the procedure in December 2004, arguing that Germany could be trusted to reduce its annual additional deficit to 2.9% by 2005. The Commission proposed an SGP reform, which the Red-Green government supported, arguing that the SGP should be applied in a more flexible way and with greater consideration to the economic circumstances and the specific economic difficulties in a Member State (Deutscher Bundestag, 2004b, 2005d). The former government regarded a strict fiscal policy as counterproductive because it would hinder economic growth and therefore wreck the preconditions for consolidating public finances. It also feared a backlash against European integration if the government had to justify further cuts in social security by referring to the SGP. Although the proposals to soften the SGP criteria led to very controversial discussions within Germany (in particular, the German Central Bank opposed any watering down) and the EU, the European Council rejected the proposals in March 2005.

The position of the new federal government towards the SGP has not changed substantially. In March 2006, the Ecofin Council requested that Germany meet the deficit target by 2007 at the latest. This compromise avoided the immediate initiation of an official deficit procedure. Due to the favourable economic development after 2005 and tax revenues higher than projected the government already fulfilled the demands in 2006. Although the deficit procedure has been terminated, continuous efforts to maintain meeting the 3% target will affect social policy reform insofar as an 'employment-friendly' shift away from contribution financing is hampered. Increasing indirect taxation beyond the rise of VAT by three percentage points in 2007 (of which one percentage point is designated to lower the contribution rate to the unemployment insurance scheme from 6.5% to 4.2%) would mean an additional threat to economic recovery. Therefore, enduring growth of the economy and of employment is essential for raising the revenues of the social insurance schemes so that contribution rates may remain stable as well as for additional tax revenues that would facilitate a further shift in the structure of financing the German Sozialstaat.

Enlargement

Opinions and discussions about Eastern enlargement have been quite mixed in Germany. On the one hand, the government conceived it as an important step towards 'reunifying' Europe. When enlargement was realised in May 2004, the Red–Green government supported and appreciated it as a historical chance to create democracy, peace, stability and economic growth in the whole of Europe (Deutscher Bundestag, 2004c). On the other hand, Eastern enlargement was perceived as a threat, giving rise to a political backlash against European integration if citizens regarded enlargement as a danger to domestic social standards. In fact, Eastern enlargement was always criticised by public opinion, not only by parties from the far Right and Left. Even the Centrist Christian Democratic Party several times issued (populist) concerns to the Bundestag about a crowding out of German workers (Deutscher Bundestag, 2005e). While the Red–Green government regularly replied that positive effects on the economic development in Germany would prevail, it admitted that some sectors, particularly those employing low-skilled workers, might come under pressure (Deutscher Bundestag, 2005f).

As to the free movement of workers, Germany has made use of the clause to restrict labour market immigration from Eastern European citizens. After the government reviewed the development in 2006, according to a recent statement, these restrictions will most likely continue for another three years, possibly until 2011 (Bundesregierung, 2006b). The government justified its intention by maintaining its aim to 'protect the German labour market against a multitude of workers from the Eastern European countries' (Bundesregierung, 2006b). This statement shows the government's enduring concerns about the negative effects of Eastern enlargement on German labour markets and social standards. The debate about prolonging restrictions for migrant workers from new Member States and the Services Directive has raised demands for introducing a statutory minimum wage to counter potential dumping processes. The reactions were mixed (initially, even the trade unions were not unanimously responsive to those proposals). The Bundestag has not passed draft minimum wage laws introduced by both the Left and the Green Party (see Deutscher Bundestag, 2006b), because the government parties disagree on this issue – the SPD is in favour of a statutory minimum wage, the CDU/CSU strongly against it.

Conclusions

The German welfare state was and still is regarded as a national project based on the established concept of a social market economy, with no explicit reference to notions of an ESM. The reforms pursued by the Red-Green and the Black-Red government over the past 10 years were attempts to modernise the German model of social market economy with its politically defined problems and within the capabilities determined by established national institutions.[7]

Nevertheless, a firm social dimension of the EU has strong support, not least for avoiding political backlash against the European project if social standards were lowered. However, the government has sometimes exploited the EU as an excuse for justifying unpopular or otherwise controversial reform proposals, for example in relation to the 'Hartz' labour market reforms. In its National Action Plans and Reports it expresses its support for most of the social policy objectives within the OMC and strongly emphasises its accomplishments. In contrast, the opposition has very often accused the government of not complying with objectives, indicators and benchmarks, insofar as different actors have used the EU as a vehicle for backing their position in the national political struggle over welfare state reform.

When it comes to the direction of reforms in Germany, particularly after 2003, the distance between the European 'third way' and the German model of social market economy has narrowed due to initiatives of the Red-Green government in its increased emphasis on self-responsibility and inclusion in the labour market (that is, activation, not compensation). However, a central objective of reconstructing the German social insurance state, that is, to decouple social security financing from employment for the sake of improving firms' international competitiveness and stimulating job growth, is still hampered by the deficit criteria of the SGP. Given the enormous share of social insurance contributions, raising taxes so that the accruing revenues facilitate a significant decrease of contribution rates has reached limits after increasing VAT by three percentage points in 2007. Moreover, the pressure to further lower the national budget deficit constrains the room for manoeuvre for extending social services that ease and enhance the inclusion of child-rearing women into the labour market. Besides increased tax funding, various retrenchments have stabilised contribution rates to social insurance schemes and contained total social expenditure. Consequently, higher burdens have been shifted to employees and private households to provide for and cope with social risks.

Most official documents examined in this chapter relate to EU initiatives that were launched during the incumbency of the Red-Green government (or even before). More generally, positions regarding EU social policy hardly changed under the new government and, in particular, the Black-Red government definitely holds on to the conviction that no further competencies must be transferred to the EU level – and on that account it is clearly in accord with the Länder. The constitutional change to reform federalism in Germany, legislated in 2006, has even strengthened the shield of the subsidiarity principle due to a more clearly defined demarcation of competencies between the federal government and the Länder governments.

The shift of the federal government from Red-Green to Black-Red, however, means a new mixture of positions to social policy-related issues at the EU level: a slight incline towards protectionism (Eastern European workers and immigration as such, the Services Directive), a more positive attitude towards a further liberalisation of markets other than the labour market, and a continued ambivalence regarding European benchmarking in social policy. *If* the Grand Coalition will hold for a while, in pursuance of a strict fiscal policy to maintain meeting the deficit criteria of the SGP, it should welcome any (informal) EU pressure and support for largely unpopular social security reforms that imply further cuts.

Nevertheless, the two parties in government have agreed on priorities for the German EU presidency in 2007 that are not dissimilar to the position of the previous Red-Green government. The Merkel government's EU presidency programme stresses that the economic and social dimensions of the EU complement each other (Deutscher Bundestag, 2006c, p 8). The conclusions from a German EU presidency conference 'Joining Forces for a Social Europe', held in February 2007, urges the EU Member States to afford the political will to implement the objectives and values inherent in the ESM and strengthen the social policy objectives within the Lisbon Strategy (Bundesministerium für Arbeit und Soziales, 2007), which is in line with a previous statement of the government: 'Social policy is and remains a central element of the Lisbon strategy' (Bundesministerium für Arbeit und Soziales, 2006, p 6).

In summary, the current government strongly supports the social dimension of European integration and pursues reform strategies that are in accordance with the EU's 'third way'-oriented objectives for social policy reform. However, it puts national autonomy first by strongly insisting on the principle of subsidiarity and rejecting any further involvement of the EU in national social policy matters.

Notes

[1] It is interesting to note that in all relevant reports of parliamentary or expert commissions or of advisory councils, EU initiatives related to social policy receive no mention apart from reference to the internal market (free movement of labour) and directives concerning the admission of medical drugs.

[2] Chancellor Merkel, in her speech on European policy in the Bundestag (Regierungserklärung), again emphasised the 'value added' for citizens as the central criterion for possibly shifting competencies between the EU and the Member State level (Deutscher Bundestag, 2006a).

[3] In 2008, the recommended rate of savings for supplementary private pensions reach the final stage of 4% of gross earnings. Those savings efforts benefit from direct subsidies or, alternatively, tax breaks in order to encourage the take-up rate.

[4] A further conflict between the government and the opposition was related to the role of the EU Commission in the Lisbon Strategy. While the government parties demanded a partnership model between the EU Commission and the government the opposition asked for a more rigorous benchmarking and ranking process in order to increase reform pressure on the government (Bundesrat, 2005; Deutscher Bundestag, 2005b).

[5] The Länder are equally concerned about the potential transfer of competencies to the EU at their expense. Such fears were clearly expressed by Wilgardt Schuchardt from North Rhine Westphalia's Ministry of Labour and Social Affairs, representing the Länder at a conference on the OMC in pensions (see Verband Deutscher Rentenversicherungsträger, 2002, pp 94-8).

[6] Due to the weak economic position of East German Länder and higher unemployment there, net interregional transfers out of public purses (federal, state and social insurance budgets) from West to East Germany continue. Recent estimates of the Economic Research Institute in Halle show that, in 2003, they amounted to 3.2% of GDP (gross domestic product) that roughly matched the total public deficit in the same year (Lehmann et al, 2005).

[7] In December 2005, the government informed on a number of welfare state reform projects it intended to deal with during the current legislature (Bundesregierung, 2005e). Except for a reform of financing long-term care insurance and (further) liberalising dismissal protection (which was cancelled), it completed the list in early 2007. The laws

on raising the statutory retirement age from 65 to 67 between 2012 and 2029, on improving employment opportunities for older workers, and on health care reform (mainly aiming at improved quality and efficiency through more competition among sickness funds) passed the parliamentary bodies in 2007, and the reform of the parental leave allowance scheme was already legislated in 2006.

THREE

The United Kingdom: more an economic than a social European

Julian Le Grand, Elias Mossialos and Morgan Long

As a country's social policy reflects its values, understanding and anticipating a country's position on social policy first calls for identifying its ideological framework. In the United Kingdom, belief in the autonomy of the individual, the need to protect and assist the vulnerable, and a focus on economic growth to provide opportunity for all defines the role of government. It is through this framework that the UK considers both domestic and European Community policies.

This chapter covers European social policy from the UK's perspective. The first section spells out some of the fundamental differences (both perceived and real) between the European social model (ESM) and the UK social model, and discusses how these fuel the UK's basic attitudes towards European social policy. The second describes recent reforms in some areas of UK social policy and discusses how European or other international models have influenced these reforms. The third section summarises the national responses to European Union (EU) social policy initiatives. There is a brief concluding section.

The European social model versus the UK model

In discussing issues of this kind, distinguishing between actuality and perception is important. There are two actualities, and two perceptions of those actualities, that we need to consider here: first, the actual ESM versus the UK's perception of that model; second, the actual UK model versus the rest of Europe's perception of that model. With respect to the first issue, not one ESM but a wide variety of models exists. The first attempt to put some order on that variety by classifying European and other industrialised country welfare states was undertaken by Esping-Andersen (1990), where he identified three types: liberal (basically Anglo-Saxon countries), social democratic (basically Scandinavia) and conservative (everyone else). Since then, others have attempted to refine or replace his classification, including Esping-Andersen himself (Leibfried, 1992; Castles and Mitchell, 1999; Esping-Andersen, 1999;

Goodin et al, 1999). The most recent – and the most useful – of these is that of Karl Aiginger and Alois Guger (Aiginger and Guger, 2006).[1] They have identified three spectra along which ESMs can differ: the balance of *responsibility* between the state and the individual; the extent of formal and informal *regulation*, especially in the labour market; and the extent and form of *redistribution*. They use these spectra to identify five different kinds of ESM: the Scandinavian (Denmark, Finland, the Netherlands, Sweden, Norway), the Continental (Germany, France, Italy, Belgium, Austria), the Anglo-Saxon (Ireland, the UK), the Mediterranean (Greece, Portugal, Spain), and the Catching-up (the Czech Republic, Hungary).

Some key decision makers in the UK recognise the plurality of ESMs. Thus a pamphlet by two leading Labour politicians, David Blunkett and Alan Johnson, states that 'there is no single European Model because each Member State has its own, specific traditions, institutions and practices. However, these differences are underpinned by shared values – solidarity, mutuality and the pursuit of social justice – which are distinctive features of European civilisation' (Blunkett and Johnson, 2005, p 1).[2] However, many other commentators and opinion formers in the UK have a perception that only one kind of ESM exists – one close to their understanding of Aiginger and Guger's Continental model.[3] In terms of the spectra of responsibility, regulation and redistribution, it is one where:

- the state bears most of the responsibility for the factors that affect individuals' welfare. This approach reflects the view that the individual is basically a product of society with little opportunity or capacity for freedom of action;
- all markets, especially the labour market, are heavily regulated. The regulation can be informal (collective agreements between social partners) or formal (labour laws on hiring, firing and working conditions);
- redistribution takes the form primarily of supporting those not in work (unemployed people, retired people). Although this form reduces poverty, it has a detrimental effect on economic growth and on incentives to work and to find employment.

Similarly, many commentators and decision makers in the rest of Europe have a perception of the UK model that is almost a mirror image of the UK perception of the ESM. It is one where:

- the individual is on his or her own in most situations, with only minimal help from the state – and then only in times of dire distress. This construction stems from a view of the individual as essentially an autonomous agent, responsible for his or her own decisions and actions;
- all markets, including the labour market, are 'free', with the inevitable consequence of worker exploitation, poor working conditions, long hours and massive differences in pay;
- redistribution is minimal, with low, means-tested benefits and with the state forcing people into work, leading to employment in low-paid, unrewarding jobs. Thus widespread poverty and inequality exist.

We do not have the space here to comment on the extent to which the UK's perception of the (Continental) ESM is accurate, and the exact nature of the social models in other Member States is the subject of other chapters. But with respect to the European perception of the UK's model and its relationship to actuality, we note the following.

There are large areas of social policy where the perception of the British welfare state as a triumph of individualism over solidarity does not hold up, notably the National Health Service (NHS), free at the point of use and funded from general taxation, and the provision of universal child benefit for families. However, in general it is probably true that there is a greater belief in the capacity of individuals to make choices, and thus in the concept of individual responsibility, than in much of the rest of Europe. This belief is reflected in government rhetoric, in popular attitudes to welfare, and in key areas of policy (such as pensions, with extensive private provision, or higher education, with growing private funding through tuition fees).

The UK has rather more labour protection than the European perception would indicate, including a minimum wage close to the average of other Member States, various legal roadblocks in the way of firing workers and many individual rights for employees. However, it is true that, with the decline in union membership, collective agreements play a less significant part in the UK than elsewhere in the EU. There is less non-legislative labour protection, and, perhaps in consequence, more people are working longer hours within wider pay differentials than in much of the rest of Europe. But there are also higher average incomes, higher employment and much lower unemployment.

Redistribution through the benefit system, much of which is means tested, is quite effective in reaching the people it is intended for. However, the government clearly believes that work is the best way to help the less well-off, partly to get people off benefits, but, more fundamentally, because it believes that this approach will enable individuals to fulfil their potential. Thus much of UK policy reforms are directed towards encouraging those receiving benefits back into work.

These differences in perception and realities fuel much of the UK's attitudes towards EU policies in general. Key policy makers in the UK are not impressed by what they interpret to be the ESM. Thus they believe strongly in the principle of subsidiarity, and display little enthusiasm for expanding the EU's role in social policy. This position is apparent both in the development of UK social policy and in the UK's reactions to European initiatives in the area, as we see in the next two sections.

Figure 3.1: Principal characteristics of the UK social model

- Based on individual responsibility and choice.
- Provides flexible, competitive markets, through which social objectives can be achieved.
- Protects the vulnerable.
- Assists individuals in need in their transition into active members of the economy.

Main principles in national reforms

This section lists some of the main areas of national reform since 1990 and discusses the extent to which these have been inspired by national factors or by the national application of broader international policy models such as the EU, Organisation for Economic Co-operation and Development (OECD) or the World Bank. The situation is complicated by a change of government in 1997 when the long-serving Conservative administration (in power since 1979 under the premierships of Margaret Thatcher and John Major) was replaced by a Labour government under Tony Blair. However, although the details of the reforms themselves differed between the governments, there were similarities of approach in many areas. Indeed, on the central question of the impact of international policy models on national policy making, little difference exists.

Health

The NHS has undergone an enormous variety of organisational reforms under both governments. These include the introduction of an 'internal market' by the Conservative government in 1990, its partial abolition in 1997 by the incoming Labour government, the introduction of a command and control regime by that government with the setting of performance targets and the use of direct management to achieve those targets, and the re-introduction of key market-type reforms by the government as the performance management regime reached its limits (Le Grand and Vizard, 1998; Le Grand, 2002). The Labour government also engaged in a substantial increase in public spending on the area.

In developing some of these reforms, policy makers have tried to learn from best practice in other countries both within the Union and outside it. However, as with other areas of domestic welfare reform, they have not been led by EU-level social policy initiatives; many of the reforms are essentially home-grown, showing little signs of influence from anywhere outside the UK. The OECD issued a couple of supportive reports on the various market-type reforms in health care, but these came after their introduction (Koen, 2000; OECD, 2004). The World Bank and other international organisations had no impact whatsoever.

The only change to show any signs of significant international influence, and then of a rather particular kind, was the last of those just listed: the Labour government increase in public spending. It came about almost by accident – during an unscripted television interview in early 2000, the Prime Minister made a public commitment to bring UK spending on the NHS up to 'the EU average' (Rawnsley, 2000). The result of this commitment has indeed been an increase in actual and planned government spending on the NHS, with the amount almost tripling in cash terms from 1997/98 to 2008/09.

Not only spending but other forms of comparison within the EU also enter into UK health debates, usually drawing attention to the relatively poor performance of the UK, for example, in waiting times, in cancer survival rates and in rates of MRSA infection.[4] Occasional flurries of interest in other Member States' systems for funding health care, including charges and social insurance, occur. However, these die down as the disadvantages of such systems – when compared to the UK system of funding through general taxation – become apparent.

But the EU is not totally irrelevant for the UK in the health arena. Helped by EU rules concerning professional mobility, the NHS has recruited doctors and nurses from the rest of the EU; now that it is paying some of the highest salaries in Europe for these professionals, such recruitment is increasingly easy (BMA, 2006). Moreover, the EU may become more significant for UK health policy. As the new quasi-market for health care develops, the system may become liable for the application of EU competition law, and the Services Directive, once implemented, may also have an impact (Mossialos and McKee, 2002b). Nonetheless, overall, it is hard to resist the conclusion that the impact of EU social policy at either the Commission level or that of other Member States on UK health policy has been relatively small – and then involving only inter-state comparison rather than anything more direct.

Pensions

Until recently the UK was relatively content about its pension position relative to other Member States. Extrapolation of future public pension liabilities for most Member States showed an alarming increase in the costs of public pensions over the next 50 years, both in absolute terms and as a proportion of national income. Those for the UK did not. Indeed, although the absolute cost would rise slightly, public pensions as a proportion of national income would actually fall, because of three related factors: the indexation of the universal flat-rate state pension to prices, not earnings (a change made by Margaret Thatcher's Conservative government in 1982); the very limited public earnings-related pension scheme (emasculated by the same government in 1986); and the growth of private pension provision (amounting to over 40% of pension provision when Labour came into power in 1997).[5]

Since the turn of the century, however, this relative complacency has given way to a growing alarm. This change partly resulted from problems with private pensions, including scandals associated with mis-selling and, more importantly, the decline in the stock market and the associated fall in returns to private pension funds. But it also arose from worries about the dramatic increase in life expectancy and its impact on the total cost of pensions (and of health and social care), along with a dawning awareness that this cost, whether publicly or privately financed, would have to be borne by the economy. To deal with these issues, the government set up the Pensions Commission, under the chair of Adair Turner, which reported in 2005 (Turner, 2005). The Turner Report recommended a rise in the retirement age from 65 to 68, a more generous flat-rate universal pension paid to UK residents (not on the basis of National Insurance contributions as currently happens), re-indexation of this pension to earnings, and a new national pension scheme (offered through employers) that would automatically enrol workers unless they requested to opt out and that would receive contributions from the employers, employees and the government. The government has now published a White Paper accepting most of these recommendations (Secretary of State for Work and Pensions, 2006).

Both the Turner Report and the White Paper consider pension policies in the light of experience in countries such as the US and Sweden. But again there is little sign of EU influence at the Commission level, or indeed of influence from any other international organisation. When there was a serious possibility that the UK might enter the Eurozone, the anti-European press raised concerns as to whether entry might make the UK in some way liable for other Member States' commitments to public pensions. However, as the likelihood of the UK soon adopting the euro has diminished (see the next section), that worry has disappeared.

Finally, both governments also introduced a variety of measures that make it easier for pensioners to continue to work and to save after retirement. The Labour government has also introduced measures that encourage those who retire early to return to work (DWP, 2006a). All these measures are consistent with the general British belief that a large part of the state's role in welfare should be to help those who help themselves and, more specifically, that the best route out of poverty is through work (at least for those who can). This belief shows up most strikingly in labour market policies, to which we now turn.

Labour market policies

The policies under review in this section fall into three categories: those that restrict the benefits that those out of work can claim; those that directly facilitate re-entry to work; and those that increase the income of those in work relative to those out of work. John Major's Conservative government (and the Thatcher government that preceded it) concentrated primarily on the first of these: restricting the benefits for claimants (Evans, 1998). Perhaps most significant were the changes to unemployment benefit, significantly renamed Jobseeker's Allowance. A six-month limit on its receipt was imposed, after which it was means tested. Lower rates were to be paid to the under-25s and a 'contract' between the claimant and the agency, formalising job search and training requirements, was to be established.

The Labour government, under the rubric of welfare-to-work, has concentrated more on the second and third type of policy: those that facilitate re-entry into work and those that increase the incomes of those in work (McKnight, 2005). Typical of the facilitation policies have been the New Deal programmes, which cover four main groups: lone parents, young people aged between 18-24, long-term unemployed people aged 25 and over and disabled people. Under these programmes, individuals receive personalised support in Jobcentres that help with job search and work preparation. In some cases entry into the programme is compulsory and highly structured (young people and long-term unemployed people); in others it is voluntary (lone parents and disabled people), although it may not remain so for much longer. Another important innovation is the setting up of Jobcentre Plus, a government agency that brings together welfare payments and job search assistance into a single point of delivery (see also DWP, 2006b).

The policies for increasing income in work include the introduction of a minimum wage in 1999 and the development of various forms of 'tax credits'. The latter are essentially a form of negative income tax, where payments are given to those in work at low earnings and withdrawn as earnings increase, but at a lower rate than the increase in earnings. So unemployed individuals receiving Jobseeker's Allowance can enter work knowing that they will not lose all their state benefits; and, although as their earnings increase they will lose some benefit, it will not be pound for pound. In consequence, both entering work and working harder once in work will yield a net benefit.

Some international influence on these policies is evident, including the experience of the Netherlands, Denmark, Canada, Australia and New Zealand. But the principal role model has been the US. It is the US that provided the rhetoric and ideological push behind welfare-to-work, although the programmes themselves are much less draconian than the more extreme North American versions. So, for instance, there is no limit on the total length of time a claimant spends on welfare as in the US. The negative income tax was a product of the fertile mind of US Nobel Laureate and economist Milton Friedman, and Bill Clinton's Earned Income Tax Credit was a linguistic forerunner of the tax credit schemes, although in structure the latter do not differ much from the older (British) Family Credit programme.

Family policies

Many of the policies aimed at helping families with children were part of the policies already considered, with the New Deal programmes and the tax credit schemes incorporating special features for dealing with children. However, a number of policies were also directed specifically at families with children, including increases in the universal child benefit under both governments, increases in the allowances to children under 11 in non-working families receiving Income Support, and increases in maternity leave and maternity allowances under the Labour government (Stewart, 2005).

In addition, the Labour government introduced a National Childcare Strategy in 1998 (DfES, 1998). This programme provides funds for the setting up of new nurseries, and, on the demand side, gives families in receipt of tax credits a childcare tax credit worth up to 70% of formal childcare costs. The government also began the Sure Start programme: local programmes of parental support and childcare for families of 0- to 4-year-olds in the most deprived 20% of areas in the country. Finally, the government introduced the Child Trust Fund: a capital grant to all newborn babies from September 2002 (larger for low-income families) to be invested to accumulate until the child reaches adulthood, when it can be drawn on (HM Treasury, 2001a, 2001b).

Was there any EU or other international influence on all these programmes? A small part of the Labour government's actions could be seen as a response to the call of the Lisbon Summit (23-24 March 2000) for Member States to take steps 'to make a decisive impact on the eradication of poverty' and the requirement to set up a National Action Plan for social inclusion (DWP, 2003). But the pressure for a Labour government to do something about the UK's dismal record on child poverty had been there since it was elected in 1997. And Tony Blair's pledge 'to end child poverty forever' was made a year before the Summit in 1999. Although Sure Start has echoes of the US Head Start programme, it is rather different in execution; two of the advocates of the Child Trust Fund were North American, but the rest were British (Le Grand, 2003). Little else shows much signs of outside influence.

National responses to the EU initiatives

The current UK government speaks of the EU in terms of globalisation and internationalism (Sherrington, 2006). This economic vocabulary frames the UK perspective on EU initiatives related to national social policy. The majority of UK government reports emphasise the need to empower people through mobility and skills training, thereby increasing the EU's competitiveness in a global market. It is in this deregulatory, economic language that the UK evaluates EU proposals.

In 'a rising tide lifts all boats' philosophy, the UK government has argued that the best use of EU initiatives is to construct policies to improve the EU's economic standing and competitiveness in a global marketplace rather than to focus on social policy objectives (HM Treasury, 2005). The UK perspective is that matters such as demographic change, social protection and enlargement can all be handled by achieving the objectives of the Lisbon Agenda. It has argued that, by increasing the EU's competitiveness in an international marketplace, the resulting economic growth and prosperity will lead to improved social welfare. Moreover, by concentrating on removing barriers to economic opportunity, the EU will then succeed in its social objectives (HM Treasury, 2005).

The best way of executing EU policy from the UK perspective is through the use of subsidiarity. Under the umbrella of subsidiarity, decisions should be taken at the level that is the closest to citizens and where the most information is available and relevant. Subsidiarity can thus be viewed as a method that embraces transparency, flexibility and the use of stakeholders. An avid proponent of this method of policy formation, the UK has argued that Member State legislation is better suited to dealing with social policy concerns (Blunkett and Johnson, 2005).

This viewpoint makes the UK government wary of EU-level regulation, a concern often mentioned in UK government reports on EU policies. The UK has implemented a number of reforms in social and labour policies, and is anxious about any EU re-regulation that may undermine these achievements. This aversion to heavy regulation explains the UK's preference for the use of the open method of coordination (the OMC) in achieving EU goals and policy objectives. Under this method of soft regulation, the UK is able to interpret EU recommendations in a way that best suits its needs and priorities. Conscious of protecting its autonomy, the UK has consistently preferred the flexibility of the OMC to rigid EU-level regulation. More generally, the UK government, as echoed in its own recent reforms, has a clear and vocal preference for a deregulatory approach to government: barriers to economic growth are removed and its citizens are empowered through education and skills training (Siegel, 2004). The result, in the UK's view, is an increase in economic competitiveness, through which fulfilling social and environmental priorities then becomes possible.

Lisbon Strategy

The UK favours the Lisbon Agenda over any other EU endeavour. The Lisbon Agenda embraces the political vocabulary of the British Prime Minister Tony Blair as it addresses economic growth and opportunity in a global competitive market (Sherrington, 2006). The UK identifies the core objectives of the Lisbon Agenda as improved competition, enterprise and innovation, and trade liberalisation. In the UK Treasury's February 2005 report, the government stated that, by addressing these issues, environmental and social objectives would become obtainable (HM Treasury, 2005).

Despite the UK's dedication to and support for the Lisbon Agenda, it has argued that EU legislation should be the last resort for obtaining its objectives; rather, market-based solutions and initiatives at the national level should have priority (HM Treasury, 2005). However, while the UK has a clearly stated preference for national autonomy and the use of best practice to achieve the Lisbon goals of 'growth and jobs', it sees the need for some EU legislation. Primary areas for EU action include reforming the Common Agricultural Policy and state aid to 'better support the overall goals of the Lisbon Agenda' (HM Treasury, 2005).

The UK has already transposed 70% of the Lisbon recommendations (Secretary of State for Foreign and Commonwealth Affairs, 2005). This readiness to achieve the Lisbon Agenda objectives becomes more evident when contrasted with the EU average transposition rate of 58%. By implementing policy reforms relating to pensions, labour and competition, the UK has demonstrated its commitment to the Lisbon Agenda.

Social Policy Agenda

While the UK has been an ardent supporter of economic reforms such as the Lisbon Agenda, it does not have a similar affection for the EU Social Policy Agenda. This position was particularly true of the Conservative government from 1979 to 1997. Not until the Amsterdam European Council in 1997 did the UK reverse Margaret Thatcher's decision to opt out of the EU Social Chapter (Sherrington, 2006).

However, even after the election of the Labour government in 1997, enthusiasm for EU social policy was distinctly limited. The UK's participation in the EU Social Chapter was linked to the objectives of the Lisbon Agenda and cloaked in the language of creating a 'dynamic, knowledge-based' economy. Former Secretary of State for Work and Pensions, David Blunkett, and Secretary of State for Education and

Skills, Alan Johnson, state in their joint October 2005 paper that the UK's intention is to use economic reform as a means of improving social conditions, not vice versa. The government therefore believes that a high level of employment is the best form of social protection. This belief is based largely on the philosophy of individual responsibility, where society's best course is presenting economic opportunities for individuals to help themselves.

Given this reluctance to use an EU approach to social policy, the UK has encouraged the use of 'better regulation that allows Member States to develop appropriate measures for their individual circumstances' (DWP, 2005a). Rather than focus on EU-wide legislation to address social concerns directly, the UK clearly prefers Member State solutions. Furthermore, the UK has consistently argued that social conditions will more readily improve through deregulation and the opening up of new markets.

Open method of coordination

As the previous outline of the UK's position on EU initiatives on national policies indicates, the UK is an ardent supporter of the OMC. Key concerns for the UK government in policy making are subsidiarity, the autonomy of the Member State, flexibility and transparency. As reflected in various government reports and in the Commission's evaluation of the OMC for social protection and social inclusion, the UK government believes that the OMC incorporates these policy criteria.

The OMC embraces the principle of subsidiarity and the use of benchmarking and best practice in the development of national policies. Subsidiarity, where policy decisions are made at the lowest level of government to best represent the will and need of the people, reflects the preferred UK style of policy making. For example, the government frequently involves stakeholders in its policy formulation to ensure effective policy implementation and outcomes. As the OMC allows for the continued practice of policy making at the lowest level (within the Member State itself), the UK government often prefers the OMC to EU-level regulation (Brye, 1993).[6]

In part, the UK's preference for the OMC stems from the view that it is a positive, flexible means of using Member State experience and evidence to develop policy options. According to the UK government, the OMC provides for more flexibility in policy reforms and implementation, the importance of which is stated in several key government reports (DWP, 2005b; HM Treasury, 2005). The OMC also allows the exchange of successful reforms, which can enable Member States to learn from one another. These attributes of the OMC enable Member States to collaborate and harmonise their policy reforms while also allowing Member States to tailor policies to best suit their individual needs.

However, the UK also values the OMC's ability to ensure the autonomy of Member States over their domestic policies by avoiding the use of EU-level targets (European Commission, 2006h). The UK has used the flexibility of the OMC to implement those parts of EU strategies that apply to its national circumstances, while rejecting others. For example, the UK government disagreed with many of the Commission's European Employment Strategy (EES) recommendations, viewing them as redundant to measures already implemented in the UK (Büchs, 2004). However, while the UK opted out of at least some of the social exclusion recommendations, the UK has introduced an exhaustive list of nationally drafted programmes in its National Strategy Report to the European Commission on adequate and sustainable pensions.

Reflecting its liberal welfare ethos, where responsibility is held at the individual level, the majority of programmes within the National Strategy 'help people to make the most of longer active lives so preventing future poverty' (Blunkett, 2005). This ethos of helping people help themselves is evident in the New Deal programmes that not only focus on those just entering the workforce but also provide assistance to encourage those who have retired early to rejoin (DWP, 2006b).

The UK is wary that, after years of many painful economic reforms in the 1980s (especially where the government fought with labour unions to introduce labour market reforms), EU regulation may force the UK to retreat on these policy gains (Brye, 1993; Blunkett and Johnson, 2005). The Thatcher government believed that its new deregulatory process would have to be reversed under the Social Charter programme (Brye, 1993). Rather than opting out of EU policies (as the Thatcher government did), the current government views the OMC as a way to avoid revisiting politically divisive issues while allowing the government to implement measures in line with EU goals. This position is possible because of the flexible nature of the OMC. Thus, in response to the 2003 Commission report on streamlining social inclusion and social protection, 'the UK defended the retention of National Action Plans [central to the OMC process] because of the visibility it gave to social inclusion within the UK' (Armstrong, 2005). Meanwhile, while the UK government supports the use of streamlining the OMC for social protection policies, it questions whether streamlining will so generalise the policies as to render them of little value (Select Committee on European Scrutiny, 2006).

Finally, the UK government also values the OMC as a means of dealing with the 'democratic deficit' within the EU. The EU is frequently cited as suffering from a democratic deficit because of the lack of separation of powers between, and complicated structure of, EU institutions. Moreover, while the EU is a democratic entity, many believe it is not as democratic as it could be. Addressing this 'deficit' is important to the UK government.

Demographic change

Issues related to demographic change were a focal point at the informal summit at Hampton Court in the autumn of 2005 during the British presidency. The UK recognises that Europe's ageing society is an issue, but, consistent with its general attitude towards social and economic policy, it defines the problem in terms of its impact on the Lisbon Agenda. Demographic change will not be a problem if there is high employment and workers are receiving additional skills to enable them to stay in the workforce longer.

The UK government sees the issue of demographic change, viewed through the scope of global competitiveness, as a matter of employment and its impact on the economy. It believes the EU cannot achieve the Lisbon targets through job growth alone. The EU will also have to focus on skills improvement and lifelong learning to ensure that the majority of society is equipped to contribute to the economy. It is through maximisation of the workforce that the EU will become a global competitor.

Services of general interest

The Commission's Green Paper on services of general interest (SGI) covers market services such as transport, energy, communication and postal services, as well as 'non-economic' social services like health and education. The inclusion of both economic and non-economic services makes SGI and EU regulation of such services a difficult matter for the UK.

The UK government is torn on the issue of SGI. It does not believe that there is a commonly agreed-on definition of social SGI (see Social services of general interest: UK response to Commission questionnaire, nd). Further, it does not believe that there is even a set definition of 'social services'. Therefore, the government does not believe that there should be an EU-wide definition of social services.

While it strongly supports the Services Directive, which will remove barriers to the free movement of goods and services and contribute significantly to the objectives of the Lisbon Agenda, the UK government does not believe in including publicly funded services, such as education, welfare and public health care. Further, the government finds that, in regards to non-economic services, Community intervention in national social services provision is not appropriate, given that the delivery, financing and organisation of public services are for Member States subject to compliance with existing Community obligations. Despite its desire to exclude some services from EU regulation, the UK does not believe that Member States should be able to have a laundry list of exemptions, as it would undermine the objective of the Services Directive.

Proposal on the Services Directive

The UK has been one of the leading advocates of the Services Directive. It was one of six Member States to sign a letter calling on the Commission to support an ambitious version of the Directive. The UK's support for the Directive lies in its intent to remove barriers to the freedom of establishment and the free movement of services, which it views as essential to creating a true Single Market and achieving the objectives of the Lisbon Agenda.

In its Services Directive Briefing, the UK government has a strong preference for using Member State social policy frameworks to avoid any undermining of its own regulatory framework for employment standards. Moreover, the government wants to reserve the right to govern all workers entering the UK. For example, it supports a version of the Directive that ensures that a service company cannot pay wages to posted workers lower than the minimum wage in the host Member State and that service providers from another Member State posting workers into the host Member State must abide by health and safety rules in the host country.

According to the Copenhagen Institute of Economics, the Directive will create £26 billion in new wealth and generate 600,000 new jobs. The UK government has used this report to argue that, under the Directive, the UK will benefit from new sources of labour, increased opportunity for British businesses and greater choice for consumers.

While an ardent supporter of the Services Directive for its potential contribution to the Single Market, the government actively pursued an exclusion for health, education and welfare services, which it viewed as non-economic services. It believes that these services belong at the individual Member State level. The government also put forward amendments during its presidency to clarify in Council text that the Directive does not include matters of taxation, financial services, electronic communications services and networks, transport services and gambling activities.

European Economic and Monetary Union

It is transparent to the British public, the British government and other Member States that the UK will not soon become a member of the Economic and Monetary Union (EMU). While once a source of heated debate in British politics, the EMU is no longer a priority for the Labour government.

The determining factor underpinning any decision on UK membership of the single currency is the national economic interest, as well as whether the economic case is clear and unambiguous. In 1997 the UK Treasury created a five-test framework to help evaluate the economic case. These tests were based on convergence, flexibility, investment, financial services and employment and growth (HM Treasury, 2006). On the morning of the Chancellor of the Exchequer's speech to Parliament on 9 June 2003 on UK membership in the EMU, the Treasury released 18 volumes of evidence supporting the 246-page assessment of the tests on joining the euro (Sherrington, 2006). In this speech the Chancellor stated that the EMU had yet to meet two of the five tests: sustainable convergence and flexibility. Only after the EMU met these tests would the issue be put forward to the British public in a referendum (Sherrington, 2006).

However, while the euro referendum was announced in the Queen's November 2003 speech, it was not included in any of the Chancellor's subsequent pre-Budget speeches to Parliament. In the 2006 Budget, the Treasury did not propose a new assessment of the five economic tests to be initiated, and the current set will be reviewed again in 2007. The matter has slipped off the government's agenda and 'mention of the euro within the UK media and political speeches is at its lowest level for four years' (Sherrington, 2006).

Any decision to forgo the pound for the euro would not be popular with the largely eurosceptic British populace. In 2003, a *Guardian* newspaper poll found that 62% would vote not to join the euro if a referendum was held. Time has not softened this position, as a MORI poll in 2005 found that 55% of Britons would vote against joining the euro. This resistance to joining the EMU was further reflected in the 2005 general elections. The leading political parties (Labour, Liberal Democrats and Conservatives) did not place Europe high in their party manifestos despite the UK then holding the EU presidency.

While some may argue that the UK's reluctance to join the EMU may have negatively impacted on its social policy, in fact it has not. Between 1997 and 2005, the government has increased public sector spending by 65%, a large part of which has been allocated to health care, education and policies that target child poverty (see spending reviews at www.hm-treasury.gov.uk; Flight, 2005).

Enlargement

A strong supporter of enlargement, the UK has consistently supported the accession of new Member States, including the Western Balkans and negotiations with Turkey (Secretary of State for Foreign and Commonwealth Affairs, 2004, 2005, 2006). As further evidence of the UK's commitment to enlargement and the free movement of people, the UK is one of only three Member States that originally lifted restrictions on Eastern European workers.[7]

Seeing an opportunity to improve its own economy, the UK government has claimed that these Eastern European workers are drawn to the UK by its competitive labour environment. The government's position is that these workers are positively contributing to the economy by filling important vacancies.

Conclusions

As we have seen, the UK has a clear position on EU social policy. It believes in the primacy of EU economic policy, as illustrated by the Lisbon Agenda, and that only by getting that policy right can social policy objectives be achieved. Any imposition of EU social policy requirements on Member States is likely to damage economic competitiveness and growth, largely because such requirements will likely assume the heavy regulatory form that characterises the perception of the ESM held by many people in the UK, as spelt out in the first section of this chapter. Despite a series of European Court of Justice (ECJ) decisions that may impact on UK social policy, such as patients' rights to care abroad (which may change the nature of the NHS), the UK perspective is that social policy is best left to Member States.

Is this attitude likely to change soon? Almost certainly not. The government is undoubtedly anxious about, and embarrassed by, its poor record on poverty and inequality. But it is much prouder of its record with respect to relatively high economic growth and relatively low unemployment. The UK government believes that this record will lead to improved social conditions in the long term. Moreover, it believes that welfare-to-work measures to promote employment are the best way to reduce poverty, and that little would be gained – indeed, much would be lost – by adopting regulatory ESMs of social policy. If the economy were to falter, and if mass unemployment were to return, then UK attitudes might change, but until then the UK will remain an economic, not a social, European.

Notes

[1] Aiginger and Guger (2006) prefer to talk of a European socio-economic model rather than a European social model, since they believe that the debate concerns economic issues, such as incentives, efficiency and competitiveness, as much as the traditional social ones of income, education and health. Although we agree with their point, for consistency we shall continue with the old terminology.

[2] David Blunkett is a former Secretary of State for Work and Pensions. Alan Johnson is currently (April 2007) the Secretary of State for Education and Skills.

[3] There is also a growing interest, especially from the Left, in the Scandinavian model as exemplified by Sweden and, increasingly, Finland.

[4] MRSA (methicillin resistant staphylococcus aureus), commonly known as the 'superbug', is used to describe strains of this organism that are resistant to one or more commonly used antibiotics. Patients in hospitals are more at risk to MRSA infection, and the British NHS has experienced a significant rise in the number of patients infected.

[5] For more details on both governments' records concerning pensions, see Evans (1998) and Evandrou and Falkingham (2005).

[6] The emphasis of policy making at the Member State level over the Community level is emphasised regularly in government reports. The UK government has clearly stated its preference for the OMC for policies dealing with pensions, social inclusion and employment (DWP, 2005a).

[7] By 31 March 2006, there were 392,000 applicants to the UK's Worker Registration Scheme, a scheme that requires workers from the eight accession countries to whom transitional measures apply to register when they take up employment in the UK. The figures are not current – any individual who has registered but who leaves employment (or indeed the UK) is not required to deregister.

FOUR

France: defending our model

Bruno Palier and Luana Petrescu

On 29 May 2005, 54.87% of French voters voted against the European Constitution. However, this French 'Non' appears to have been less against Europe in general and more against the perceived threat of an 'ultra-liberal' Europe, which would lead to the loss of jobs to foreign workers (both in France and abroad) from outsourcing, thereby creating a social dumping that would endanger the French social model. Since France views itself as having a strong commitment to 'solidarity',[1] it still believes that it has a 'French social model' to defend. It thus frames its position towards European social initiatives with this preoccupation in mind.

The European social model versus the French model

From a comparative perspective, France can be characterised as having a Bismarckian or 'conservative corporatist' welfare system: most of the social rights are earned through work, by paying social contributions; most of the benefits are contributory (proportional to former wage); most of the financing is based on social contribution; and most of the benefits are managed within insurance funds, where the social partners have a seat (and a say). This system is complemented by various benefits aimed at the 'socially excluded' (such as *revenu minimum d'insertion*, RMI); France now has eight minimum incomes covering 10% of its population and an important set of family benefits, one of them being universal.

This system has experienced many difficulties for nearly 20 years, specifically social exclusion (due to high unemployment and the absence of social rights – especially to health – for those long-term unemployed), permanent financial deficit, high non-wage costs associated with the high level of social contribution and high difficulties in implementing changes, partly because of the system's mode of governance, which includes the representatives of 'insiders' such as wage earners' trade unions.

Within France, French citizens do not associate their social protection system with any kind of conservatism or corporatism (in contrast to the comparative classification of the French welfare system), but generally relate their social model to the concept of solidarity and the Republic. They believe that their model has a universal aim ('universal' in France means equally covering all the French – which it does not – and becoming a model for all human beings). Each time a reform is proposed in France, people view it as an attack on permanent jobs and the *sécurité sociale*, and it is therefore perceived contrarily to the ideal French social model that each French person wants (that is, a permanent job and social security). From a French point of view, everyone should be an insider, thus enjoying full and comprehensive social rights.

Since Jacques Delors was among those who conceptualised the idea of a European social model (ESM) in the early 1990s, the French idea is that the ESM should look like the French social model, perceived as high-quality jobs guaranteed for everyone (with a high minimum wage, high employment protection, high social protection). The idea that the French social model may no longer be functioning or may not be a model for other European countries is just entering French discourse. The more recent electoral results were disturbing: in the 2002 presidential election, the Left dropped out of the second round of the elections; in 2004, almost all French regions were won by the Left from the Right, and, in 2005, the French said 'Non' to the European Constitutional Treaty. These results, in addition to important and sometimes violent social movements (for example, against pension reform in 2003), contribute to a sense that the French model is in crisis.

However, beyond the internal cleavages and debates, a rather strong consensus is against 'ultra-liberal' globalisation and the possible threat that an 'Anglo-Saxonised', market-led Europe would pose for the French (and European) social model. Thus, there is an attempt to fiercely fight the first version of the Bolkestein Directive or any apparent threat to public services, social protection systems and so on. Therefore, the French position towards Europe in general and European social policy in particular is a great vigilance against anything perceived as threatening protected employment and social protection, and a consensus to seek a more social Europe. This consensus, however, is quite formal, since as soon as concrete reforms are offered, fresh opposition and cleavages appear in the French debate – because the definition of what makes a good social protection system and relevant social policies is not only non-consensual in France but also not really discussed.

The ambiguities of the French position towards European social policy probably rely on the discrepancy between the ideal and the reality in France. These ambiguities also derive from the framing of social issues from a very dual perception of economic and social policies as either neoliberal (that is, North American, thus bad) or social (that is, French, thus good). That more than two approaches exist in Europe is not really perceived in France, and some complex issues, such as flexicurity, are just starting to be discussed.

Beyond this paradoxical situation of the French public debate, which may explain the French position at the European level, the French welfare system has implemented many reforms and moves. Since these reforms have usually been poorly explained to the French citizenry and not openly negotiated with the social partners, they are often perceived as neoliberal cutbacks and associated with European economic constraints.

Main principles in national reforms

The French labour market has experienced various reforms since 1997. In the area of active measures, the main programmes represent the *Nouveau départ* (New Start), which helps unemployed people after six months of unemployment. One example of labour market reform is the return to work action plan (*plan d'aide et de retour à l'emploi*, PARE), which introduced in 2000 a new support scheme to help unemployed people find jobs by means of a personalised action plan (*projet d'action personalisé*, PAP). The PARE simultaneously links the payment of benefits to the efforts of jobseekers to find new occupations or undergo a professional reclassification.

These schemes constitute a shift in France, moving labour market policies away from passive measures, which constituted income-maintenance policies, focusing on the protection of jobseekers against job losses, towards active measures seeking to integrate all categories of jobseekers (Daguerre and Taylor-Gooby, 2003). This reorientation – in particular the indication of the new concern for prevention and the contractual relationship between the jobseekers and the public employment service, linking service supplies to the increased requirements for unemployed people – does not fit with traditional French policies but seems to follow the main ideas promoted at the European Union (EU) level. The coherence between the labour market policies introduced since 1997 in France and the EU guidelines is also confirmed by the latest evaluation reports of the European Employment Strategy (EES) (DARES – DGEFPP, 2005).

Moreover, the government has tackled some incentives problems. The main innovation, established in 2001 and extended in 2003, constitutes an income tax credit (*prime pour l'emploi*, PPE), which consists of a state bonus linked to earnings.[2] This measure aims at increasing the incentives for relatively low-paid workers to take up work by granting an income tax rebate or a refund if the income is less than a given level. In addition, the minimum earned income (*revenu minimum d'activité*, RMA) has been introduced in 2003 to compensate for the deficiencies of the RMI. This new measure grants financial assistance to employers hiring people who have received the RMI for more than two years, therefore allowing the employment of people at low costs. The main objectives of this programme are to encourage a return of long-term unemployed into the labour market through financial incentives for RMI recipients. Furthermore, it involves a sorting process among minimum wage beneficiaries to select those able to work. The introduction of the income tax credit PPE, as well as the minimum earned income RMA, belong to a new consensus that considers unemployment as the result of two factors: labour market rigidities and the impacts of social policies that discourage both unemployed and inactive people from searching for and accepting jobs because of disincentive problems. This interpretation has been diffused by Organisation for Economic Co-operation and Development (OECD) and EU Commission reports (Erhel et al, 2005).

However, the influence of the European guidelines remains limited in two main fields: first, the integration of older workers into the labour market and, second, the area of lifelong learning. For the labour market situation of older workers, French policies are inconsistent. On the one hand, the priority is on the development of a more gradual transition from work to retirement, for example, through part-time early retirement schemes such as progressive early retirement (*pré-retraite progressive*, PRP).[3] On the other hand, older workers continue to receive encouragement to leave the labour market through generous redundancy payments that are justified as parallel to activation measures, such as the replacement allowance for employment (*allocation de remplacement pour l'emploi*, ARPE) or the early retirement for selected workers scheme (*cessation anticipée d'activité de certains travailleurs salariés*, CATS). These schemes allow employees over the age of 57 to withdraw from the labour market if they have undergone hard working conditions (for example, assembly line work, night work). These schemes, which are managed by the social partners, appear more attractive than a gradual withdrawal and thus lead to the relative failure of part-time retirement programmes, as several studies have shown (see, for example, Erhel and Zajdela, 2004).

In fact, both the relative failure of part-time early retirement and the creation of new full-time schemes such as ARPE and CATS result from the opposition of social partners and employees, who stress the concept of solidarity in the French social model, as well as the resistance from companies, which perceive competitive constraints when employing older workers. Unions regard early retirement as a matter of social justice and social progress, since it compensates workers who have undergone hard working conditions. For companies, the full-time retirement schemes represent a way of modernising work organisation and renewing the labour force. Additionally, the unemployment benefit system provides functional equivalents to full-time early retirement, which hinders the development of a part-time transition scheme to retirement (Erhel et al, 2005).

As regards lifelong learning, the influence of the EES is also rather limited, despite important organisational reforms and some reports on the subject. Generally, this area is characterised by two main difficulties: first, great inequalities, since the most qualified are most likely to receive further training. Second, the lack of a real lifelong perspective, leading to a reinforcement of the age problem, as older workers are usually under-trained as a consequence of the development of early retirement options since the 1980s. As a first step towards improvement in lifelong learning, the Aubry Laws allow negotiations for making time for further training through individual 'training accounts'; however, this measure has had very little success (CGP, 2001). In the fall of 2004, the social partners signed an agreement (*droit individual à la formation*), which guaranteed 20 hours of vocational training for any worker, whatever his or her employer.

As for pension policies, the French government introduced the Fillon reform on 24 July 2003. Its main attributes included the extension of the contribution periods, irrespective of the employees' occupational sector, and the newly introduced system of bonuses (*surcote*) for retirement after the legal retirement age of 60 and sanctions (*decote*) for retirement before 60, as the required period of contribution would not be complete. By introducing these systems of bonuses and sanctions, the reform Act encouraged people to work longer, thereby corresponding to the EU policy of active ageing. Moreover, since pension regimes were to be aligned in the private and public sectors, this instrument was well in line with the EU objective of equity. Additionally, by developing some supplementary private pension plans as a compensation for the diminution of the public pension, the Fillon reform followed the main orientations of the EU (Erhel et al, 2005, p 230).

The debates on social exclusion in France go back to the early 1970s. Since then, a large academic community, political debates and finally legal Acts have emerged, such as the 1998 Act against social exclusion and the RMI, proposed by François Mitterrand, which came into force in 1988 and represents the occupational integration minimum income that entitles its beneficiaries to benefits in kind, especially for families with children. These developments are additionally reflected in the existence of the Direction générale de l'action sociale and the Direction de la recherche, des études, de l'évaluation et des statistiques, created in 2000 by the then Minister of Social Affairs, Martine Aubry, to work on issues of social exclusion. These measures reveal that research, discourse and institutional capacity building were initiated in France well before the launch of the open method of coordination (OMC) inclusion. Therefore, the French position is that France influenced the OMC inclusion, not the other way round (Erhel et al, 2005, p 231).

National responses to the EU initiatives

During the campaign in France on the Constitutional Treaty, many EU economic issues were discussed, such as the single market, the Economic and Monetary Union (EMU) and the Bolkestein Directive. In the meantime, very few public debates were launched on EU initiatives closer to the social policy areas, such as the EES or the OMC. Therefore, we present the administrative reaction to these policies while reflecting the more open and public debate on the former.

Lisbon Strategy

In France, the Lisbon Strategy is not central to the public debate, for many reasons. One is that when it was adopted (in spring 2000) France was more focused, first on its presidential elections and, second (within the Ministry of Social Affairs), on preparing for the forthcoming French presidency of the EU, where the Nice Summit was prepared. French officials were more concerned about the preparation of the new Treaty and some hard laws than about the development of soft laws. Moreover, when a further step in the Lisbon Strategy was adopted in Barcelona, with some new benchmarks, France was living under 'cohabitation' (that is, the Prime Minister was socialist when the President was right-wing), leading to a confusion about the French position on these targets. People thus heard about the Barcelona Summit only through a political controversy in which Prime Minister Jospin accused President Chirac of taking contradictory positions in Barcelona and back in France. Thus, in the French debate, hearing that France wants to become one of the most competitive knowledge-based economies is relatively rare, as

French investment in research and education is not very high compared to that of its neighbours.

Open method of coordination

French actors usually deny that EU recommendations trigger any direct, causal influence on national policies, instead attributing reforms to national factors. They are more inclined to see France as having influenced European-level policy orientation (Erhel et al, 2005, p 228). Nevertheless, this attitude does not mean that the effect of European integration is null. National actors use various OMC tools in their national policy-making processes. From either their use of OMC instruments or their participation in the OMC, a leverage effect is observable, one that manifests in four ways: the rationalisation of policies, horizontal cooperation, vertical cooperation and legitimisation of procedures.

For the field of employment, covered by the EES guidelines, the National Action Plans constitute an important element, since they bring together all the different measures, their implementation, their evaluation and their evolution. Thus, the Plans provide the opportunity for highlighting the contradictions of diverse policies layered over time, and sometimes an opportunity to rationalise them (Coron and Palier, 2002). National actors view the Plans as helping them to develop some programmes of action and to rationalise national policies, making them a resource that facilitates their work at the national level.

A further leverage effect can be observed in the horizontal cooperation, that is, that between the different ministries. In France, one of the main difficulties is the dispersion of the ministries and the directions each ministry pursues. However, the compilation of the National Action Plans requires the involvement of different parts of the administration, such as the SGCI,[4] the Ministry of Employment and Solidarity and DARES, the service in charge of statistics and studies.[5] Therefore, the EES and in particular the National Action Plans allow the various ministries to cooperate in putting forward policy objectives and simultaneously promote greater coordination among them (Coron and Palier, 2002).

Moreover, the Plans function as a vector of vertical cooperation, that is, that between the Ministry of Employment and actors at the regional and local level, as a result of efforts to strengthen the local dimension of the public employment services. Finally, the OMC can increase the legitimacy of actors and orientations, for example, when the government uses OMC tools, such as the reference to European dynamics or to other countries, to justify unpopular reforms (Erhel et al, 2005, p 237).

A similar picture is revealed in the area of social inclusion policies. French actors see France as the point of origin of EU orientations on social inclusion, not as absorbing EU impacts. However, even though social and professional inclusion is regarded as a national imperative with a long tradition in French policies, external impacts are observable. The National Action Plans – viewed as a resource that facilitates national work and therefore interpreted as the main documents of reference in France – have become a means of rationalising national policies and developing action programmes (Erhel et al, 2005, p 234). Moreover, since the compilation of the Plans is part of the interplay between different ministries, directorates and authorities (for example, the Conseil national des politiques de lutte contre la pauvreté et l'exclusion and the Conseil national de l'insertion par l'activité economique, where administrations, delegates and social partners convene), it has helped improve inter-ministerial coordination. Therefore, by commonly creating the Plans, the collaboration between the different ministries, especially the Employment and Social Affairs Ministry and the Economic and Financial Affairs Ministry, has been increased (Erhel et al, 2005).

The use of OMC tools has also led to a move towards decentralising the social exclusion programmes at the departmental level. Furthermore, the threat of poverty, especially with the arrival of the new Member States, has become an important issue. National actors use OMC arguments to legitimate unpopular national reforms. However, OMC inclusion is not well known in France, despite a sensitisation campaign in 2003. At the level of government services, the OMC information has been circulated at technical meetings and via the intranet of the Ministry of Employment, Social Cohesion and Housing (Ministère de l'emploi, de la cohesion sociale et du logement, 2006a, p 7).

In the field of pensions, while French policy makers do not claim to have influenced European orientations, they argue that the OMC for pensions occurred too late in France for consideration in the reform process. Indeed, the pension reforms had already been announced long before the launch of the OMC, and their necessity has been demonstrated by several experts' reports as well as by the work of the Pensions Advisory Council (Conseil d'orientation des retraites, COR), introduced in 2000 and reinforced with the national pension reform in 2003. The OMC for pensions has therefore played an accompanying role in the French reform process, confirming the French pension situation as already assessed by the ministries and the COR. However, the OMC for pensions is well known by policy makers and the social partners (Ministère de l'emploi, de la cohesion sociale et du logement, 2006a, p 2). Similar to other policy fields, policy actors use the OMC tools to serve national interests; the main objective is preserving a sufficient level of pensions and defending this stance at the EU level to preserve the French pension system.

Services of general interest

The French authorities welcome the publication of the Green Paper on services of general interest (SGI). They stress the importance of SGIs for the cohesion between Member States and their citizens, as well as for the bond between citizens and the EU. In particular, they regard the services of general economic interest (SGEIs) as key factors for keeping the economy functioning well, completing the European internal market and keeping the EU territory economically attractive.

Moreover, to keep SGEIs in the EU satisfactorily sustainable in the long term, the French authorities consider a cross-cutting legal instrument at the EU level essential. This instrument should help to create an optimal interface between the EU approach and each Member State's method of implementing SGEIs. However, the French standpoint emphasises the principle of subsidiarity, leaving the authority to determine, organise and finance SGEIs for the Member States, according to their cultural, historic and geographical features, and management method.

For the institutional framework, the French authorities view the creation of a regulator at the EU level as problematic because, among other things, it would not improve the implementation of EU rules according to the specific features of every Member State (Représentation permanente de la France, 2003). However, while the French authorities see the responsibility for identifying the economic or non-economic nature of the services as lying with the Member States, the French national funds in charge of the mandatory health insurance (CNAMTS, CCMSA and CANAM)[6] want the character of the SGI clearly differentiated by a 'permanent criteria body' at the EU level. Nevertheless, the systems of health insurance, as well as their financing criteria, should depend on the exclusive competence of the Member States, leaving the EU the role of mere cooperation and coordination of the social protecting systems (CNAMTS et al, 2003).

Demographic changes

As regards the Green Paper on demographic change, France welcomes the Commission's initiative to engage in a debate about demographic change and the need for promoting a new solidarity between the generations. The ongoing ageing of the European population constitutes a major threat to economic growth, employment, social cohesion and the long-term development of the Lisbon Strategy. The EU has already introduced a number of measures in response to Member States' demographic changes, especially in the framework of the EES and structural policies aimed at modernising the social security systems.

Nevertheless, the French authorities suggest that the EU pays more attention to the economic consequences of these demographic changes. In particular, the effects on the dynamic of the European economy, its innovative capacity and its financing structures should be major topics of the debates within the Green Paper on demographic change. These debates should, however, allow for the specific national situations and should benefit from the diverse experiences and measures introduced in the Member States. In this context, the French authorities propose a number of objectives: better economic and social inclusion of young people, policies supporting older people, a better reconciliation of work and family, and the promotion of women's rights. Moreover, the French authorities propose to cooperate in demographic analyses and to launch an annual conference on demographic developments (Représentation permanente de la France auprès de l'Union Européenne, 2005, pp 2-3).

The representative of the French social security institutions to the EU (REIF)[7] agrees that the balance between work and family responsibilities remains a major explanatory factor for fertility. In this context, both companies and public authorities should support policies providing childcare and childcare access (REIF, 2005, pp 3-4). Furthermore, REIF confirms the rejuvenation of the host populations through immigration, as well as the positive economic effects of the increased demand for goods and services and thus for labour. Therefore, REIF stresses the importance of integrating migrants into the labour market, teaching and educating them, and giving them access to housing and social and health care services (REIF, 2005, pp 7-9). As for integrating young people, REIF stresses not only socialising them through access to recreational and cultural structures and insuring their health and academic education but also supporting parents in their educational function. Moreover, it emphasises that better integration of young people necessarily occurs through their acquisition of knowledge and skills that allow them to find and keep jobs. To this end, individual student support needs improvement, teaching methods need modernising and access to the knowledge society needs advancement (REIF, 2005, pp 9-11).

Debate on the Economic and Monetary Union, EU enlargement and the Services Directive

This section deals with France's stance on the EMU, the enlargement issue and the proposal on a Services Directive. This grouping of topics most appropriately reflects the discussion in France. Indeed, the proposal on the Services Directive, the EMU and EU enlargement represented major topics during the campaign for the referendum on the European Constitution in May 2005. In reply to President Chirac's announcement of a referendum, France's political parties opened up the debate around European integration, linking the European Constitution to topics such as Turkey's membership and the liberalisation of services.

After the early 1990s, European integration included the adoption of the single currency and imposition of the Maastricht criteria. With Maastricht, French governments were obliged to control the public deficit (including the social security deficit) and the inflation rate, and therefore to control the growth of social expenditure. After 1992/93, the Maastricht criteria meant including the retrenching of social expenditure in the strategy of reducing public expenditure and public deficits. Commitment to the single currency led to the imposition of sectoral reforms in unemployment insurance in 1992, in the pension system in 1993 and in health care in 1995 (the highly controversial Plan Juppé). One could argue that these reforms would have been necessary without Maastricht (since the major problems are not linked with Europe but with domestic developments), and that Maastricht was a scapegoat for avoiding blame. However, the Maastricht process apparently helped the government, at least rhetorically, to impose reforms otherwise seen as not feasible, especially in conservative corporatist welfare systems. Consequently, the Maastricht criteria (and thereafter the Stability and Growth Pact, SGP) have been perceived in France as one of the causes of the retrenchment of the French welfare state, to which the population is very attached. Thus French citizens have an increasingly negative perception of the EU.

However, no common stance exists within the political debate on these issues. Instead, divisions between the parties and cleavages within the mainstream parties of both the Left and the Right have obstructed a coherent European policy standpoint. On the mainstream Right, European integration has always been a difficult question. While the Christian Democrat Union pour la démocratie française has demonstrated an element of consistency in its broadly pro-integrationist position, the Rassemblement pour la République revealed discrepancies in its European outlook. Similarly, the Union pour la majorité présidentielle supported the ratification of the EU Constitution with a great majority, although some internal voices (representing republican, social, national and Gaullist ideas) opposed it (Dupont-Aignan, 2005). On the anti-establishment, non-mainstream Right, the Front National, Philippe de Villier's Mouvement pour la France, the Mouvement nationale républicain and Charles Pasqua's Rassemblement pour la France all opposed the EU Constitution, in line with their eurosceptic positions.

On the mainstream Left, the referendum gave rise to Socialist Party disagreements on policy orientation and personalities (Hainsworth, 2006). Although it officially supported the Constitutional Treaty, different strands within it, such as the Nouveau parti socialiste or the Nouveau monde, openly campaigned for a 'Non' vote. Likewise within the Greens, which officially supported the EU Constitution, 'Non' supporters promoted their views actively on joint platforms. Similarly to the Right, the smaller, less mainstream Left parties opposed the EU Constitution. These included the Parti communiste français, the Ligue communiste révoltionaire and the Lutte ouvrière.

All in all, the 'Non' camp represented a mixture of different small-scale parties and strands of mainstream parties. The issues that were put forward in this context included the liberalisation of services in the EU through the European Commission's Bolkestein Directive, which was seen more as prioritising corporate profits than as protecting workers' interests and that symbolised further unemployment, social dumping and a threat to France's social model. Consequently, concerned about its possible assistance to the 'Non' camp, President Chirac successfully intervened and impeded the introduction of the Directive (Hainsworth, 2006, p 204).

Furthermore, EU enlargement appeared to constitute a new battleground for the eurosceptics in their opposition to Europe. Despite a major consensus on the need for EU incorporation of Central and Eastern European countries, concerns related to potential economic dilution and further unemployment were raised. During the referendum campaign, the principle of free trade was interpreted by the 'Non' campaign as the servant of an ultra-liberal Europe and therefore more in line with the 'Anglo-Saxon' model.

As to EU enlargement, the French government follows a rather careful line to the 'transitional restrictions' on the movement of the labour force from the new Member States. As the first two-year transition period expired on 1 May 2006, the government declared its intention to pursue a gradual controlled lifting of the restrictions on the free movement of workers from the eight new Member States. This partial opening concerns seven sectors characterised by a short supply of labour. For the rest, France has maintained restrictions, requiring work permits for those wanting to work on French territory (Ministère de l'emploi, cohésion sociale et du logement, 2006b).

Further topics that helped promote opposition to the Constitutional Treaty included unemployment through outsourcing, economic liberalism versus a social Europe, and the safeguarding of public sector services. The fear of the 'Polish plumber', representing low-paid workers (from new EU Member States) who might take over French jobs, has played a central and effective role in the campaign against the European Constitution.

However, the cleavages around European topics have been related to the traditional Left–Right divide based on socio-economic classes. This new division, already evident during the Maastricht referendum, is rooted in a culture of protest and opposition, a culture that involves defending social gains in a nationalistic setting (Perrineau, 2005).

Conclusions

On the whole, France has experienced a wide range of reforms, including active labour market measures or instruments aimed at making work pay. In both areas, the indication of the new concern for prevention and the contractual relationship between jobseekers and the public employment service seems to follow the main ideas promoted by the EU. Similarly for pensions, new instruments aimed at the extension of working and contribution periods, the alignment of pension regimes for the private and public sector and the diminution of public pensions follow the main EU orientations. For social inclusion policies, although they have a long tradition in France, some external effects triggered by OMC tools are observable. In contrast, the influence of the European guidelines remains somewhat limited for both the integration of older workers into the labour market and lifelong learning measures. The relative failure of part-time early retirement and the creation of new full-time schemes result from the pressure from social partners, companies and employees who stress the competitiveness constraints or the concept of solidarity as a principal part of the French social model.

However, a look at the French policy-making process makes it difficult to observe any direct effects of European recommendations.

Nevertheless, this difficulty does not mean that no link exists between the national and the EU level. European orientations do not necessarily appear as causal influences on national policies but rather as resources for national actors. Even though French policy makers deny the European influence, national actors have used various OMC tools in their policy making at the national level. This use of OMC instruments has triggered a leverage effect that is manifested in four different ways: the rationalisation of policies, both horizontal and vertical cooperation, and the legitimisation of policies. As for EU initiatives such as the Green Papers on SGI and demographic changes, the French government fully supports these approaches. But despite the agreement to improve the cooperation between Member States and the EU in these areas, France emphasises the principle of subsidiarity, leaving the authority of policy determination at Member State level according to the cultural, historic and geographical features of each Member State.

Still, topics such as the EMU, EU enlargement and the proposal on the Services Directive are rather controversial in France. Within the framework of the EU referendum campaign in May 2005, divisions between the parties and cleavages within the mainstream parties are clearly noticeable. The main divisions around European issues have been less related to the Left–Right division than to the vision between those who see themselves as having benefited from the European integration (white-collar employees and professionals working in the open private sector, elite members) and those who perceive themselves as having lost something (for example, blue-collar workers).

Speculating on the future positions of the French government concerning the ESM, Europe and social policies is difficult. Traumatic political events have occurred frequently in France since the early 2000s, showing the degree to which France is shaken by the consequences of its adaptation to a globalised economy (Culpepper et al, 2006). The electoral campaign before the referendum showed two clear trends: marketisation and the refusal of the social consequences of globalisation – two elements very often associated with European economic integration – and a certain movement back to protectionism (protecting French firms, French jobs, French social protection schemes). This last trend is reinforced by the current Prime Minister (Dominique de Villepin, 2005-), who argues for 'economic patriotism'.

In this context, one may fear that France will always defend the status quo, contesting reforms that it views as threatening its social model and as reinforcing the EU 'bureaucracy' (often denounced by the former

Prime Minister J.P. Raffarin) and/or as favouring a neoliberal Europe. Unless the EU proposes alternative solutions to 'ultra-liberal' ones, any progress towards more EU institutional involvement in social policies and reform may be extremely contested in France. The only hope for change is if the developments at the European level could be presented in France as having been instigated by French officials.

Notes

[1] Another term for solidarity is *fraternité*, one of the three words associated with the Republic: *liberté, égalité, fraternité*.

[2] This premium is made up of a variable part, depending positively on the time worked and negatively on the wage, and a fixed part, taking into account the family circumstances (number of children, spouse's income and so on) (see Ministère de l'emploi et de la solidarité, 2001).

[3] This scheme allows employees aged over 55 to transform their full-time job into a part-time position with a wage of 80% of their previous salary. The costs of the early retirement are then shared between the employer who, since May 1997, pays a financial contribution depending on the proportion of the hard-to-place unemployed people hired instead of the retired worker; the Union Nationale pour l'emploi dans l'industrie et le commerce (UNEDIC), by giving older part-time workers an allowance amounting to 30% of the previous wage; and finally the retired older worker who accepts a reduction of 20% of their monthly wage.

[4] General Secretariat for Inter-ministerial Cooperation on European Affairs, which has recently become the SGAE (Sécrétariat général des affaires européennes).

[5] Direction de l'animation de la recherche, des études et des statistiques.

[6] National Health Insurance Fund for Salaried Workers (CNAMTS), Central Fund of the Agricultural Mutual Insurance System (CCMSA), National Health and Maternity Insurance Fund for Non-salaried Workers in the Non-agricultural Professions (CANAM).

[7] REIF (Représentation des institutions françaises de sécurité sociale auprès de l'Union Européenne) brings together the French general scheme, including CNAMTS for health insurance, CNAV for retirement, CNAF for the family and ACOSS for collection, as well as occupational schemes in charge of compulsory social insurance

(CCMSA for the agricultural scheme, CANSSM for the mining industry scheme, CANAM for health insurance for self-employed professionals, CANCAVA for retirement pensions for craftspeople and ORGANIC for retirement pensions for those who worked in private trade and industry).

FIVE

Italy: between indifference, exploitation and the construction of a national interest

Stefano Sacchi

Italy is generally considered a warm supporter of the European integration process. While the positive attitude of Italians towards the European Union (EU) has somewhat declined in recent years, it remains high enough to allow justifying and legitimising domestic strategies of state modernisation through pointing at EU membership imperatives. Paradigmatic in this regard is the impressive sequence of (mainly social policy) reforms in the 1990s, allowing Italy to enter the Economic and Monetary Union (EMU) through the main door. Still, Italy's implementation record is poor, and its participation in day-to-day EU-level decision making is generally haphazard. Social policy is no exception.[1]

This chapter shows how Italy's official response to various recent social policy initiatives has generally been inattentive, left to the voluntarism of civil servants commanding few organisational resources and lacking political guidelines – and legitimacy – on which to orient their actions. In some cases, however, Italy has responded to social policy initiatives, either criticising them or trying to influence their development at EU level. This response has occurred when the envisaged initiatives were at odds with the government's domestic policy agenda, or when they could be exploited precisely to promote and legitimise this agenda. Whether this type of response implies a path-shift in Italy's participation in the EU social policy process, or merely signals a cynical attitude on the part of the government that ruled Italy for the first half of the current decade, is an interesting question that will be covered in the conclusions to this chapter.

The European social model versus the Italian model

A founding Member State of the European Community, Italy has always been considered (and has considered itself) as one of the most europhile Member States, with a generally positive attitude towards first the European Community and then the EU. Between the mid-1970s and the late 1990s, a positive evaluation of Italy's membership in the European Community/EU ranged between 60% and 80%, a higher figure than the European average (about 60%).[2] However, while still a majority, this consensus has since been declining. This downward trend, only momentarily reversed in the early 2000s, possibly due to the initial enthusiasm for the euro, has now brought Italian citizens' attitudes towards the EU roughly in line with the European average (both the EU25 and the EU15): 56% of Italian respondents think that Italy's EU membership is a good thing, in contrast to 54% in the EU25 and 55% in the EU15 (Eurobarometer, 2005). By the same token, the share of Italians who think that Italy's membership is neither good nor bad has risen to 24% in 2005, again in line with the European average.

Roughly the same story, albeit with different timing, applies to the question of whether Italy has on balance benefited from being a member of the European Community/EU: the share of Italians replying in the affirmative was about 70% in the early 1990s, as opposed to 50% in the Community as a whole. However, the figure dropped to little above 50% in the early 1990s, and has remained constant, matching both the EU25 and the EU15 average (Eurobarometer, various issues). Thus Italy can now be seen as the average EU country when it comes to its citizens' attitudes towards European integration, a shift from its own record of support of the integration process and clearly at odds with its self-perceived europhilia.

When it comes to social policy, Italian citizens' attitudes towards the EU tend to be more positive than the EU average. In 2005, the share of Italians who thought that the EU played a positive role in various aspects of social policy (fighting unemployment, pensions, health care) was higher than the EU average (both in the EU25 and the EU15); conversely, the share of those with a negative perception of the EU's role in such fields was lower than average (Eurobarometer, 2005).

However, these perceptions tend to vary with the economic cycle. More stable are Italians' attitudes towards competence allocation between the EU and the national level in social policy, where they share a rather favourable attitude towards joint EU–national decision making. Respondents in the affirmative to the question of whether the fights against unemployment and against poverty should be decided jointly with the European Community/EU rather than by the national government alone have always been a large majority in Italy (a higher figure than the European average), and this share has actually increased with time while remaining stable in the EU. Even for health and social welfare issues, the social policy domain in which European citizens are less keen on joint decision making, the share of Italians favouring shared competences has always floated at about 50%, as opposed to between 33% and 40% in the EU. At the same time, however, Italians give less weight than Europeans overall to the fights against unemployment and poverty as EU priorities.

This positive outlook on the role of the EU in social policy is reflected in lower-than-average fears about the possible detrimental impact of European integration on social protection at the national level: only about 40% of Italians are worried that 'the building of Europe' might lead to the loss of social benefits, while about 50% are not worried, as opposed to reversed shares in the European population as a whole, both in the EU25 and in the EU15 (Eurobarometer, 2005).

Italy and the European social model

The concept of a European social model (ESM) can be understood in two ways: either as the social model of the EU as a political entity in its own right or as the basic commonalities between the social models of the EU Member States, as highlighted by Saari and Välimäki (see Chapter Fourteen, in this volume).[3] As for the former understanding, consistent with citizen support for EU intervention in social policy, the stance of Italian governments has generally favoured expanding the competences of the EU in this field, both extending the catalogue of activities falling within the EU's scope of action, and loosening the majority principle towards the adoption of qualified majority voting. Such a consistent stance, however, has generally been one of passive support.

As for features in common with the other Member States, Italy's social model displays two characteristics partly at variance with most of the other Member States. On the one hand, it has a higher income inequality than the EU25 average; on the other, it shows some distinct imbalances in the allocation of social protection expenditure across functions. The former feature dates back to the early 1990s, when, as a consequence of the economic downturn, the income distribution changed and never returned to a more egalitarian shape. As for imbalances within the social protection system, while the share of social protection expenditure from GDP (gross domestic product) is only slightly lower than the EU25 average, considerably more Italian resources are devoted to risks connected with old age than in all other Member States, while needs connected with the family, unemployment, housing and social exclusion tend to remain dramatically under-covered (Eurostat, 2007). Social protection is thus service-lean; unemployment benefits are available only to a segment of the active population – those employed in the primary labour market under a standard contract – and their replacement rate is low except for workers dismissed from large companies. Anti-poverty policies are scanty, mainly geared towards two categories: elderly people and disabled people. Italy shares with Greece and Hungary the questionable peculiarity – within the EU25 – of not having a minimum income scheme as a safety net for the poor.

Main principles in national reforms

Italy has undergone many important social policy reforms over the past 15 years (Ferrera and Gualmini, 2004; Madama and Maino, 2005; Jessoula and Alti, 2007). Some of them have emerged as a direct result of European hard law, such as European Court of Justice (ECJ) rulings or the adoption of Council directives. Others are, at least partially, the result of EU-level influence, in the form of soft law, on social policy models and procedures. Most of them, however – in the 1990s in particular – are connected to an overarching form of pressure exerted by Italy's EU membership: the need for public finance restructuring and cost containment. This need has accompanied Italy since the early 1990s, not only in the government's pursuit of EMU membership but also within the constraints of the Stability and Growth Pact (SGP).

The constraints imposed by prospective and then actual EMU membership have been powerful stimuli for successive governments to push through measures of welfare retrenchment and rationalisation. Opportunities opened up for a strategy of welfare reforms geared to achieve three objectives: public finance soundness, social equity and efficiency. These were the guiding principles of the two main health care reforms and four pension reforms of the past 15 years. Cost containment was not a factor in labour market reforms, which were guided instead by compliance with EU law and by the principles of labour market flexibility and of enhancing the skills and capacities of individuals. By the same token, social assistance reforms came about through recognition of social protection imbalances.

The first reforms to be enacted, those of the Amato government in 1992, were strictly linked to the Maastricht criteria. The Amato pension reform occurred after the lira was first devalued and then pulled out of the Exchange Rate Mechanism (ERM) of the EMU, in the currency crisis following the French and Danish referenda on the Maastricht Treaty. Expenditure on public pensions had reached 12.8% of GDP in 1992 and was projected to reach almost a quarter of Italy's GDP in 2040. The Amato reform introduced several restrictive changes by, among other things, elevating the retirement age. It also harmonised the rules for public and private employees. Although the reform's savings effects were not at all negligible, the gradual phasing in of some of its provisions (a concession to trade unions) and, critically, Italy's adverse public finance conditions made the Organisation for Economic Co-operation and Development (OECD), the International Monetary Fund (IMF) and the European Commission advocate a new, more incisive, pension reform.

After the first Berlusconi government failed to pass a reform bill in 1994, a technical government led by Dini managed to enact a new pension reform in 1995. The reform, negotiated with the trade unions, modified the pension formula, with a shift from earnings-related to contribution-related pension benefits for new entrants in the labour market, the provision of a flexible retirement age and the tightening of eligibility conditions for a seniority pension. Although often cited as a model reform all over Europe, the Dini reform could not immediately produce all its potential savings effects on the state budget because getting the consent of the trade unions called for its gradual phasing in. But the EMU deadlines were approaching, particularly after Prodi (who succeeded Dini as Prime Minister in 1996) failed to convince Spanish Prime Minister Aznar to join forces to obtain a more flexible interpretation of the EMU convergence rules. Thus, to get into the EMU without delay, the Prodi government had no choice but to proceed to yet another pension reform. However, the proposals put forward by a commission of experts triggered so harsh a confrontation within the ruling majority that Prodi could only adopt minor changes that still entailed an immediate budget saving of 0.2% of GDP, thus making an important contribution to Italy's compliance with the EMU requirements.

As a consequence of the Amato, Dini and Prodi reforms, the long-term financial sustainability of Italy's pension system is now much less of a problem than 15 years ago: public pension expenditure as a percentage of GDP is projected to increase by roughly two points over the next three decades. However, two problems remain: one of sustainability in the short run, before the Dini reform gets thoroughly phased in; the other of adequacy of pension benefits for the younger cohorts to whom the Dini reform applies, under which benefits are calculated with the new, less generous contribution-related formula. To deal with both problems, the Berlusconi government in 2001 obtained a parliamentary mandate to make adjustments to the public pension pillar, and to introduce reforms to enhance the supplementary pension pillar so as to compensate for lower future pension benefits. The government explicitly framed the latter issue in terms of the adequacy of the pension systems objective agreed on at the Gothenburg European Council in 2001 (see Presidency Conclusions, Gothenburg, 15 and 16 June 2001, para 43).

As the reform languished for some time, Berlusconi seemed willing to propose, as a priority for the Italian presidency of the EU in 2003, some form of EU-wide cooperation on pension reform, harder than the one envisaged under the open method of coordination (OMC) for pensions. Two governmental advisors put forward a draft proposal for a 'Maastricht for Pensions', which, however, did not cut much ice either at the national or the EU level, so the issue was dropped. After making changes to its original reform bill, the Berlusconi government passed its pension reform under a confidence vote in 2004. It introduced more stringent rules on seniority pensions and retirement age, to be phased in by 2008, thereby creating an annual saving of 1% of GDP between 2010 and 2025. Due to the change in government in 2006, however, the fate of the reform as it stands is uncertain, with the trade unions calling for its reversal, and the government unable to forego the savings it entails.

Health care has undergone various reforms in Italy during the 1990s. Their framing has been cast more in terms of potential effectiveness and efficiency gains than of compliance with EU requirements or pressure. However, the need to abide by the SGP has spurred institutional innovation in this policy field, so that a domestic stability pact was devised for keeping tight reins on health care expenditure. Since the establishment of a universal national health service in 1978, health care in Italy has entailed shared competence between the state and the regions. Due to the absence of fiscal federalism until the late 1990s, health care financing has always been plagued by the common pool resource problem. In 1992 the Amato government enacted a thorough reform of the national health service, both in organisational and financial terms. Another reform was enacted in 1999. The organisational content of these reforms is clearly unrelated to EU-level policy dynamics; their cost-containment content, however, is closely linked with the efforts first to qualify for EMU membership and then to respect the SGP.

Sweeping labour market reforms, which were less directly related to immediate public finance imperatives and less driven by cost-containment motives than pension and health care reforms, have been enacted in Italy since the mid-1990s. However, European policy models and procedures have undoubtedly had a great impact on domestic reforms of employment policies and the labour market in general.

To secure the trade unions' support – needed to adopt massive budgetary manoeuvres and to signal a renewed commitment to joining the EMU to international markets and agencies – the governments of the 1990s relied on acting in concert with the social partners. This strategy led to the signature of social pacts, including labour market policy reform.

The European Employment Pact (EEP), signed by the social partners and the first Prodi government in 1996, entailed the institutionalisation of an ongoing strategy of local development, based on territorial pacts and area contracts, best practice later adopted at the EU level with the provision of territorial employment pacts. This strategy of activation of local resources, path-breaking in the Italian context, was first devised when the European Commission took a negative stance towards the traditional policy intervention toolkit for fostering investments in the South (the 'extraordinary intervention for the Mezzogiorno'), considered as unlawful state aid in Commission decision 93/254/EEC of 9 December 1992.

Likewise stemming from the 1996 Social Pact, an important labour market reform was enacted in 1997. It moved towards the Essen priorities and, more importantly, the pillars of the renewed European Employment Strategy (EES), being defined precisely in those months. The reform envisioned making the labour market more flexible, relaunching part-time and temporary contracts that until then had had very little success in Italy, due to the many legal limitations on their use. The reform also envisioned an overall rebalancing between passive and active labour market policies; the end of public monopoly over employment services – a development accelerated in anticipation of the ECJ ruling in *Job Centre II* (Case C-55/96) that would declare such a monopoly incompatible with Treaty provisions; and the devolution of powers to the regions and provinces for active labour market policies and employment services.

As for the EES, its impact on Italy's employment policy field has been rather important: on the one hand, its emphasis on active labour market policies and the importance of employment services has influenced Italian policy, to the extent that expenditure on active labour market policies surged from 25% of total outlays for employment measures in 1996 to more than 50% in 2003 (Ministero del Lavoro, 2005). On the other hand, the procedural requirements of the EES have induced a noticeable change in Italy's policy-making modes and structures in employment policy, contributing to institutional capability building within the Italian public administration, particularly those related to planning and monitoring tasks (Ferrera and Sacchi, 2005). Moreover, the second Berlusconi government, elected in 2001, extensively used the EES and the commitments stemming from it to justify its 2003 labour market reform, introducing innovations in employment services and new flexible work contracts.

We have already sketched the peculiarities of the Italian welfare state in the family and social inclusion policy field. While tight budget constraints left precious little room for new costly programmes, the issue of poverty and social exclusion came to the political fore in the mid-1990s. The European influence was felt, albeit only at the level of ideas: the experts comprising the commission advising Prodi over welfare reform were clearly aware of the 1992 recommendation on sufficient resources, the work within the poverty programmes and the EU-level policy discourse on social inclusion and family support. They put forward proposals to reform family benefits and introduce a fully fledged anti-poverty strategy. Only some of the proposals were adopted, including a pilot minimum income scheme started as a two-year experiment in 1998. The experiment was then extended for two years, until the Berlusconi government discontinued it in 2002 (Sacchi and Bastagli, 2005). Means-tested maternity and family benefits geared towards those women or families who have no access to insurance-based family benefits were also introduced in 1998.

A long-awaited law reforming Italy's social assistance sector was enacted in 2000. While its adoption is unrelated to EU-led motives, its drafters were aware of the ongoing EU debates steered by the European Commission that would lead to the launch of the social inclusion process in 2001. The latter, however, has had very little impact on Italy's social inclusion policy, either on the policy model itself or on policy-making modes and procedures, for two main reasons (Ferrera and Sacchi, 2005). One is a 2001 constitutional reform that by devolving competence on social assistance policies to the regions has thoroughly upset the framework set up only a few years earlier and taken away from the central government basic coordination resources. The other is the Berlusconi government's policy agenda, which framed social inclusion policy mainly in terms of work inclusion and scattered interventions aimed at raising transfers for select groups, such as elderly people.

National responses to the EU initiatives

Reviewing Italy's official responses to various EU social policy initiatives in recent years is no easy task. Italy's favourable attitude towards EU involvement in social policy all too often translates as a substantial lack of interest towards specific initiatives, coupled with little organisational investment, manifesting as poor implementation at the national level and little documentary evidence. The level of politicisation of the concrete issues involving social policy initiatives at the EU level is negligible, as opposed to declarations of principle on the ESM, thus parliamentary debate is non-existent.

Moreover, the initiatives that this chapter covers occurred almost entirely within the tenure of the second and third Berlusconi governments (June 2001–May 2006), which, in terms of policy action, can be considered the same government, particularly for social policy. Generally speaking, the government made little political or organisational investment in EU social policy initiatives, and official responses to such initiatives were left to voluntarism on the part of a restricted circle of liaison officers between Rome and Brussels, with little or no guidance from political echelons of the government. Only on a few occasions has Italy reacted, or even acted, at the highest political level, to influence EU social policy initiatives or launch new ones. This has mainly happened when such EU initiatives ran counter to the Italian government's policy priorities, as can be seen with the EES, or could be used in order to further domestic reforms, such as in the case of pension policy coordination. Once reforms at the national level have passed, interest in the specific initiatives has faded.

The old Lisbon Strategy

For the social aspects of the old Lisbon Strategy, the most remarkable official reaction on the part of Italy was the 2002 Italian impact assessment of the first five years of the EES. After having analysed the impact of these five years on Italy's employment policy, the Italian report criticised some aspects of the EU strategy itself, offering proposals for improving it. The new EES adopted some of these proposals after 2003, before the whole Lisbon Strategy was changed in 2005. This impact report marked probably the first time that the Italian government reacted in an official document (rather than passively) within the context of the EES and the Lisbon Strategy. The report highlighted some specific limits of the EES, such as an excessive emphasis on active labour market policies, important but not sufficient per se. Moreover:

> The reference to public employment services as the ideal
> tool for solving the structural problems of the Italian labour
> market has also been excessive. The limit of the strategy has
> also been the lack of concern for the need for a geographical
> network and the interaction with other types of economic
> and social policies. ... [L]ittle consideration has been given
> to the regional aspect of Italian employment problems and
> the interaction between implementing employment policies
> and the socio-economic context of the different territories.
> (*Impact evaluation of the European Employment Strategy. Italian
> employment policy in recent years: Impact evaluation*, Final report,
> nd, pp 4, 8)

The proposals of the Italian government had been both general and
specific. The most important general proposal was that of better taking
subsidiarity into account within the EES, considering more thoroughly
the differences among Member States, their institutional peculiarities
and their priorities. An important consequence of this approach was that
the exclusive focus on public employment services needed loosening,
allowing each Member State to define the mix of public and private
in employment services (one of the most important aspects of the
2003 Italian labour market reform), and the reconsideration of the
proactive and preventive approach. In addition, the report called for
a better consideration of two issues that would in 2003 be included
in the list of employment guidelines within the new EES: undeclared
work and regional economic disparities.

Still in the context of employment policy, the stance of the Italian
government towards quality in work is noteworthy. In June 2001, the
Commission issued a communication proposing various dimensions
to the concept of quality in work and indicators for assessing such
dimensions, for adoption at the Laeken European Council of December
2001 (European Commission, 2001a). In the October 2001 White
Paper on the labour market, the government enthusiastically upheld
the proposal:

> The Italian government will support at the Laeken
> European Council the integration of the principle of quality
> at work within the objectives of the EES, in the logic
> of mainstreaming. This should not be a mere formalistic
> support, but rather the convinced application of a new
> method in order to debate with the regions, local authorities

and the social partners the issues of work and employment.
(Ministero del Lavoro, 2001, pp 59-60)

However, the White Paper reframed the quality issue almost uniquely
in terms of the flexibility and desegmentation of the labour market and
the fight against undeclared work – the two priorities of government
employment policy at the time. More generally, the White Paper
defined quality in work in terms of the individual's labour market
chances, thus disregarding all the other dimensions in favour of
emphasising the flexibility side of flexicurity (Ministero del Lavoro,
2001, p 59). The Laeken Summit approved a list of indicators based
on 10 dimensions proposed by the Commission.[4] The issue of quality
in work thus received a broad connotation in the Community debate,
encompassing the 10 dimensions, and was included as the second of
the three overarching objectives of the new EES. Italy then tried to
reduce the salience of quality in work, to the extent that the Joint
Employment Report 2003/04 noted that Italy's 2003 National Action
Plan for employment did not explicitly cover such issues (Council of
the European Union, 2004).

The new Lisbon Strategy

Under the new Lisbon Strategy, Member States were asked to submit
a three-year National Reform Programme by October 2005, focusing
on growth and jobs and taking into account 24 integrated guidelines
divided into macroeconomic, microeconomic and employment
guidelines. The Italian National Reform Programme, called the Plan
for Innovation, Growth and Employment, focuses on five categories
taken as priority goals, against a background of monetary and financial
stability:

• extending the area of free choice for citizens and companies;
• granting incentives for scientific research and technological
  innovation;
• strengthening education and training of human capital;
• upgrading tangible and intangible infrastructure;
• protecting the environment (Dipartimento per le Politiche
  Comunitarie, 2005).

Italy's National Reform Programme displays some interesting
features. Foremost, by focusing only on the microeconomic set of
guidelines, it implicitly challenges the current articulation of the

integrated guidelines: it considers macroeconomic guidelines as subsumed under the stability programmes (and thus already accounted for), while considering employment as endogenous to all the other priorities (and thus stemming from growth induced by pursuing the envisioned priority actions). Furthermore, Italy's plan challenges the appropriateness – or indeed the meaningfulness – of setting quantitative targets for Research and Development (R&D) spending, irrespective of a country's production and economic structure, and prods the European Commission into a more careful consideration of policies aimed at combating Italy's North–South structural divide (identified as a productivity divide), within a suboptimal currency area such as the EMU.

Given the challenging character of Italy's National Reform Programme, it is little wonder that the Commission was fairly critical of the document in its January 2006 Annual Progress Report, lamenting that Italy's programme did not set targets or timetables, and insisting on a more orthodox approach. The October 2006 Implementation Report (prepared after the Berlusconi government had lost power to the government led by Prodi) reverted to an orthodox stance, also covering employment policy issues (Dipartimento per le Politiche Comunitarie, 2006a).

Open method of coordination and the Social Policy Agenda

Italy, with Belgium and France, was one of the warmest supporters of the application of the OMC in the field of pensions (Natali, 2006). On the one hand, the exchange of information on pension reform strategies gave Italy a chance to present itself as a best practice example, thanks to the Dini reform. On the other hand, the OMC on pensions was perceived to be helpful for tying up loose ends and problems within the Italian pension system. In this vein, during its EU presidency in 2003, Italy made some proposals for a strengthened procedure that should have led to closer coordination, in between soft and hard law, on pension reform.

As we have seen, the Berlusconi governments' pension reform was stalled in Parliament in 2003. The government then tried to use Italy's presidency semester to upload the pension issue to the European level, subsequently exploiting the external constraint to pass the reform bill. Two advisors to the government (the Prime Minister's economic advisor, and Italy's representative to the Social Protection Committee, SPC) drafted a note on a 'Maastricht for pensions', sketching out a proposal for a strengthened procedure within the OMC for pensions, entailing sanctions for those Member States that would not reach country-specific targets (Brunetta and Cazzola, 2003). Prime Minister Berlusconi seemed keen on an even more structured process, resting on stringent criteria, for the retirement age in particular.[5] However, the proposal did not garner much sympathy from other Member States, and was therefore dropped after the Brussels European Council of October 2003. For the same reasons, during its presidency the Italian government supported the idea of streamlining the social protection and social inclusion processes within a single OMC process, to place the OMC on pensions on a firmer base (Consiglio informale dei Ministri del Lavoro e degli Affari Sociali, 2003).

Given the streamlining, and to get input from the Member States and the stakeholders on the OMC on social protection, in February 2005 the European Commission prepared a questionnaire on the experience of both the social inclusion process and the pension reform strategy process, to be returned by June 2005. In March 2006, the Commission issued a document with the results.

Italy's response to the questionnaire is rather unbalanced (with the exception of the discussion on the role and significance of indicators and targets), insofar as it considers only the social inclusion process, making no reference to the OMC on pensions. The response thereby signalled a lack of Italian interest following the 2004 pension reform. Likewise, for social inclusion, the Italian response tended to be incomplete. While Italy responded that 'the OMC is playing a strategic role in defining a new welfare policy, above all in the field of social inclusion', in the aftermath of the sweeping constitutional reform that devolved social assistance competences to the regions, not much evidence is given about the alleged positive impact of the OMC on such a governance system, except for quoting the White Paper on welfare, a fuzzy document issued by the government in 2003 that is of limited help for policy purposes, and for stating that 'the OMC can be a very positive tool in a country such as Italy characterised by a heterogeneous development in the social inclusion processes'. The most interesting proposals in the Italian response come in the field of indicators – the need for an indicator of absolute poverty in particular – and for working methods, with the idea of creating thematic working groups within the SPC and boosting comparisons between Member States facing similar challenges. Some critical remarks are also made in the Italian response on peer review exercises and the Community action programme for social inclusion, with a view to improving their functioning.

All in all, the overall impression is that while the field of pensions was neglected after the reform passed, that of social inclusion tended to be left to the voluntarism of liaison officers, both in Rome and Brussels, who had to cope with the OMC exercise with little guidance or interest from top civil servants or political leaders. The same can be said of Social Policy Agenda 2005-10, on which Italy took no official position. Still, the informal position of the Italian representatives in Brussels was that, as opposed to the Social Policy Agenda 2000-05 (praised as a wide-ranging document involving all the stakeholders), the new Social Policy Agenda was not much more than a checklist of Commission objectives in the social field.

Demographic change

In March 2005, the Commission issued a Green Paper on demographic change, with a questionnaire on various aspects of the phenomenon, facing the challenges related to them, and the possible role of the EU in coping with such challenges. Italy issued a response in October 2005, prepared by the services of the Welfare Ministry and of the Ministry for European Affairs, with contributions from other ministries and stakeholders.

The Italian document presented the challenges originating from demographic change, as they were perceived in Italy, and reviewed the governmental policies of the past few years covering – directly or indirectly – such challenges. However, the document seems to be stuck halfway between a general analysis of the overall challenges and a catalogue of policy responses coming from the recent Italian experience, so that no innovative policy solutions to be adopted either at the Community or the Member State level are envisioned. In particular, the possible role of the EU in coping with demographic change is not clearly sketched out, at least in terms of actual measures or initiatives, except for the recognition of the mutual learning potential entailed by common analysis and information exchange at the EU level: given that some Member States (Italy, Spain, the new Member States) are now experiencing problems that other Member States (France, the Scandinavian Member States) once faced, more knowledge of policy responses adopted by the latter could be helpful for the former.

Services of general interest

In 2003, the Commission issued a Green Paper on services of general interest (SGI), inviting feedback from public authorities and all stakeholders. As Italy did not react to the Green Paper, no national official position is available.[6]

Taking stock of the responses, in May 2004 the Commission issued a White Paper on SGI, in which it announced a future communication on social and health SGI. The White Paper stated that further work in this area would account for EU policies related to social and health service provision, and would also describe the ways in which social and health services are organised and function in the Member States. In the interests of so doing, the Member States – through their representatives in the SPC and the High Level Group on health services and medical care – would share in the preparation of the communication(s).

A group of volunteers within the SPC drafted a questionnaire on social SGI, asking the Member States to reply voluntarily to various questions about the organisation and financing of social SGI in the national context, national definitions of social SGI, the influence of EU law on domestic social SGI, and the envisioned steps at the EU level. Given the nation-specific understanding of the concept of social SGI, Member States were free to choose those specific instances of social SGI they deemed appropriate.

Italy's response was drafted by a team of civil servants from the Welfare Ministry, with the help of a leading expert in EU social security and labour law. It focused on social services and health care services, describing the organisation of provision and financing methods in Italy. The document then provided definitions of social SGI from Italian law that could be of some help in clarifying the concept at the EU level.

The document also reviewed the two cases of potential conflict between European Community law and national arrangements in the field of social SGI (apart from the *Job Centre* case, on public monopoly of employment services): the *Sodemare* case (Case C-70/95) and the *INAIL* case (Case C-218/00). In both rulings, the ECJ upheld the existing regulations. In *Sodemare* it upheld the decision of the region of Lombardy to allow only non-profit organisations (NGOs) to participate as providers in the social assistance system that gives these parties the right to public reimbursement for their services; in *INAIL* the ECJ upheld the public monopoly in mandatory insurance against work injuries. Italy's response to the questionnaire then provided information on a case of balancing the market and solidarity principles in the field of social SGI, that of Law 328 of 2000 on social assistance reform. This regulation, in particular, allows only non-profit providers to participate in managed competition mechanisms, thus complying with the ECJ orientation in *Sodemare*; moreover, it states that the criteria of choice between providers in managed competition must be based not on the lowest price of service provision alone, but rather on the best mix of cost and quality.

Finally, the Italian document favoured the adoption at the EU level of a social SGI definition that should, however, not lead – at least for the time being – to harmonisation. Rather, it called for the application of the OMC to social SGI, with the help of a dedicated committee. Once again, Italy's official position apparently boils down to be that of a restricted circle of liaison officers acting from a voluntaristic élan, receiving no instructions from higher echelons within the public authority or from political leaders.

Proposal on the Services Directive

Italy has officially backed the Commission proposal on a Services Directive since its early stages. In the past some concerns about the effective applicability of the procedures entailed by the provisions on posted workers were voiced within the civil service (the Welfare Ministry in particular). Moreover, Italy joined the majority of the Member States in rejecting Article 23 of the original proposal, about the moot issue of the need for preventive authorisation for health care treatments. Nonetheless, Italy's official position, as posted on the website of the Ministry for European Affairs, has always been full backing of the Directive.

Italy's supportive stance of the Services Directive proposal includes both the Berlusconi government and the Prodi government beginning in May 2006. However, the object of their support has been different: the original proposal, before amendment by the European Parliament, for the Berlusconi government; the modified proposal, agreed on by the Council of Ministers on 29 May 2006, for the Prodi government.

The Minister for European Affairs in the Berlusconi government, Giorgio la Malfa, considered the original proposal 'a great step forward in the application of the Treaty', and highlighted the link between the Directive and economic growth. Such a stance was fully shared by the Minister for European Affairs in the Prodi government, Emma Bonino, a Left libertarian and former European Commissioner, who as a European Member of Parliament voted against the agreement, considering it too watered down. However, as a member of the Prodi government, she had to mediate between the various stances within the majority supporting the government, comprised of political parties belonging to all the major European parties. The outcome of the mediation has been that of supporting the draft proposed by the Austrian presidency and agreed on in May 2006.

Italy's official position on the Council-approved draft was therefore one of support: 'The Italian delegation has upheld the presidency's compromise, considering that a further delay would not have made the various positions any closer, by now entrenched, of the different Member States. Albeit within its limits, the approved proposal can still prove an effective instrument in order to create an internal market for services, with positive effects on growth and employment' (Dipartimento per le Politiche Comunitarie, 2006b). Given the reactions to the deal struck in the Council of the far-Left parties within the Prodi government, opposition to the Directive, finally approved on 12 December 2006, will likely re-emerge in the implementation stage at the national level. Whatever happens, the original text of the Services Directive would have opened a rift within the parliamentary majority of the Prodi government, whereas the compromise allowed it to postpone potential conflict.

European Economic and Monetary Union

Italy has backed the EMU project since its very early stages and indeed has used it as an external constraint for passing difficult reforms – maybe even for state-rescuing purposes. The government used this strategy particularly during the 1990s, leading to an impressive cycle of reforms that brought Italy's primary budget surplus from being near zero in 1990 to about 4% of GDP in the late 1990s and early 2000s. This momentum slowed down in the 2000s, and the adverse economic cycle and the government's economic policy decisions led to a virtually null primary budget surplus (as a percentage of GDP) in 2005. Italy, foreseeing the possibility of being in the same situation of non-compliance with the SGP as France and Germany, supported the suspension of the excessive deficit procedure against these two Member States during its presidency of the Council in November 2003.

No serious debate on the social consequences of the common currency has taken place, despite substantially increased prices of some goods and services whose consumption is fixed in the short run and typically pertains to the middle classes. This increase has been accompanied by a sizeable horizontal income redistribution across socio-economic classes, to the advantage of self-employed people, managers and retired people, and the disadvantage of workers and employees. Whether economically justified or not, a perception of impoverishment spread among the middle classes.

Given the sluggish economic growth, some political forces within the coalition supporting the Berlusconi government, and most notably the

Northern League, started to ride the tiger, postulating a link between the euro and economic problems and sometimes even advocating a return to the lira, as in the summer of 2005. The Berlusconi government seemed increasingly keen on blaming the euro, to the extent that during the 2006 election campaign Prime Minister Berlusconi occasionally used anti-euro arguments to harm his competitor, Romano Prodi, under whose government Italy had joined the EMU in 1998. Prodi has always defended Italy's EMU membership, pointing out positive effects such as reduced and stable mortgage interest rates. Still, the share of Italian citizens who believed that adopting the euro has been advantageous dropped from 57% to 43% between 2002 and 2005, as opposed to a more modest drop (from 54% to 51%) in the Eurozone. Conversely, in the same period the share of those who believed that the change has been disadvantageous soared in Italy (from 29% to 43%), as opposed to the lesser rise in the Eurozone (from 32% to 39%) (Flash Eurobarometer, 2002, 2005).

The Prodi government emerging from the May 2006 elections included as Finance Minister a former member of the European Central Bank board, Tommaso Padoa Schioppa. This government seems more determined than its predecessor to abide by the SGP, and reduce its budget deficit (4.1% of GDP in 2005).

Enlargement

Italy has always favoured enlargement. In 2001/02 the Berlusconi government repeatedly advocated the rapid expansion of EU membership to Romania and in particular Bulgaria. The Prime Minister and his foreign ministers also envisioned an EU including Turkey (a stance harshly opposed by the Northern League, a core party in the ruling coalition) and, prospectively, Russia.

Still, when it came to the free movement of workers after enlargement, Italy introduced transitional provisions provided for by the Accession Treaty and thus applicable to all new Member States except Cyprus and Malta.

Data published by the European Commission show that before the latest enlargement Italy had been virtually unaffected by work-flows from the 10 new Member States: only 0.1% of the Italian workforce came from these Member States (European Commission, 2006g). However, in one of its latest decisions before the new majority coalition took over in May 2006, the Berlusconi government decided to prolong the transitional regime until 30 April 2009, under the same restrictive provisions adopted for 2004-06 (Welfare Ministry, 2006). The new government reversed this decision at the end of July 2006, allowing complete freedom of movement for workers of the 10 new Member States (Ministero della Solidarietà Sociale, 2006).

Following the 2007 enlargement, however, work-flows from Bulgaria and in particular Romania are likely to be substantial, as Italy is among the preferred destinations of nationals of these countries (Traser, 2006). The Italian government has thus introduced one-year transitional provisions regulating access to the labour market for nationals of Romania and Bulgaria (Ministero dell'Interno and Ministero della Solidarietà Sociale, 2006). These provisions apply for dependent workers, while there are no restrictions on self-employment. Also, some sectors such as agriculture, hotel and tourism services, domestic work and care services, construction, engineering, managerial and highly skilled work, and seasonal work were opened up as of 1 January 2007.

Conclusions

This chapter has dealt with Italy's responses to EU social policy initiatives over a time roughly coterminous with the tenure of the Berlusconi governments in the 2000s. An explicit comparison with the stances of previous governments is hampered by the concentration of important EU social policy initiatives in the past few years – and would fall beyond the scope of this chapter. Still, the Berlusconi governments' substantial lack of interest in social policy issues, apart from a labour market flexibility agenda, is well documented at the national level and clearly translated into Italy's inactivity at the EU level (Ferrera and Sacchi, 2005). This lack of interest came on top of these governments' somewhat diffident, when not overtly hostile, attitudes towards the EU, a new feature in Italian politics. However, this overall attitude did not rule out exploitation of EU-level initiatives as legitimisation mechanisms for the government's domestically driven policy agenda or as flagships for its actions (for example, corporate social responsibility). On the other hand, Italy has created a novel capacity for critically analysing EU-level decisions, highlighting their glitches and pitfalls from the Italian perspective and suggesting improvements, as is clear in the impact evaluation of the EES, or Italy's National Reform Programme.

Can all this indicate a new approach, one that is more aware and less across-the-board acquiescent towards EU-level decisions? Or does it simply show a cynical attitude, in which the government deems EU activism useful for furthering the domestic policy agenda but then discards it once its usefulness is over? While the latter is most probably the more realistic account, there may still be signs of discontinuity with a past marked by a shallow europhilia, never willing or able to discern which courses of action are in Italy's national interest, and which are not, and should be opposed within EU decision making.

Even in the new, difficult environment characterised by reduced support for the integration process, some clear signs of Maastricht (and post-Maastricht) fatigue, and a new domestic constitutional architecture that makes nationwide policy coordination laborious, Italy can still look at the EU as a precious resource for legitimising reforms, while paying extra attention not to fall victim of the perverse game most joyfully played by national governments in contemporary Europe: that of claiming credit for the EU's achievements, while shifting blame for unpopular decisions to the supranational level and in so doing eroding the legitimacy bases of the EU itself.

Late 2000s, Italy is far from being out of the woods: public finance is in distress again, with a primary budget surplus close to zero and by far the highest debt to GDP ratio in the Eurozone; the Italian welfare state is still strongly unbalanced, to the benefit of old risks and the neglect of new social risks and risk categories; and the new constitutional structure is conflict-prone and conducive to policy stalemate and clashes over competence between the state and regions. Against this background, the EU can still be an agent of state modernisation, in the framework of a more aware, structured Italian membership, rather than one marked by unthinking acquiescence, all too eager to pass the buck whenever possible. This is possibly the best turn Italy can give the EU: more serious participation aimed at integrating its own national interest within a deliberative arena, refraining not only from turning to the supranational level only for instrumental purposes but also from acquiescing to everything, while implementing little. In this regard, looking at Italy's response to EU social policy initiatives in the past few years can teach us a lot, for better or, more probably, for worse.

Notes

[1] See Giuliani (2006a) on Italy's poor implementation record and its causes. For a thorough discussion of the lights and shadows of Italy's European policy see Giuliani (2006b). Giuliani and Piattoni (2006) analyse the current predicaments of Italy's membership of the EU, while the contributions in Fabbrini and Piattoni (2007) provide a refreshing view on Italy's role in EU decision making across various policy fields, challenging the widespread view that sees Italy as a consistently weak actor in EU decision making.

[2] See Eurobarometer (various issues). Question: 'Generally speaking, do you think that Italy's membership of the European Community/EU is a good/bad thing; neither good nor bad; I don't know'. Data have been available since 1973.

[3] Such commonalities can be taken to be: an extensive level of basic social protection against a wide array of social risks for all citizens; a high degree of interest organisation and coordinated bargaining; and a more equal wage and income structure than in non-European contexts (Ferrera, 2002).

[4] The 10 dimensions agreed on at Laeken were: intrinsic job quality; skills, lifelong learning and career development; gender equality; health and safety at work; flexibility and security; inclusion in and access to the labour market; work organisation and work–life balance; social dialogue and worker involvement; diversity and non-discrimination; and overall work performance.

[5] However, it is to be noted that the Welfare Minister, Roberto Maroni, tried to obstruct the proposal, for reasons linked to the electoral constituency of his political party, the Northern League. Since the majority of early retired people are in the more industrialised Northern regions, where the Northern League receives its core support, provisions intended to raise the effective retirement age were not well received by the leaders of such a party.

[6] Comments came from two Italian regions: Regione Calabria, in its capacity as coordinator of the regions on labour and vocational training issues, and Regione Friuli Venezia Giulia.

SIX

Poland: redefining social policies

Irena Wóycicka and Maciej Grabowski

Defining Poland's official position towards European social policy initiatives is difficult, because as a result of parliamentary elections in the autumn of 2005 the right-wing Law and Justice Party took power and announced a radical political transformation. The former left-wing liberal government declared support for modernising the European social model (ESM), focusing on employability and vocational activation. Instead, the present ruling elite seem to emphasise the need to 'maintain the European social model based on solidarity'. This emphasis may signify a major shift in the approach to adapting Polish solutions to the concept of the ESM: a weakening of the commitment to implement modernisation processes in favour of maintaining existing solutions in Poland.

The slogan of social solidarity, as opposed to liberalism, was one of the pillars of the parliamentary campaign of the winning party. However, so far the present government has not incorporated this position into its social programme. Thus social policy is at an intermediate stage, that is, abandonment of the earlier approach is not accompanied by a clear indication of the scope of change.

The European social model versus the Polish model

The social model of Poland, shaped by the reforms of the transformation period, is a mix of conservative-corporate elements and elements of a liberal model (on typologies, see Esping-Andersen, 1999). The model comprises both the Bismarckian tradition of the 19th and early 20th centuries, and the most contemporary reforms dominated by liberal trends.

Poland's spending on social protection at about 23-24% of GDP (gross domestic product) is roughly at the average European level. Social transfers equal around 18% of GDP and are among the highest in the European Union (EU). Spending is dominated by cash benefits, replacing employment earnings (pensions). By contrast, expenditure on social services is very low (Wóycicka, 2003). The main reasons for the relatively high poverty rate experienced by Poland are unemployment and poor economic activity. The past 16 years in Poland have been characterised by an increasing number of economically inactive citizens, high unemployment and fast differentiation of income. These outcomes obviously result from a rapid and exceptional restructuring of the economy, with the overlapping of processes generated by the globalisation of the economy and those of the transformation of the system.

The Polish social policy system does not fulfil the EU modernisation requirements and is not capable of facing the challenges of Poland's major social problems: the lowest employment level among Member States, the highest unemployment and the resulting scale of poverty. These challenges should make Poland one of the major advocates of modernising the social model towards employment growth. Although on the level of declarations Poland has expressed a commitment to these reforms in documents relating to the Lisbon Strategy and the European Employment Strategy (EES), even the governments that declared the need for change achieved poor results because of insufficient social support or a lack of strong determination.

Poland's EU membership has fulfilled years of the Polish people's aspirations and ambitions, to whom being an integral part of European culture was a cornerstone of national identity. It is thus obvious that Poland views the EU not only in pragmatic categories but also as a community of values: 'Within the EU one can speak of common values, which set apart the models applicable in EU Member States from the models applicable in other of the world's regions. These values are: social solidarity, meaning assistance to the people in difficult circumstances, social dialogue and acceptance that social policy should be a prominent consideration in carrying out the economic policy' (Ministry of Foreign Affairs, 2005, p 1).

When assessing Poland's internal policy, the lack of equilibrium between the economic and social spheres should be underlined. It was not long ago when parliamentary electoral politics were dominated by issues relating to the need to improve the competitiveness of Poland's economy and to consolidate public finances. Strong emphasis was placed on modernising the social system, foremost understood as a means of reducing social expenditures, reducing labour costs and providing stronger work incentives. But the government underestimated the issues of social cohesion. A definite reform programme under the Hausner Plan (Council of Ministers, 2003) was not implemented, as the reforms met with strong opposition even from the government's supporters.

A radical political change resulting from the recent parliamentary and presidential elections has changed domestic policy priorities. The former emphasis on restoring financial equilibrium and improving economic competitiveness has diminished. However, no actual progress is observable in the policy on combating poverty and social exclusion. Meanwhile, the pressure to maintain the existing social solutions has increased, especially with regard to maintaining costly group privileges, that contributes to the present low employment of older people at a productive age, and high, non-wage labour costs.[1] Thus, following the recent parliamentary and presidential elections, Poland's policy has deviated from a commitment to the modernisation of the social model despite general verbal political declarations suggesting otherwise.

A key role in the Polish social model is that of the subsidiarity principle, reflected in the Constitution. It impacted on the country's administrative reform, which led to the establishment of three autonomous levels of local administration. It was also manifested in the special position of families as social policy subjects.

Universal legislation limits the autonomy of the respective levels of state administration, which does not cause any particular formal restrictions in fulfilling Poland's EU membership commitments. However, in practice the reform process partly depends on voluntary cooperation between local and central government institutions.

Poland holds the view that within the EU one cannot speak of a single, supranational social model. Poland's sceptical attitude towards harmonising the ESM results from fears of the noticeable pressure from certain older Member States to increase social spending and labour costs. Awareness of the immense gap in economic development and the need for catching up give rise to Poland's concern that the imposition of uniform social standards within the EU will make its economic competitiveness deteriorate. Stressing the rule of subsidiarity, Poland clearly opposes any attempts at harmonising social policy beyond its present frames. In particular, Poland is opposed to the idea of harmonising tax and contribution rate burdens. Poland emphasises that proposals regarding social policy should take into account the specific issues of certain Member States in which GDP is markedly lower than the EU average. The need to accelerate the economic growth of those Member States, something that is in the interest of all EU members, is in conflict with expectations of higher social spending. In this context Poland also points to their proportion of social spending to GDP as similar to the EU average (Ministry of Foreign Affairs, 2005).

Consequently, the Polish government regards the open method of coordination (OMC) as a means for Member States to attain jointly agreed objectives, promote learning from best practice, and mobilise national activity in reducing the development gap. Still, Poland clearly opposes pursuing the jointly agreed objectives by means of shifting from 'soft' to 'more rigid' methods of coordination (Ministry of Social Policy, 2006).

As one of the poorest EU Member States, Poland perceives EU solidarity as a chance for robust support in making up for the results of immense neglect, particularly in its infrastructure. Nevertheless it stresses that 'from the perspective of the Member States representing a lower level of economic development, an extremely vital role in implementing the Lisbon Strategy falls to the European cohesion policy' (Council of Ministers, 2005a).

Main principles in national reforms

Over the past 16 years Poland has moved from a social model characteristic of the communist system to one rooted in democracy and the market economy. The prime driving forces behind changes to Poland's social model since 1989 have been the political and economic changes taking place in the aftermath of the collapse of the communist system. Political reforms concerned the creation of the foundations of a democratic system, such as individual rights, civil liberties and political liberties. They also extended to the process – rooted in the constitutional principle of subsidiarity – of decentralising the public administration.

The shape of the Polish social model was also strongly impacted on by economic reforms. Changes to the economic system aimed at restoring the market economy (economic liberty, privatisation, macroeconomic stabilisation and market competition) led to significant reductions in public sector employment. The role and importance of state-owned enterprises was radically reduced: they became subject to restructuring and privatisation. The social services that the public enterprises and public administration once provided have been largely privatised or liquidated.

Global processes have also influenced changes in the social model, particularly the rapid technological changes connected with Poland's catching up in technology terms and increasing external competition.

In addition, almost from the outset of the transformation process Poland was in regular dialogue with such international institutions as the International Monetary Fund (IMF), the World Bank, the Organisation for Economic Co-operation and Development (OECD), the International Labour Organization, and the European Communities, all of which played a significant advisory and funding role in carrying out social reforms. Poland also received technical assistance from many countries in Western Europe.

The reforms created the social mix model, dominated by partly privatised social security insurance, which provides employment-related benefits (pensions). Family allowances are means tested and, along with welfare assistance, serve as benefits for alleviating poverty. The share of social spending – in the form of benefits addressed to the needy – is low. The social services sector is poorly developed, burdening families with many social policy responsibilities.

The process of the changes in the social model over the past 16 years comprises three phases (see also Golinowska, 2005).

From 1989 to 1993: this was the period of the transformation crisis, the rapid growth of unemployment and a decrease in incomes. In social policy it was a period of building the social safety net for the population most threatened by the transformation process. During these first years of transformation, new labour market and social assistance institutions emerged and the first pension reform was carried out. Its major element was the new benefit formula, linking the amount to the duration of employment and the amount of contributions (plus their regular indexation).

The basic objective of the reforms was to counteract the rapid increase of both unemployment and poverty. The institutions and the precepts of reforms from those years dealt both with local traditions and with the experiences of Western European countries. For instance, the changes in programmes for the employment of disabled people consisted of combining French solutions with institutional traditions shaped before the Second World War. The new Act on Social Assistance was related, in an updated form, to the 1923 Social Assistance Act, particularly for the major role it gave social workers and social work. The pension reform process went in the direction of a greater insurance element in its benefits formula, drawing on Continental models of social insurance.

From 1994 to 2001: this was the period of planning and designing market-driven reforms. Even though the governments of the time were from the Left and the Right ends of the political spectrum, the reforms were liberal. Concepts from both the World Bank and the OECD helped shape these reforms.

After several years of discussions and presentations of various concepts, the government enacted a pension reform, aimed at dealing with the challenges facing an ageing population. The reform's main features consisted of introducing a multi-pillar system, partially privatised, and replacing the earlier pay-as-you-go system in the public pillar by a notional Defined Contribution system.[2] The reform was based on a general idea that the World Bank has promoted since 1994 and was later modified. The World Bank (1994) also provided significant support for organisational and intellectual development of the reform and its public promotion in Poland. The Office of the Government Plenipotentiary for Reform of the Social Security System (1996-99), established for the purpose of developing and implementing pension reform in Poland, also received technical assistance from the Swedish government.[3]

In the other reforms of these years, the impact of the external environment was more general, with a greater intellectual input than organisational or financial. The reform of unemployment benefits was driven by internal considerations, such as high unemployment, fiscal pressures, low effectiveness and insufficient funding of active labour market policies. The reform radically limited access to unemployment allowances, both to cut down the disincentives to work, and to reduce unemployment. After 1994, family benefits also became subject to fundamental reforms. These reforms were driven by many different, frequently contradictory and inconsistent processes. First, a traditional Bismarck-type model of social benefits appeared inefficient given the massive unemployment and rising poverty in the first stage of transformation. To better handle the benefits, the government needed to decouple benefit eligibility from employment status. Second, fiscal pressures led to savings in social expenditures, in turn leading to income thresholds defining eligibility for benefits (Balcerzak-Paradowska et al, 2003).

From 2001 to 2005: this is a period dominated by the impact of the EU accession on Polish social policy. As an accession country, since 2003 Poland was encompassed by the OMC on employment and social policy. The Polish government and the European Commission drafted the Joint Assessment of Employment Priorities in Poland (JAP) in 2001, and in 2003 the Joint Inclusion Memorandum (JIM), which constituted the first in-depth assessment and recommendation for Polish social policy in the context of European integration.

This period was characterised by social reforms concentrating on reformulating the existing social policy model towards a more active social policy. This process has also been reflected in the strategic documents and legislative activity of the Polish government (Ministry of Social Policy, 2003). However, despite covering many areas of social policies – social assistance, employment policy and the positioning and role of non-governmental organisations (NGOs) – the legislative changes were not fundamental. Recognition of the role of activation programmes came mainly under the impact of internal problems – high unemployment persisting even at a time of high economic expansion and related poverty. On the other hand, they also reflected an increasingly European edge of social policy. This resulted in abandoning the 'Polish' model of social assistance in favour of more universal approaches, in reality constituting the first step towards setting up a standard of minimum income guarantee.[4]

National responses to the EU initiatives

The documents allowing for reconstruction of the attitude of Polish authorities to the EU initiatives come from the period before the recent parliamentary elections. The only official document relating to the EU initiatives is the National Reform Programme for 2005-08, adopted in December 2005, with a delay due to the election calendar (Council of Ministers, 2005b). Consistent with the integrated guidelines of the Lisbon Strategy, the National Reform Programme also includes seven employment-related guidelines. Although the proposals address the fundamental challenges of the Polish labour market and improving skill levels, the proposed implementation measures, and sparse specification of the planned reforms, raise serious objections (European Commission, 2006i). The document can hardly be regarded as decisive on the shape of reforms to be carried out by the government, given that a newly formed government had written it in haste. Moreover, the new government has not yet presented any detailed implementation plans.

Mid-term review of the Lisbon Strategy and renewed Social Policy Agenda

In February 2005, the Commission published its position on reforming the Lisbon Strategy. The former Polish government adopted *Poland's position for the mid-term review of the Lisbon Strategy* (Council of Ministers, 2005a). This position fully accepted the reorientation of the Lisbon Strategy through combining the issue of macroeconomic stabilisation with the improvement of the competitiveness of the economies and employment growth. The Polish government supports the philosophy of the renewed Lisbon Strategy in relation to the social model, which is no longer a constitutive factor of the new Lisbon Strategy. The Polish government did not see the dangers that emphasising economic growth, employment and macroeconomic equilibrium may have an effect on limitations in achieving the social policy objectives. The former government emphasised the imperative of public finance consolidation, accelerating economic development and improving the situation of the labour market. Therefore, Poland was in favour of reshaping the Lisbon Strategy. In its view, only under conditions of such fast growth would sustaining the ESM be possible.

Poland's position towards reforming the Lisbon Strategy fully corresponded with its government's internal policy objectives, which strived for (albeit without a noticeable effect) carrying out a comprehensive reform of public finances through reducing social spending. The position also corresponded with Poland's economic interests in completing the building up of a common market for labour and services. Poland, like the rest of the new EU Member States, was covered by a transition period for free access of workers to European labour markets.

In the scope of building up the European market, the position of the Polish government accentuates the need for completing the construction of an internal market, especially for services and labour. Poland emphasised formulating migration policies as best facilitating the movement of employees within the EU. It stressed the need for effectively using European labour resources, particularly young people, and expressed the hope for the early elimination of the existing administrative barriers to the movement of the labour force. Within this context, Poland underlined that immigration from non-EU countries should only supplement the European labour market.

In its *Position for the mid-term review of the Lisbon Strategy* the Polish government emphasised the need to bolster employment-oriented policies. Notable in the Polish position was the emphasis on the need to modernise social protection to eliminate barriers to employment. The Polish position also clearly stresses the need for better handling of social expenditure to reduce public spending and the tax wedge.

In its position on the new Social Policy Agenda, the former Polish government presented its main national priorities. Its position on the European Social Policy Agenda is dominated by the view that social inclusion policy should be pursued primarily through ensuring access to jobs. Nonetheless, Poland was somewhat reticent about measures that would result in strengthening income support to those in need.[5] Obviously taking into account the situation on the labour market,

Poland wished to have the new Social Policy Agenda include actions to support employment of people with low educational status, pointing out that efforts in this direction so far have proved insufficient to ensure the employment of most of them.

Open method of coordination

In March 2005 the European Commission sent Member States an evaluation questionnaire on the open method of coordination (OMC) in the area of social protection. Poland responded that the OMC was useful primarily in formulating strategic policy goals, mainly by defining common objectives at the stage of identifying key social problems and in standardising the monitoring and statistical systems. Poland emphasised the OMC's role of exchanging experiences among the Member States, although the diversity of economic and political modalities and of social expectations in different Member States meant that few were applicable to Polish legislation and practice (Ministry of Social Policy, 2005).

The Polish government believes that the common goals incorporated in the EES for 2004-10 and in the area of social protection correspond with Polish priorities and speak to all the national policy priorities. Nonetheless, their implementation will require extending legislative actions, as well as more extensive information and public debate, if the reform process is to include the interested parties, social partners and NGOs.

Poland has its reservations regarding the goals relating to anti-poverty policies and social exclusion. In particular, it points out that the diversity of social problems in the various Member States means that defining specific groups of people to whom policies are targeted would not always be appropriate to the situation of a given state. As a result, a situation could develop where the position of specific groups of people threatened with exclusion (for example, people with disabilities, people involved in agriculture) would change little, while excessive attention would go to marginal issues (for example, in Poland, problems of national and minority ethnic groups). Poland also has reservations about the applied poverty index, which it sees as inappropriate to the situation of poorer Member States, while at the same time proposing the development of an EU basket of basic needs (Ministry of Social Policy, 2005).

Although the application of the OMC on social inclusion increased the attractiveness and participation of social partners, Poland views the level of public acquaintance with the OMC as insufficient. Poland spoke for leaving the OMC fundamentally unchanged, while still noting that without more robust regulations it may prove insufficient for attaining the set goals.

National strategic documents adopted by Poland under the OMC confirm that the common objectives and guidelines meet the fundamental challenges of Polish social policy and the labour market. In August 2004 the Polish government adopted, under the OMC, the National Action Plan for social inclusion for 2004–06, and in August 2005 the National Strategy Report on adequate and sustainable pensions, both of which presented the national strategies and policies in these two areas. The National Action Plan for social inclusion applied a multidimensional approach towards poverty and exclusion, as a clear signal of retracting from the earlier dominant social policy approach, based mainly on redistribution of income. The pension strategy responded to all common objectives and correctly identified most of the challenges facing the Polish pension system. However, it superficially treated issues related to ensuring the adequacy of pension benefits. The projections in the report were based on Wóycicka (2003) and showed the high probability that replacement rates for old-age pensions (counted together from the first and second pillar) would be far below the level considered in Poland as adequate.[6] Yet the report passes over this finding without reaction, failing to present any remedial measures for improving the adequacy of future benefits.

Demographic change

In March 2005 the European Commission (2005c) adopted the Green Paper on demographic change. Following internal consultations, Poland responded to the questionnaire attached to the Green Paper. The response stated that efforts to overcome the effects of demographic processes should be taken up at the EU level, but that these should not lead to any harmonisation of the social policies and employment policies of Member States.

Poland's position on the shape of family-centred policy reflects its intention of continuing its present family-oriented policy, based on the subsidiarity principle and consisting of limited state intervention and geared primarily to supporting poor families. On the other hand, Poland recognises the need for bold actions to reduce the very high unemployment among young people and to improve the difficult housing situation, thereby enabling the establishment and development of families.

The Polish government believes that social policy should focus on support for the family. Poland is, therefore, opposed to individualising entitlement to benefits connected with raising children as a measure for more equitable division of household and family duties between men and women.

Poland's position on the development of nursing services, including for children, elderly people and long-term care, is based on the subsidiarity principle. The role of the public sector in developing such services should be limited to shaping the structural framework for market-based solutions. The Polish government is also against reducing VAT rates for nursing services, preferring assistance for the poorest families. It stresses the role of families in providing long-term care.

The main instrument for ensuring intergenerational balance is an increase in employment. The need to increase employment mainly entails groups of young workers, people of pre-retirement age and people with disabilities, with a relatively low priority assigned to increasing the employment of women. Although the latter may be a consequence of emphasising the role of families in the provision of nursing services, it may also be connected to the employment rate of women, which, although reduced, is still higher than in many other Member States.

Poland favours improving the flexibility of labour markets and abandoning the policies of defending existing jobs, to the benefit of improving the adaptability of employees and employers. A strong accent, certainly connected with internal modalities, has been put on increasing the employment of older people. Poland underlines the need of both modernising social protection (here Poland particularly emphasises the benefits of Defined Contribution systems and stresses the need to focus on finding employment for people with disabilites) and flexibly adapting remuneration to productivity, development of skills and competency, adapting labour conditions and organisation, and by gradual movement into retirement. Seeing (and experiencing) difficulties in reaching social consensus on programmes for increasing employment, Poland perceives an important role for EU governing bodies in supporting social consensus.

Poland believes that immigration should not be perceived as a means for dealing with demographic problems. It nonetheless continues to be reticent about increasing immigration from third countries, while calling for reducing restrictions on labour migration within the EU.

Services of general interest and the proposal on the Services Directive

The European Commission issued the Green Paper on services of general interest (SGI) in May 2003, nearly a year before Poland's accession to the EU (European Commission, 2003f). In May 2004, the Commission published a White Paper (European Commission, 2004c). Poland twice stated its position on SGI, including answers to the questions put in the Green Paper and a position on actions proposed in the White Paper (Council of Ministers, 2005c). The general message of the Polish position is the conviction that adopting comprehensive regulations for SGI would be difficult and unfounded, given the differences between regulations applicable in different sectors (including different solutions in directives) and in different Member States. The point is that, first, many sectors potentially representing SGI have specific funding frameworks and rules for rendering the service defined in sector directives. Second, introducing the term 'economic services of general interest' would de facto require determining which services are to be governed by market rules and which are to be exempted. Controversies surrounding such a definition have meant that the said initiative currently stands little chance of success.

The Polish government considers the draft Services Directive on EU internal markets as a considerably more important European Commission (2004b) initiative, on which the Council of Ministers adopted a position in March 2004. Following internal consultations, Poland spoke out for the fewest possible exemptions from application of this Directive, effectively requesting a single exemption for health services funded by the public authorities. The frequently reiterated position of the Polish government is to not weaken the country-of-origin rule and to ensure effective elimination of administrative barriers to delegating employees. When the European Parliament voted on the Services Directive in February 2006 the country-of-origin rule was considerably weakened.

The Services Directive is particularly important for Poland because the basic principle defined in the Treaty of the free movement of services is being implemented with much more resistance than, for instance, the principle of free movement of goods. Polish service firms are highly competitive, particularly those providing labour-intensive services in such areas as security and construction services. Ensuring real access to the services market would have similar effects on the implementation of the rule of free movement of employees. As indicated earlier, free movement of labour is subject to restrictions under the terms of the

Accession Treaty. For these reasons the proposal for an internal market Services Directive met with the approval of Member States such as Poland and with grave fears from Germany and Austria. These fears are based on the same rationale as those that led to treaty restrictions on the free movement of people. For Poland, greater freedom would lead to a better use of labour resources.

Polish reticence about the proposed directive on SGI stems, as may be inferred, from two actual considerations. The first is the conviction that parallel consideration of the two proposed Services Directives makes more likely the reduction of the effectiveness of the provisions in the Directive on the EU internal market for services. The second is that SGI in Poland are subject to limited market pressure. The introduction of competition in these areas could trigger restructuring and consolidation processes, and therefore also potential problems for the domestic labour market. Moreover, the idea of regulators for network sectors at the EU level finds no Polish support for the same reasons. Poland is also disinclined to transfer its prerogatives to the EU level.

European Economic and Monetary Union

The Provisions of the Treaty setting up the European Community (Article 116) obligates Member States outside the Eurozone to present a convergence programme. Poland's last such convergence report (up to 2010) went to the Commission on 19 January 2006, and the Commission issued its comments on 1 March. The Commission criticised the report for its expected excessive public finance deficits and instituted the excessive deficit procedure.

The question of controversy between the Commission and the government remains a different definition of the contribution to private (mandatory) pension funds. While imposing pension system reform in 1998, which led to partial privatisation, Poland assumed that the costs connected with transferring part of the pension contributions to private pension funds (accounting for 1.5-2% of GDP annually) would not enter the public account, thus increasing the budgetary deficit.

During the first stage of the dispute with the European Commission, Poland made efforts to have Eurostat allow the contributions transferred to the pension funds to be charged to the public sector.[7] Later, when this attempt failed, Poland asked at the Ecofin Council meetings to apply mitigating criteria for this part of the budgetary deficit, as it resulted from the pension system reforms. But this argument was not accepted. Therefore, from April 2007, Poland experienced a substantial increase in its public finances deficit. This increase will not only greatly hamper a reduction of the budgetary deficit but also probably delay Poland's entry into the Eurozone.

Enlargement

The results of Poland's negotiations with the EU need to be the starting point of an evaluation and formulation of opinion on national answers to European initiatives connected with social policies. These, after all, reflect Poland's fundamental point of view and the fears of other Member States (Council of Ministers, 2002). In the area at hand, the most important points of agreement concern the free movement of people, the free movement of services, social policy and employment, education, training and young people (see Appendix XII of the EU Accession Treaty).

For the free movement of people, Poland adopted a seven-year transitional period restraining Polish citizens from taking jobs in the other Member States, except for those countries that have waived this restriction. After Poland's accession, three Member States have waived that possibility: the UK, Ireland and Sweden. In addition, Germany and Austria have reserved the right to restrain the provision of services in certain fields by Polish companies for a similar period. In negotiations Poland has received the right to apply the reciprocity rule, which it has invoked and continues to apply. In effect, citizens of Member States (other than those just specified) do not have the right to the free movement of people in Poland.

In the area of social policy and employment, Poland applied for and received derogation until 31 December 2005 to the application of Directive 89/655/EEC on minimum safety and health requirements for the use of work equipment by workers. The main argument concerned the costs of adjustments to be borne by Polish firms. In the negotiation chapters on education, training and young people, Poland declared for the adoption of EU legislation in its entirety.

Negotiations have revealed the main scope of possible disputes or contradictory opinions on future initiatives of the European Council or Commission. These relate mainly to the free movement of employees and deregulation of the market of services. The intentions outlined during negotiation are reflected in Polish government positions on new Community initiatives.

The European Commission annually reviews the Lisbon Strategy adopted at the European Council in 2000. One aspect of this review relates to transposing the Lisbon directives into national legislation. As of 1 June 2005 Poland had adopted 58 of the 63 'Lisbon' directives.

For social policy this refers to Directive 2002/14/EC, setting up the framework for informing and consulting employees in the EU. In effect, Poland did not delay in adopting Community regulations on social policy. Therefore, the common legislative body in the area of social policy does not exert an excessively negative effect on the Polish labour market.

Conclusions

A look at the differences in the level of economic development shows that the Polish social model does not differ substantially from the social models elsewhere in the Member States. However, it does differ substantially from that of the ESM. During the pre-accession period and in the early years after accession, intensive adaptation processes took place in Poland, both in terms of adopting European legislation and the OMC. Poland has no basic problem accepting the objectives outlined in the Lisbon Strategy and the Social Policy Agenda as these objectives cover the fundamental challenges of social policy and the Polish labour market.

The basic problem for Poland is its large-scale economic inactivity, high unemployment and resultant poverty. Poland expects the European context to bolster domestic policies in dealing with such problems. The short period of Poland's EU membership, however, does not allow us to assess the impact of EU social and employment policies on the Polish national social model. In stressing the adequacy of the most common goals to the Polish circumstances we need to consider the big distance between words and facts. Poland is facing weak internal support for the social and economic reforms it needs for accelerating employment growth.

The lack of visible political and social consensus in Poland does not allow for a coherent and sustainable implementation of the reforms. Although the government promoted initiatives for increasing employment and macroeconomic stability, the absence of determination in pursuing the internal reforms and lack of social support has made reform progress poor and incoherent. However, despite these weaknesses, progress should be visible both in problem identification and in reforms taking into account the European dimension. This progress is without any doubt an effect of Poland's inclusion in the OMC, which allows for a perception of Poland's problems in the context of the European experience and challenges.

Understanding and defining the challenges facing Poland's economy and society differs, according to actual political trends and the ruling coalition. As a consequence, the concept of the ESM is also redefined – from the liberal to the conservative and right-wing. Whereas the rationale of the renewed Lisbon Strategy was supported by the former left-wing and liberal government, the new government seems to put more emphasis on the social dimension.

Poland shows evident reservation about the question of harmonising social policy in Europe and the application of more rigid requirements within the OMC. Such reticence may reflect the fear of imposed solutions, which would reduce the competitiveness of the Polish economy. Yet the huge development gap between Poland and the older Member States means that the fundamental priority for Poland is the fastest possible reduction of that gap. The great distance in development also manifests in both the type and scale of social problems in Poland, often out of proportion when compared with other Member States.

Poland, obviously enough, wants to eliminate restrictions on the movement of employees stipulated in the Accession Treaty. This change, according to Poland, would allow a more effective use of labour resources within the EU. Similarly, the highly competitive character of Polish services makes Poland a natural champion of eliminating barriers to their free movement.

The unstable political situation after the 2005 parliamentary elections means that the issue of a high budget deficit may continue. The minority government has so far failed to take actions that would aim at reducing the deficit and accelerating employment growth. However, some prospects remain for lowering the high tax wedge, which is one of the major reasons for the continuing high unemployment in Poland.

Despite over a year having elapsed since the last parliamentary election, the position of the Polish government on both EU and domestic social policy remains unclear. Although placing more emphasis on the social dimension, the first government action gives rise to the assumption that the new government will maintain and extend the existing system of middle-class social privileges, instead of eliminating social exclusion and poverty. This government puts much less emphasis on economic competitiveness and macroeconomic equilibrium, and will focus on a strong support for deregulating EU markets, especially the labour and services markets. Poland's reticence about strengthening coordination in the area of social policy will probably remain and expand.

Notes

[1] The case here is that of postponing the decision regarding the abolition of the right to early retirement for many professional groups. Because of these privileges, among others,, Poland spends the most among the

EU Member States on social benefits replacing income for people at an older productive age (4.6% of GDP) and has one of the lowest average ages of withdrawal from the labour market (55.1 years for women and 58.1 years for men in 2001).

[2] The main features of the reform were:

- Workers' contributions were divided between two old-age pension pillars: the pre-existing public, pay-as-you-go scheme and a new system of privately managed individual savings accounts.
- The new private pillar is pre-funded, with the savings invested and managed by private pension funds. The government guarantees a minimum pension from both pillars together and a minimum rate of return for the pre-funded pillar, if other measures to ensure good returns fail.
- The public scheme was transformed from a Defined Benefit scheme with substantial redistribution towards low-income workers to a notional Defined Contribution scheme in which benefits will be based on each worker's own contributions. The amount of pension will be calculated by dividing the accumulated contributions paid by the average statistical life expectancy of the worker's age cohort at the normal retirement age (gender-neutral life tables will be used in this calculation). Thus, benefits will decline automatically in response to increased life expectancy (unless the individual keeps working and delays retirement). Individual accounts will be established to record each worker's contributions. Past contributions will be adjusted at the rate of 75% of the real growth of wages, which are subject to contributions.
- Starting from 2008, all early retirement entitlements will be eliminated (special provisions enabling early retirement to continue for a relatively narrow group of occupations are foreseen).

[3] 'The pension reform in Poland was planned along similar lines as the pension reform in Sweden (from 1994) and an ongoing reform of the pension system in Latvia....The Office of the Plenipotentiary in Poland had identified a need for technical assistance support to be able to analyse and discuss different alternatives for the detailed design and implementation of the pension reform' (Öström, 2003, p 6).

[4] Polish social assistance was based on social work provided by social workers, aimed at the activation and motivation of economic and social self-reliance of a person and his/her family. The cash and in-kind benefits provided by social assistance should be adjusted to the specific, individual needs of a beneficiary. The new Act establishes the

minimum amount of the social assistance benefit at the level of 20% of the individual poverty gap, to be increased up to 50% in 2008.

[5] Poland has reservations on the proposed debate on the effectiveness of national minimum income guarantee systems (see Polish Government, 2006).

[6] ILO Convention 102, ratified by Poland, defines such a level.

[7] One should point out here that if Eurostat accepted the Polish government arguments, then the effects of the pension system reform, consisting in alleviating the burden on the public sector to partly finance the pensions in the long run, would be totally eliminated.

SEVEN

Spain: starting from periphery, becoming centre

Ana Guillén

The European Union (EU) means a lot to Spain. It bears a symbolic value of belonging and identifying with an advanced and modern geographical area. Such a feeling is deeply grounded in historical reasons: Spain was and felt apart for centuries, probably since the decline of the empire, but much more so during the 40 years of the Francoist dictatorship (1939-75). Thus Spain has been an enthusiastic and respectful Member State. Nonetheless, its acute consciousness of backwardness (much more subjective than objective) has also pushed Spain into proving at all times that it is also a deserving Member State, very able to do its homework properly. This belief does not preclude an absence of criticism or occasional disenchantment; even the best marriages have well-kept secrets, disagreements and a certain dose of indifference.

The present socialist government (PSOE) claims that a significant shift in international relations has occurred since its victory in the March 2004 general elections. While the conservative Partido Popular (PP), in office from 1996-2004, was most respectful of the EU social and employment guidelines and norms, its decision to support George Bush and Tony Blair in the Iraq war was interpreted by the socialists as giving the EU the cold shoulder. As soon as PSOE was back in office, in 2004, public discourse changed sharply, with the declared aim of recovering good relations with the EU, especially Germany and France. The new government clearly showed its coldness in official activities with and declarations towards the US, and a parallel warming towards EU Member States, considered its 'natural allies'. Spanish troops were withdrawn from Iraq in June 2004, only a few months after the elections. Likewise significant of the new government's orientation is that, to show its reinforced European vocation, the Spanish Parliament confirmed the European Constitution as early as February 2005 and a successful referendum was held in May 2005. It is in this climate that the opinions of the present Spanish government should be judged.

As to sub-national levels of government (as with other Member States), Spain is a deeply decentralised country. Autonomous regions and governments hold their own views on EU policies, especially in the social policy areas where they have competence, that is, health care services, education, social services and housing. Political decentralisation in Spain has an asymmetric character; that is, powers and responsibilities are gained in bilateral negotiations with the central state at different points in time, so that some autonomous regions enjoy broader powers than others. This situation is especially true of certain 'historical nationalities' (Catalonia, the Basque Country). Spanish regions have opened their own representation offices close to EU institutions and have fought, without much success, for their language to be treated as co-official within the EU. This chapter, however, analyses the positions and opinions of the central government, provided that no major disagreements between the central and autonomous governments on the broad issues treated here have been ascertained.

The European social model versus the Spanish model

In general, Spain has always favoured being part of the EU. After 40 years of dictatorship and isolation, joining the EU and integrating into it has remained a permanent goal. In the social policy field, the most popular geographical point of reference has also stayed throughout the 30 years of democratic rule, that of emulating the Scandinavian model (particularly the Swedish model). Popular aspirations in this respect have been and remain shared by political elites, especially by socialist governments (in office from 1982 to 1996 and from 2004 to the present), with one caveat: as the origins of the Spanish welfare state are Bismarckian, what the government has pursued in terms of change towards a social democratic model has affected the welfare services rather than economic transfers. Income maintenance has remained mainly tied to labour market participation, although several non-contributory programmes (retirement, minimum income, unemployment) have also been created to narrow protection gaps. By contrast, the tendency for welfare services has been that of turning social insurance programmes into universal ones, as in the creation of a national health service in 1986 and the universalisation of compulsory education in the 1980s. Both the socialist governments and the unions are behind these moves.

At present, the Spanish welfare state constitutes a mix of the three welfare state regimes of Esping-Andersen (1999): conservative in income maintenance policies, social democratic in the field of health care and education, and liberal (universal and means tested) in care and social services and family policies. One of the main reasons for the 'liberal' component lies in the lack of development of care policies and family policies in the last years of the dictatorship in the 1970s; 'selective universalism' is obviously less expensive than full universalism. While health care and education were fairly well developed and turning them into a universal protection scheme (as the population wanted) was economically feasible, the effort towards universalising care and family policies would have been much greater. Lack of citizen pressure and demand (now increasing rapidly, but not during the 1980s and 1990s) may be another reason. Finally, the democratic governments showed little desire to be identified with the proclaimed pro-natal and pro-family – although not very generous – policies of the dictatorship.

The main characteristics of the Spanish welfare state can thus be summarised as follows:

- It is a mix of traditional conservative, social democratic and liberal models.
- Eligibility criteria are based mainly on labour market participation or dependence on a worker. However, health care and education have de facto reached universal coverage, even for immigrants, and likewise for retirement pensions. Low income level has also become a criterion for access to social services, family policies, minimum income, housing and social inclusion policies.
- It is deeply decentralised, with autonomous regions in welfare services, minimum income and social inclusion policies. Municipalities also play a relevant role in providing some of these services, especially those concerned with care and social inclusion. But Spanish citizens do not lose their social protection rights when they move from one autonomous region to another. Contributive income maintenance policies such as invalidity and retirement pensions and unemployment subsidies remain in the hands of the central state.
- For financing, a progressive separation of financing sources between social contributions and general taxation has taken place, in accordance with the mix of traditional models. Moreover, the separation of financing sources was officially sanctioned by the 1995 Toledo Pact on the future of the pension system. Thus, social contributions are to be used only for contributory economic transfers, while non-contributory transfers (minimum income, family subsidies, non-contributory unemployment subsidies), and welfare services are to be financed from general revenues. The process is close to full separation.

- As for management, despite the Bismarckian origins of the Spanish welfare state, separate social funds have never existed. Social security is a single institution managed by the public administration. Doctors and health professionals (including primary care) have always been salaried public employees. Unions and employer organisations have never played a decisive role in the management of social protection institutions, as in France or Germany.

Overall, Spain has acted according to its EU enthusiasm. As EU documentation shows, Spain's process of economic adjustment towards joining the Economic and Monetary Union (EMU) has been exemplary. The same commitment is true for compliance with the Stability and Growth Pact (SGP). Thus Spain's compromise with EU integration lies not only with the assets (EU funds) but also with the liabilities.

Therefore, it is hardly surprising that Spain greatly favours the concept of subsidiarity, grounded on the idea that each level should take care of whatever it can best fulfil in a flexible way. Spain is against the idea of a strict division of responsibilities/competencies between the national and EU levels because it could limit the process of European construction and integration. The principle of subsidiarity should not disrupt the integration process.

There is no clear general position in Spain on the principle of proportionality. Its adequacy is considered differently according to different policy issues. As a country of medium weight among Member States, Spain views proportionality as making sense – but only when a stronger weight in decisions is coupled with a higher level of implication (contributing accordingly).

Likewise, Spain is in favour of an expanding EU role in social policies. Brussels is seen as a crucial actor for the promotion of higher standards in Member States. This can be achieved by passing hard, normative EU recommendations and providing financial support for the less developed states. As the fifth economic power within the EU, Spain sees its role as salient in helping foster the European social model (ESM). Spain thinks that the EU's role should be enhanced. For example, in Spain's view, when the Commission and the Parliament take a decision on social policy, that decision should have broader public impact than at present (that is, more transparency, more 'shaming' and more impact on the media and the public discourse). The EU should make specific recommendations to particular Member States in Spain's view.

Spain is highly aware of the existing heterogeneity among member welfare states, and about the consequent difficulties for converging in social protection levels. Nevertheless, it is clearly in favour of sharing a broad pool of common European values. It views the ESM as a set of common principles and values, a common vision with different articulations, protecting old and new social risks in every Member State. The Commission's role should be enhanced for establishing at least a common denominator in institutions and European policy processes. Brussels is seen as a good place for experimenting with and promoting exports of social policy models and developing social policy instruments. The EU economic model is increasingly facing problems because of the slow development of the social model, leading to difficulties in the free circulation of workers and the development of European citizenship. The Commission is seen as the crucial actor in achieving an appropriate interplay between internal markets and social policy models.

Spain perceives its social model (as compared to the ESM, in this case understood as the averages of Member State social standards) as having achieved very good levels in certain policy areas (such as health care, pensions), and lagging behind in others (social care, family policies, housing policies, minimum income). As already noted, if we understand the ESM as EU social policies (acquis communautaire, recommendations, open method of coordination – OMC), Spain thinks that the EU should be much more active and efficacious.

Main principles in national reforms

The analysis of the recent evolution of Spanish social policy shows how domestic factors have been most influential. However, external factors have also played a salient role. Rather than being inspired purely by national factors and circumstances, recent reforms of the Spanish welfare state represent in many cases a domestic application of broader international policy models. The same also holds true for the 1980s. While the influence of the World Bank or the International Monetary Fund (IMF) has been minor, that of the Organisation for Economic Co-operation and Development (OECD) and (especially) the EU has been major.

The influence of the EU on domestic social policy has stemmed from the transposition and implementation of EU legislation. The conditions for macroeconomic convergence (for joining the EMU) have significantly affected the evolution of social policies. Structural and cohesion funds have eased reform, changing attitudes and developing administrative and managerial capacities. EU recommendations, White Papers and the OMC have helped reshape the domestic discourse on social policy reform, by changing perceptions and attitudes, and by helping policy makers to use blame-avoidance strategies.

All Council directives on labour and working conditions, gender equality, free movement of workers, and health and safety at work have been transposed into Spanish legislation (European Commission, 2000f, pp 251-65; Valiente, 2003). Nonetheless, in most cases, national legislation had already contemplated the provisions of directives. Therefore, the acquis communautaire and its transposition into domestic legislation can hardly be held responsible for the redesign of Spanish social policies in the 1990s.

Some have argued that the worse-off Member State economies have been able to profit from the structural and cohesion funds in the better-off Member State economies. Spain has been and still is the country that benefits most from structural and cohesion funds in absolute terms, although other Member States (for example, Ireland, Portugal and Greece) benefit more in per capita terms. Whether such funds have been used for ameliorating social protection networks or, conversely, for following a social dumping/devaluation strategy has already been the subject of research in Southern Europe. Such research shows that the financial support offered by the funds has generated growth, wealth and employment, not social dumping (Guillén and Matsaganis, 2000; Guillén and Álvarez, 2001). This support has also helped trigger social policy initiatives at the national, regional and local levels and to give the problems of certain social groups enhanced visibility (for example, long-term unemployed people). However, the significant reductions of incoming financing flows, to start in 2007, have not been received by the Spanish population as a shock; moreover, such reductions do not seem to have diminished the traditional pro-European inclination among Spaniards.

Understanding what happened in the 1990s is difficult without understanding the developments of the 1980s. From the mid-1980s to the early 1990s, the Spanish welfare state underwent a major transformation through the adoption of a national health service, the universalisation of education and pensions, and the introduction of minimum income schemes (the latter at the regional level). Domestic factors were highly influential, especially the ideology of the party in office (social democrats were in office for four consecutive legislatures), the process of political decentralisation towards the autonomous regions, pressures from the unions, and public preferences. Still, the reforms were also in line with the European Community's social discourse of the time, which focused on the fight against poverty and social exclusion and insisted on the reduction of gaps in access to social protection.

A significant degree of Europeanisation was achieved between 1982 and 1993, in terms of the reform of welfare goals and institutional arrangements, and of welfare inputs and outputs (Mangen, 1996; Guillén and Álvarez, 2004).

When the austerity era began and rationalisation became a must, the expansion and search for universalism of the Spanish welfare state was relatively recent. The population was therefore extremely reluctant to accept retrenchment. In this context, the government used Brussels' new doctrine of blame avoidance on many occasions. For example, passive unemployment protection was severely restricted in 1992. The reasons for this move were totally rooted in domestic circumstances, such as the sharp increase in fixed-term contracts producing continuous entries to and exits from the labour market and peaking costs of unemployment subsidies. However, according to *El País* (22 June and 18 July, both 1993) the government identified the recommendations of the White Paper on *Growth, competitiveness and employment* (European Commission, 1993a), together with the OECD doctrine, as one of the reasons for the restriction of passive unemployment protection.

In health care, where universalisation had just been attained, rationalisation measures proposed by a parliamentary commission in 1991 were strongly opposed by the unions and the population in general. Therefore, the government sought to create efficiency in the health care domain quietly and incrementally, always making sure not to affect the recent equity gains. For instance, the Spanish national health service is the only one in the EU not to have introduced any out-of-pocket payments in the past two-and-a-half decades. Adjustment in this field was mainly achieved by not letting public expenditure grow above GDP (gross domestic product), as the Convergence Plans prescribed.

For pensions, the public debate centred on a choice between making the public pension system viable or privatising it. The government decided to pursue the former strategy, as agreed by the Toledo Pact of 1995, which came about first among political parties with parliamentary representation, later joined by the social agents and the banking sector. Including 12 sets of rationalising recommendations, it was renewed in 2003, so that it still guides pension reform. Some of the Toledo Pact recommendations were implemented in the 1997 restrictive pension reform, as agreed in the Social Pact achieved the previous year. Again, the government cited Brussels, saying that Spain had an adverse demographic situation that called for welfare reforms. From then on what has occurred is rather an amelioration of the lowest pensions, widows' and orphans' pensions and contributory conditions of atypical workers (for example, fixed term, part time and/or marginal workers).

Finally, participation in the European Employment Strategy (EES) and the OMC, and the preparation of the National Action Plans, have helped make public policies in the corresponding realms more transparent. In those social policy fields in which Spanish autonomous regions have exclusive responsibilities, preparing the Plans pushed regional policy makers into some positive efforts for transparency and standardisation of indicators, as well as better coordination among regional executives. Much remains to be done, however.

In sum, the insistence of the European Community on the need to fight poverty, promote social inclusion, close the gaps of social protection and pursue gender equity has been important in the reorientation of the Spanish welfare state over the past two decades. At the other extreme, EU statements in the 1990s on Spain's need to rationalise social protection and improve efficiency have also been very influential, helping national governments legitimise cost-control measures.

The influence of the OECD in reforming Spanish social policies is also clear (Álvarez and Guillén, 2004). In its annual reports the OECD has been much more insistent on proposing reforms in economic policies than in social policies. However, these two realms are connected. In the early 1990s the OECD emphasised the necessity for making public management more efficient and recommended analyses of costs and benefits for different social programmes. Furthermore, in the 1990s the OECD insisted on the dual character of the Spanish labour market. The existence of strong protection for open-ended full-time contracts, while non-core workers enjoyed much lower levels, was considered negative. Redundancy payments were considered both too high and unjustified, given the high levels of unemployment protection, which in turn hindered participation in the labour market by raising the reserve salary. The need for insisting on the development of activation policies was also noted in OECD annual reports. OECD worries about the financial balance of the pension system were voiced both in the 1980s and 1990s. Although welcoming the Toledo Pact, the OECD wanted even stricter rationalising measures. As for health care, the OECD saw a need for greater efficiency especially in cost control on public pharmaceutical spending.

Considering that the government followed most of the OECD recommendations, one has to conclude that Spain appears highly receptive to them. Nonetheless, very different amounts of time elapsed between OECD proposals and actual action. In general, action was swifter when it suited political, electoral and economic circumstances. Moreover, some OECD recommendations are very generic, thus defending the great influence on domestic decisions is easy, as in the case of some efficiency-seeking measures of the 1990s.

National responses to the EU initiatives

The timing of the most significant boost in welfare development in Spain coincided with the period in which the country became a full member of the EU.[1] Spain has been particularly exposed to EU influence since negotiations for accession began. Such influence was twofold: first, it constituted a basis for legitimising the new democratic regime and, second, it helped strengthen institutional capabilities. The EU was fundamental to consolidating democratic institutions and it served as a benchmark of the kind of society to be achieved. Hence, a respectful position towards any arguments and ideas stemming from the EU has been the norm in the Spanish public discourse, including EU initiatives related to social policies.

However, when facing adaptive pressures from the EU, the response is not always immediate, especially if there is a need to comply with national needs, national and sub-national public debates, cultural and historical trajectories, and the positions of vested interests. Spain is a democracy, so internal politics matter most. Few Spanish politicians are ready to admit that their actions have been triggered exclusively by EU recommendations with the exception, of course, of those occasions in which EU policies allow for blame-avoidance strategies. But even if the process of mutual accommodation shows innumerable intricacies, the EU influence on Spanish policies is hard to deny. However, disagreements or lack of response sometimes occur. Despite being enthusiastic Europeanists, Spaniards are also very conscious of the price to be paid. In short, Spain's relation to the EU can be compared to a normal marriage, as opposed to a perfect, idealised one.

Lisbon Strategy

The government of the PP, in office when the Lisbon Strategy was launched, subscribed to its objectives fully. The PP thought that the Lisbon Strategy meant the consolidation of the idea that Europe would be unable to reach full employment if the necessary (liberalising) structural and economic reforms failed to be carried out. Thus labour market policies aimed at promoting activation and economic policies grounded on zero deficits were a national priority (Comparecencia del Ministro de Trabajo y Asuntos Sociales, 2003). The PP government defended, with a marked liberal orientation (together with the UK and the support of both the Portuguese presidency and the Commission), the liberalisation and enhanced competitiveness of the electricity, hydrocarbon, aviation, railroad and telecommunications markets. Furthermore, among the proposals that Spain defended at that point were the reduction of state financial support to certain production sectors, increased use of financial instruments such as risk capital, the widening of the use of the internet, and the definition of sustainability criteria of public pension systems (Consejo Económico y Social, 2000, p 165). In other words the PP government clearly favoured prioritising employment creation through the liberalisation of production and the rationalisation of social protection, especially in the pension sector.

Reformed Lisbon Strategy 2005

By 2005, the position of the new socialist government had changed substantially. As the Spanish Prime Minister stated at the informal summit at Hampton Court, Spain believed that the relaunching of the Lisbon Strategy should revolve around three main axes: increasing flexicurity, enhancing the dynamism of the state as a catalyst of public policies, and increasing global cooperation, that is, promoting a viable economic and social model allowing for a rise to the top in social protection along the lines of the Scandinavian model (Rodríguez Zapatero, 2005a).

The Spanish government believes that Spain has contributed and continues to contribute actively to revising the Lisbon Strategy and manifests its wish for a 'nationalisation' of the process. This means introducing the Lisbon Strategy as a basic guide of national economic policies, which has been translated in the Spanish case into an ambitious National Reform Programme.

In the National Reform Programme, the Spanish government preferred a reorientation towards the economic pillar, among the ones proposed by the Kok report (Kok, 2004), with a complement of the social and environmental pillars. The main objectives were two: first, full convergence with the EU25 in terms of per capita income by 2010 (97.2% in 2004); second, to reach an employment rate of 66% in 2010 (61% in 2004) (Ministerio de la Presidencia, 2005).

The *Joint report* has evaluated as positive for the Spanish Programme such aspects as budgetary stability, emphasis on investment on Research and Development (R&D), and quantitative objectives (especially for infrastructures) (European Commission, 2005h, 2006a). The main weaknesses included insufficient measures to fight job precariousness or promote women's labour market insertion, and lack of competitiveness in the retail sector. The *Joint report* positively valued two initiatives: first, the invitation to the autonomous regions to join a permanent forum of discussion; second, the establishment of a National Evaluation Agency to follow and control the National Action Plan implementation process.

The Commission highlighted in January 2006 several illustrative examples of Spain's policies in support of the growth and job creation strategies (European Commission, 2006j). First, in the R&D and innovation pillar, the Commission pointed out that Spain was considering reducing taxes for firms investing in R&D and that it was developing specific programmes aimed at increasing the number of researchers in enterprises. In addition, Spain planned to introduce monitoring and evaluation systems to improve the effectiveness of public R&D spending. Second, for the improvement of the business environment and the functioning of markets, Spain planned to launch simplification programmes with a focus on improving legislation on tax, audit and fiscal measures, setting up business, insolvency and labour and consumer protection. Third, for employment, financial sustainability and demography, Spain strengthened the link between contributions and benefits and allowed early or late retirement with corresponding changes in benefits. Fourth, for energy and environmental technologies, both national and regional policies for wind power were showing results, with wind accounting for 6.5% of Spain's electricity output.

Spain's strategy for social policy reform is best expressed in Section 6 of the National Reform Programme, on 'Labour market and social dialogue'. The Spanish government, and in particular the Ministry of Labour and Social Security, defines its strategy in terms of achieving a balance between labour market and social policies. In other words, they wish for productive workers but not exploited ones. The extension of reconciliation between work and family life (Concilia) to all workers beyond public employees points in this direction (Ministerio de la Presidencia, 2005). Section 6 of the Programme has been designed as a necessary counterbalance to the sections devoted to the development of physical, human and technological capital (Sections 2, 3 and 4) and to measures for enhancing productivity (Section 5).

Social Policy Agenda

The Ministry of Labour and Social Affairs welcomed the Social Policy Agenda 2000-05 as established by the 2000 Nice Summit and the common indicators established by the Laeken Summit in 2001. The belief was that social cohesion was essential to allow for economic development, that poverty needed eradication and that enhanced European collaboration in the promotion of social inclusion could help in such a direction.

The Social Policy Agenda 2005-10 contains all the elements that the Spanish government considers fundamental. On the whole, Spain thinks that the new Agenda includes clearer measures than previously but that they are not totally clear. On the positive side, Spain finds that the best aspect of the Social Policy Agenda is its emphasis on immigration, low fertility and population ageing and that such problems and challenges for social policies are treated in an interrelated way. The Commission's position on permanent training, education, equality of opportunities, protection of dependent people, poverty and postponing the retirement age are among the issues best treated, according to the Spanish analysis (interview, Spanish civil servant, 2006).

On the negative side is a lack of concreteness of actions in many areas, such as labour market insertion measures for the young, women and long-term unemployed people. Examples of best practice have not been drawn from the Social Policy Agenda. In Spain's opinion, the Commission has not committed itself. For example, they have not defended the idea of activation and inclusion in a dynamic single market (interview, Spanish civil servant, 2006).

Open method of coordination

Spain finds soft decision-making instruments, such as the OMC, useful for ameliorating social protection policies through the dissemination of best practice and the evaluation of National Action Plans. However, it wants greater impact and clarity, that is, in the line of enhancing the impact of joint reports (more naming and shaming). Streamlining is also desired, provided that it is understood as enhanced coordination and increased efficiency (interview, Spanish civil servant, 2006). In relation to the advancement in the OMC strategy, the Spanish Prime Minister has proposed to produce specific recommendations to Member States linked to EU funds for their accomplishment. In other words, the EU should financially back some national initiatives to ease their attainment.

In general, Spain views the OMC as an asset, but an insufficient one. The results of the evaluation process and recommendations tend to have a very low impact on the national media and on the supranational public debate. Thus, as a decision-making process the OMC lies rather at the administrative level, not the political one. Politicians and top civil servants do not feel much pressed by it. In sum, the Social Policy Agenda is one step forward, but only a small step.

Spain thinks that the OMC has helped to achieve progress in the national policy-making process and at the European level (European Commission, 2006h). For pensions, the OMC has led directly to the study of approaches by the minister, parliamentarians and social partners on different issues, such as information provision, active ageing and the role of the second pillar. Spain believes that its national discussion on pension reform benefited from its coinciding with the preparation of the first National Strategy Plans for pensions.

In general, common objectives are still in line with key policy priorities, and they cover the most important challenges as identified in the recent joint reports. Nonetheless, Spain has suggested that future inclusion objectives could say more on poverty and exclusion linked to migration and minority ethnic groups, stress equality between men and women, pay more attention to preventing poverty, and deal resolutely with the phenomenon of homelessness.

Regarding the adequacy of indicators for monitoring progress towards the common objectives, Spain wishes to see the development of a 'global' indicator for progress towards greater social cohesion in the context of the new Lisbon Strategy. For pensions, Spain would like better verification of the expenditure projections that are carried out by the Economic Policy Committee (EPC) Working Group on Ageing Populations Working through reference to national data.

Spain thinks that consultation among different government departments and levels, on the one hand, and involvement of stakeholders, on the other, has increased as the OMC process has developed. A new inter-ministerial commission was created to oversee coordination. Because Spain is a deeply decentralised country, it emphasises building the National Action Plans on the basis of strong regional contributions. In this respect, Spain has highlighted increased cooperation with regional and local authorities while also emphasising the need for further improvement. Efforts to increase awareness have included the distribution of the National Action Plan and EU15 best practice to relevant non-governmental organisations (NGOs).

Spain has welcomed the promotion of mutual learning through the Annual Round Table and the annual meeting with people experiencing poverty. However, Spain feels that the Round Table should be less structured by its organisers, to allow a greater opportunity for civil society organisations to express their views. In the field of pensions, Spain found the two national launch seminars in preparation of the national strategies for pensions very valuable.

Finally, Spain feels that the integrated approach to economic, employment and social progress set at Lisbon needs to be maintained. It has made the following suggestions for work on health and long-term care: the process should be light, involving the EPC working with the Social Protection Committee (SPC); it should be based on the principle that everyone is entitled to health care; it should pay particular attention to policies for meeting the challenge of providing long-term care; and it should cover the provision of benefits in kind and in cash.

Demographic change

The Green Paper on demographic change is a very sensitive document for Spain, because a legal proposal for establishing a universal scheme for dependent (elderly and disabled) people is now under parliamentary consideration. Spain sees this legal proposal as the building of the fourth pillar of the welfare state.

Protection of dependent people is the responsibility of the autonomous regions, with a highly heterogeneous provision. A more fully fledged scheme for protecting dependent people has been on the agenda for almost a decade. However, the first step was to gather information on existing needs (both of caregivers and those being cared for), an aspect in which the National Institute of Social Services had a leading role starting in the mid-1990s. This was the starting point of the public debate on enhanced protection for dependants, continued under the conservative government (1996-2004) and intensified under the present government until a Social Pact with the social partners was reached in December 2005. The Social Pact highlighted the salience of socio-demographic changes in Spain and their consequences for dependent people and their caregivers.

The idea of the Pact was always to avoid passing a scheme producing too much expenditure, leading to the need for applying cost-control measures. Financial sustainability was and still is one of Spain's main worries, especially for the Treasury, given great uncertainties about the increase in dependent people (see Cabrero, 2004). The financial contribution of the central state has already been fixed, to preserve the scheme even if the Socialist Party loses the next general election. Negotiations with the autonomous regions on their financial contribution are still under way.

The new legal proposal on the protection of dependants has been inspired by the German model, given that Spain is deeply decentralised. Another reason for this inspiration is that the government wished to establish this policy as a universal right while also letting citizens know that such a right entails duties and cost-consciousness. Implementation will take place from 2007 to 2014, aiming at providing first for severe dependencies and then for medium and moderate ones.

Spain considers the proposals related to the postponement of the retirement age and partial retirement as the main assets of the Green Paper on demographic change. According to Spain, reference to the fourth pillar of the welfare state (protection of dependent people) has been missed out of the Green Paper on demographic change, and this omission is viewed as its main liability.

Services of general interest

The report of the public consultation on the Green Paper of March 2004 did not include any response by the Spanish government, headed by the PP, at that point. The reason lies most probably in its coincidence with the general elections, celebrated on 14 March 2004. Neither can any reaction from the regional governments be ascertained. Several Spanish enterprises responded and so did an association of Spanish, Portuguese, Italian and French local administrations. The latter defended both social and economic services of general interest (SGIs), regarded as common objectives of the EU, saying that they were key elements for the reinforcement of economic, social and territorial cohesion. SGIs should allow the citizens of less developed regions to enjoy access to the same services as other regions and should reduce regional disparities.

However, the new socialist government, elected in March 2004, quickly produced a response to the questionnaire on SGIs. The document was elaborated by the Ministry of Labour and Social Affairs in the autumn of the same year (Ministerio de Trabajo y Asuntos Sociales, 2004). For Spain, social SGIs, as opposed to other SGIs, should be grounded on guaranteed access and equal treatment. Their essence lies on the solidarity and equity principles with the aim of preserving social cohesion. The definition, organisation, financing and supervision of social SGIs are in the hands of national authorities and should remain so. A strict differentiation among economic and non-economic SGIs at EU level could be a complicated matter and could be devoid of added value. Hence, such differentiation should be carefully weighed. So far, the absence of differentiation has not hindered the development of SGIs. Potential application of the OMC to social SGIs is regarded as positive, provided the principle of subsidiarity is respected. The passing of EU legislation should wait until a common decision is adopted on whether social SGIs can be treated as economic or whether they require ad hoc regulation because of their specificities.

Proposal on the Services Directive

The present Spanish government claims that the previous PP government (1996-2004) did not reach a clear position on the proposal of the Services Directive. Although the socialist government now in office first opposed the Services Directive, its position has changed in the past year to one more oriented to the EU strategy.

In December 2005, the Minister of Industry, Tourism and Commerce reported to Parliament right after the celebration of the EU Council of Ministers of Competitiveness (Comparecencia del Ministro de Industria, Turismo y Comercio, 2005). He claimed that Spain understood that a step ahead in the freedom of circulation of services was positive and important for generating economic activity and creating more employment and more wealth. Therefore, Spain supported creating an internal market of services, but only if such creation respected the ESM and social cohesion. The minister pointed out that Spain had asked for an exclusion from the Directive for game services, fiscal services, private security and those related to nuclear energy, and was still studying the application of the Directive to the audiovisual and health care sectors. The exclusion of non-economic services was defended by signalling dangers of a lowering of social protection standards derived from liberalisation.

One week before the vote on the Directive in the European Parliament, the media reported that Spain shared the same position as the UK, the Netherlands, the Czech Republic and Hungary. Spain had sent a letter to the Commission (in particular to Charlie McCreevy, Commissioner of the Internal Market) supporting the passage of an effective Directive, guaranteeing free competence and decreasing the power of Member States in practice: 'we (the government of Spain) firmly share the view of the Commission. The arguments in favour of reform and increased competitiveness are stronger than ever' (*El Mundo*, 12 February 2006, p 42). At the moment, despite some divergent positions among ministries, the government claims that it will strongly pursue a consensus.

European Economic and Monetary Union

Spain continues to greatly favour the EMU. At the beginning of the 1990s, there were fears and reservations about whether Spain would be able to comply with the Maastricht criteria. However, Spain saw the process of macroeconomic convergence as an opportunity for deepening the modernisation and globalisation of the Spanish economy (Pérez Díaz and Torreblanca, 1999). As Miguel Sebastián (currently Head of the Economic Bureau of the Prime Minister) has noted, 'Europe has been the driving force of economic policy in Spain over the last four decades'. Obviously, the process had begun much earlier than the early 1990s, with the preparations for accession to the European Community and accession itself, which entailed the implementation of policies aimed at increased competition, deregulation, industrial restructuring and privatisation of public enterprises. Such initial changes not only made Spain's membership possible but also allowed it to become a founding member of the EMU. However, the convergence of the Spanish economy with that of the EU in real terms slowed down for a decade while the necessary reforms (to join the EMU) were put in place (Balmaseda and Sebastián, 2003, pp 216-17).

Doménech and Taguas (2003), in an analysis of the effects on GDP growth of lower inflation, a shrinking public deficit and a more open Spanish economy resulting from the EMU, conclude that the long-term impact of the EMU can be estimated to lead to a 3.3 percentage point increase in the rate of private investment and a 10.4% rise in per capita income. This estimate does not account for the short-term costs of the policies applied to secure compliance with the Maastricht criteria, which some experts calculate to amount to around one third of the long-term benefits (Balmaseda and Sebastián, 2003, pp 216-17).

As for the present state of the SGP, regarding the deviance of some members from it, Spain sees the role of the Council as problematic, provided it is to punish its own members. Spain thinks that enhanced instruments should be endorsed by the Commission with the aim of making its coercive power more effective (Rodríguez Zapatero, 2005a, pp 13-17). However, Spain is also very aware of the strong rejection that this strategy generates among several Member States.

Enlargement

Enlargement is related to several issues that may become a source of worry, such as the loss of financial influxes from the EU and relocations of production. However, Spain clearly supported the most recent enlargement – the incorporation of Bulgaria and Romania (and also that of Turkey) – as long as these Member States fulfilled EU requirements.

As to decreases in financial influxes from the EU, the Prime Minister declared that the conclusions adopted by the European Council on 15-16 December were positive for Spain in several respects (Rodríguez Zapatero, 2005b). First, Spain continues to be a net receiver of funds for 2007-13 (16,181 million euros). Thus Spain will be the second net receiver (after Poland) in absolute terms. Second, the agreement preserves all the rights of Spanish regions with per capita incomes below 75% of the EU average. Moreover, the 'specificity' of the Canary Islands has been maintained through the assignation of specific funds. Third, not only is the amount of EU funds coming into Spain positive but also its orientation, for example, financing lines devoted to crucial issues for Spain such as investment in R&D and immigration.

As for relocations there are social worries in Spain, especially with regard to external relocations to countries with lower labour costs, for example, Eastern European countries. Nonetheless, the European Observatory has shown that only 4.75% of job losses can be attributed to offshoring for 2000-05. Spain thinks that the EU should help new Member States reinforce their social protection programmes, so that conditions of workers become more similar and social dumping is avoided. Moreover, to enhance transparency, Spain believes that the EU should foster the modernisation of public administration and the development of institutional capacities in incoming Member States. Furthermore, to facilitate the presence of Spanish firms in their territory, Spain should increase its economic competitiveness and reinforce the relations with new Member States (Consejo Económico y Social, 2004). Spain has decided to suppress all restrictions on admissions of workers from the 10 incoming members in May 2006 (*El Mundo*, 11 March 2006, p 42).

At present, the Spanish government has declared that Spain is ready to become a net contributor in the mid-term, so that its position lies more on the political than on the economic side of enlargement. Nonetheless, it also defends the view that enlargement should not avoid the deepening of the European integration process. The constitutional project should be taken up again as a political project allowing for successful enlargement. Spain has defended the growth of the European budget (interview, Spanish civil servant, 2006).

Conclusions

Belonging to the EU and feeling an influential part of it was important for Spain long before becoming a Member State, and remains so. The development of social policies has been significantly influenced by the EU in public discourses, procedures and outcomes. Spain thinks European integration should be enhanced rather than slowed down. However, Spain is also critical of the EU doctrine included in its published documents. Soft decision instruments are thought to bear too low an impact. Thus, Spain thinks that the EU should be more assertive. Besides, the EU has not been able to influence certain policy areas in great depth in Spain, a salient area being family policies.

Future developments of social policy are very likely to follow the same trend as in past decades, that is, to respect EU guidelines by taking them into account when designing the reform of social protection policies. Both documents issued recently by the Ministry of Labour for the preparation of the National Reform Programme show such characteristics (Ministerio de Trabajo y Asuntos Sociales, 2005a, 2005b). These documents also propose a reform of social policies for the short term. They are not a dramatic departure from existent policies, except for the new regulation protecting the enhanced efforts at the reconciliation of work and family life and an accent on gender equality (with new legislation under parliamentary debate). Spain's intention is to continue the search for equity and efficiency in actual policies.

Note

[1] Some of the information in this section has been drawn from interviews with top officials at the Prime Minister's Economic Bureau. The interviews were carried out in January 2006.

EIGHT

The Czech Republic: tradition compatible with modernisation?[1]

Martin Potůček

As with other national models, the Czech social policy model is an outcome of historical legacies, decisions made at different times by various actors, filtered by street-level implementation capacities and mirrored by public reflections of its operations and effects. Up to now, it has been able to resist the one-sided, hard-line reforms happening in some other post-communist countries. Its piecemeal development can be characterised by its functional adaptation to societal, political and economic changes, which preserved its core functions: universal access to basic social and health services, and preventing the most vulnerable people from falling into poverty. Even with the impact of the European Union (EU), domestic factors and actors have played a decisive role in this development.

The European social model versus the Czech model

The Czech-Slavic Social Democratic Party was founded as early as 1878. Since then, social democratic, radical socialist and later communist political movements have always been present in the political life of the country. The Czech Lands were significantly influenced by Bismarck's conservative corporatist social policy model even before the First World War. In the interwar period, Czechoslovak democracy put its stakes on the social dimension of individual and societal existence by advanced social legislation that became a pattern for Greece. The atrocious authoritarian behaviour of the communist regime after the Second World War was, in the eyes of many citizens, partially compensated for by the delivery of core social services to everybody – and by full (over-) employment as a chronic functional feature of the centrally planned economy. Pre-1989 Czechoslovakia was described by communist propaganda as a showcase example of a country with well-organised health and social services (even in the context of the Soviet bloc). The reason for the final collapse of communism was not so much the mediocre, technically outmoded quality and sometimes limited availability of social services as the sorry state of the economy.

Because the final stages of the country's preparations for EU entry and the first years of full membership coincided with the Czech Social Democratic Party emerging as the only, or the most influential, political force in government (July 1998–June 2006), the government's attitude towards the EU and its policies was quite favourable. There is an apparent cleavage between the political parties that are pro-European and that participated in the executive branch of the government (the Social Democrats, the Christian Democrats and the Union of Freedom) and the opposition parties that took an appreciably more reserved or even openly critical attitude towards the deepening of European integration (the Communists and the Civic Democratic Party). Most of the general public supports the country's EU membership, including most Civic Democratic Party members (in contrast to their leaders).

There is one both nationally and internationally thrilling element in the policy debate on the EU, its future and its social dimension: the stance of Czech President Václav Klaus, an outspoken critic of the EU's present shape and developmental tendencies. Klaus warns against the tendency to embrace or even strengthen the coordinating and consultative mechanisms apparent in EU policy making. In his lecture 'From integration toward unification', presented to the Czech Learned Society on 15 May 2006, he pointed out that the liberalising effect of European integration had waned, whereas the present harmonising and standardising processes would necessarily lead to top-down steering and the bureaucratisation of human lives. Klaus believes that this homogenising and unifying tendency should be replaced by a return to the liberalising phase.[2] In reaction to the lecture, a group of 66 outspoken Czech scientists wrote an open letter to Václav Klaus on 24 May 2006. In 'The letter of the scientists to the President' ('Dopis vědců prezidentovi', *Právo* [daily newspaper], 25 May 2006), they did not share his critical view of the European integration process (compared to the previous integration attempts within the Soviet bloc). They opposed both his idea that EU membership was associated with a democratic deficit and his proposal to reduce collaboration within the EU to the Customs Union. They did not fear that European integration might result in the loss of Czech national or cultural identity; after joining the EU they saw neither signs of economic problems nor the irresistible pressure of Brussels' bureaucracy.

As a neoliberal thinker, Klaus finds it difficult to accept the contemporary institutional and functional shape of Czech social policy (see Potůček, 1999; Klaus, 2005, p 1).

The present condition of the Czech social model may be characterised as popular support for its main functions (although the public remains rather critical of the quality of services), the high efficiency of redistribution towards the most vulnerable (with social and health public spending at 19.1% of GDP in 2005, and with the percentage of the poor, that is, people with incomes below 60% of the national medium income, at 8% in 2002), and the universal although modest (and in some situations even unsatisfactory) delivery of core social and health services.

By and large, the European social model (ESM) (as defined above) and the Czech social model (as it has evolved up to now) are fully compatible in terms of history, culture, institutional frameworks, attitudes of the population and political legitimacy.

Main principles in national reforms

In general, the EU has played an active role in supporting and mediating modernisation in the new Member States. Its positive influence is identifiable in various fields. Most noteworthy is the EU's assistance to institution and capacity building (for example, PHARE projects), and specifically designed modernisation efforts – a reform of public administration, regulatory reform, training of professionals (including civil servants), implementation of new methods of public management and administration, collaboration in the field of education, and so on.

The history of systematic preparation of the candidate countries for accession started with the launching of the Copenhagen criteria of accession (1993). These criteria were designed more as a technical (economic and political) instrument from above than as an appropriate tool to steer people's living conditions in the candidate countries. In other words, legal, economic and political issues prevailed. Candidate countries were asked to reform their national economies to be able to compete – and be compatible – with the market economies of the present Member States. They had to build robust, reliable institutions of political democracy. They were asked to adjust their legal and administrative systems to the acquis communautaire. The fast progress in both economic and political adjustment to these requirements has been astonishing and deserves high evaluation.

Nevertheless, genuine social goals were at the very bottom of the list of priorities – limited to the preservation of individual human rights and the building of a loosely defined framework for social policy making. The containment or reduction of poverty and income inequalities, labour rights, a living wage and the alleviation of the fate of the marginalised groups – in other words, the fight against social exclusion – did not form an integral part of the Copenhagen criteria reform agendas. Most national social policies in the candidate countries in the early and mid-1990s consisted of the withdrawal of the state and the improvement of efficiency by the privatisation and marketisation of the services. These steps were to be completed by the reduction of coverage and standards for all social benefits except social assistance, a well-targeted safety net for the poor (Ferge, 2001).

The European Council launched the economic nucleus of the Lisbon Strategy in March 2000, enriching it with a social dimension in Nice in December 2000. Soon after, the environmental dimension followed in Gothenburg in June 2001. It was a stream of new political initiatives stressing the importance of human resources, quality of life, social cohesion, in short, the 'social fabric' of contemporary societies. The Czech Republic was asked to take part in the Lisbon Strategy negotiations only after the 2002 Barcelona Summit, when the new Member States had completed their preparations for entering the EU (until then organised under the logic of the Copenhagen criteria). The Czech Republic's fully fledged participation in the Lisbon Strategy started only with its accession to the EU in May 2004. Thus, social policy moved to the top of the EU political agenda of enlargement as late as a decade after the establishment of the Copenhagen criteria of accession.

Meanwhile, neither the governments of the candidate countries nor the EU institutions were able to prevent the rent-seeking institutions of the global financial market (inspired by the influential ideology of the Washington Consensus and the corresponding policies of the International Monetary Fund [IMF] and the World Bank in the 1990s) from trying to implement radical changes in various social policy fields. The World Bank indeed was seen as the major agenda-setting actor in economic and social policy making in the region (Ferge, 2001; Orenstein and Haas, 2003).

What has the specific impact of this interplay of influences been on social policy formation in the Czech Republic?

Pension reform. After minor changes to old-age pension legislation in the early 1990s, a significant legislative change occurred in the framework of the compulsory structure of social insurance with the passing of a new law on old-age pensions in 1995. An increase in the statutory retirement age limit was approved, to be introduced incrementally until 2007. The statutory retirement age for women, originally 53–57, was raised to 57–61 (depending on the number of children), while for men it increased from 60 to 62. The law conceives the old-age pension as twofold: one component is a fixed amount paid to all and the other component depends on the number of years worked and the working income received. The law is built on the principle of substantial redistribution of accumulated finances to people with a lower level of earnings. Old-age pensions for people with higher working incomes are affected by a regressively acting calculation formula.

Since 1995 a public discussion has taken place about the reform of the entire concept of the old-age pension system. It was initiated by experts from international financial institutions, that is, the IMF and the World Bank, which strongly recommended that the country opt for compulsory private co-insurance. This new type of old-age insurance would complement the pay-as-you-go public scheme that would gradually lose its importance in the total amount of redistributed resources. These institutions argued that this change was inevitable, due to demographic trends (ageing of the population) and the demand for investment in the national economy that would be satisfied by the newly established and privately run for-profit pension funds. By contrast to Poland, Hungary and (recently) Slovakia, which introduced this model, the Czech Republic resisted the pressure. Two main factors can explain this significant difference:

• The country was not in as deep a fiscal crisis as other Central and Eastern European countries and was less dependent on loans from these organisations.
• There were strong political opponents of this idea, namely the consecutive Social Democrat-led governments and the trade unions that stressed the risks of such a reform, due to the fragility of financial markets and institutions and the huge demand for additional financial inputs within the following two decades.

A special government task force composed of representatives of the whole spectrum of political parties, experts and civil servants in 2005/06 prepared a draft of the principles of pension reform. Nevertheless, Parliament did not approve the document. Czech pension reform is at a halt again, with little prospect of seeing a political consensus about its concept and content due to the deepening polarisation of the political scene before and after the general election held in June 2006.

Active and passive labour market policies. The Employment Act came into force at the start of 1991. The state employment policy, in accordance with this Act, is geared towards balancing labour supply and demand, productively using the workforce resources, and securing the rights of citizens to employment. These rights are interpreted as those of people who want and are able to work and are actively seeking employment. These people have the right to have work brokered for them in suitable positions, the right to re-qualification (as needed) for such work, and to material security before starting a job and after losing employment. By 1990 a network of regional labour offices was created for administering state employment policy in the regions.

The relevance of the EU as a partner in employment policy making became visible only with the innovation of domestic employment policy making, which started with the annual preparation and implementation of the National Action Plans for employment, guided by the European Employment Strategy (EES) at the end of the 1990s (Ministry of Labour and Social Affairs, 2004a). Inspired by and consulted on with the Commission (in applying various schemes that were effective in other countries), this EU activity represents an added value – even if the Czech Republic, along with other Member States, still faces an unacceptably high level of unemployment. Nor is the state of preparation and implementation of the national documents' standards advanced: poorly defined goals and responsibilities, lack of programme evaluation, poor inter-sectoral coordination and missing links to budgetary resources leave room for further improvements (Jabůrková and Mátl, 2006).

Social inclusion. In 2002 the European Commission asked all the governments of the candidate countries to prepare a Joint Inclusion Memorandum (JIM) to identify key problems and policy measures for combating poverty and social exclusion. The agenda of social inclusion was formally set with the preparation and approval of this document by the representatives of the European Commission and the Czech government in 2004 (Ministry of Labour and Social Affairs, 2004b).

The preparation and approval of the National Action Plan for social inclusion 2004-06 followed suit (Ministry of Labour and Social Affairs, 2005a). This document summed up other valid and prepared policies, action plans, strategies, programmes and governmental decrees relevant to social inclusion. The weakness in the document was the lack of explicit goals, a poorly defined responsibility for implementation and missing links to the budgetary process (Atkinson et al, 2005; Potůček, 2007). Significantly, the Ministry of Finance ignored the whole preparatory process.

Family policy. The government articulated and approved of an explicit family policy only in 2005 (Ministry of Labour and Social Affairs, 2005b). Its stimuli were manifold: a chronically low fertility rate (about 1.2), ideological factors (Christian and Social Democrats in power as government coalition partners), and the EU programmatic and political initiatives. Domestic factors, however, were decisive.

Health policy. The Bismarck legacy shaped the reform of the Czech health services after 1989. Despite good reasons for the transformation of the over-institutionalised state-owned communist health care system into a more flexible, national health service-like one, professionals and the older general public overwhelmingly preferred the system of compulsory health insurance financed by employees, employers and the state. The decentralisation of health care, the establishment of public Health Insurance Funds, the privatisation of most practitioners' facilities and some (smaller) hospitals, and the modernisation and improvement of care delivery followed suit. The EU's impact on the progress of this reform was very limited.

Genuine national programmatic initiative. An interesting example of the original 'national initiative' was 'The social doctrine of the Czech Republic' (Sociální doktrína České republiky, 2002). Its aim was to build a broad national consensus on the orientation, goals, priorities and corresponding instruments of Czech social policy. Five preparatory conferences in 1998-2000 constituted a 'joint venture' of the academic community concentrated around the non-profit Socioklub, the Ministry of Labour and Social Affairs and the Senate (the upper house of the Czech Parliament).

The 'social doctrine', the work of a group of experts from various fields and political affiliations, was mentioned in the coalition agreement statement of political parties in power in July 2002 as the starting point for the further development of government social policy and its priorities and approaches until 2006. Nevertheless, until its resignation in 2004, the government failed to find sufficient capacity and motivation for consequent steps: real social policy decisions stemmed mostly from either urgent problems or strong demands from various pressure groups.

In sum, the EU's role in shaping domestic social policies should not be overestimated. The obvious discrepancy between the Copenhagen criteria of accession (covering a very limited part of the social welfare agenda and installed in 1993) and the Lisbon Strategy (stretched as an explicit programme for the candidate countries as late as 2002 and politically and administratively executed only since 2004) opened considerable space for other, more active and influential international actors, that is, the World Bank and the IMF led by the neoliberal ideology of the Washington Consensus of the 1990s (Potůček, 2004). The situation has been slowly changing from the beginning of this century: the EU has helped put social policy issues higher on the political agenda, with institution building and the transfer of skills and money from the old Member States.

National responses to the EU initiatives

As Centre-Left governments have been in power since 1998, the reception and reflection of EU-related initiatives associated with national social policy were favourable in principle. Problems in communication, cooperation and reception have resulted chiefly from a shortage or lack of experience on the part of civil servants and other actors in pursuing public policies in general and EU policies in particular. Another systemic feature was the rather poor involvement of civil society in these processes: bureaucrats at the central level of government stage-managed the scene.

Lisbon Strategy

As previously mentioned, the Lisbon Strategy, developed under the auspices of the older Member States, had no relevance to the accession process. Nevertheless, between 2002 and 2004 it inspired the creation of national political programmes. A new coalition government under Prime Minister Vladimír Špidla, leader of the Czech Social Democratic Party, came to power in July 2002. The coalition agreement and the new government's declaration comprised all the Lisbon Strategy goals. The Office of the Government's Department for European Integration (Odbor pro evropskou integraci), which had existed since 1998, was renamed the Department for EU Issues (Odbor pro záležitosti EU) in May 2003. Together with the Inter-ministerial Commission for the Implementation of the Lisbon Strategy Goals (Meziresortní komise Úřadu vlády ČR pro naplňování cílů Lisabonské strategie) it supervises its implementation in the Czech Republic.

The original Lisbon Strategy was amended at the Gothenburg Summit in 2001, conceptualising sustainable development as consisting of three pillars: economic, social and environmental. The Czech government approved a strategy of sustainable development in 2004 (Office of the Government, 2004). Following a government crisis in 2004, Vladimír Špidla resigned. His successor, Stanislav Gross, installed a new Deputy Prime Minister for the Economy, Martin Jahn. One of his tasks was to prepare a *Strategy of economic growth* and *National Reform Programme 2005-08* (see, respectively, Office of the Government, 2005a, 2005b). Both documents were approved in 2005 and submitted to the European Commission. Simultaneously, the new European Commission redefined the Lisbon Strategy by prioritising economic growth, education, research and development, and fighting unemployment. Significantly, the Czech National Lisbon Programme consists of three parts: macroeconomic (notably continuing public finances reform), microeconomic (measures strengthening and increasing competitiveness) and employment (labour market flexibility, inclusion in the labour market, and education). Thus the 2005 programmatic shift at the EU level found a favourable response in the Czech Republic.

The Czech scholarly community has discussed the nature and implementation potential of the Lisbon Strategy in general and in the Czech Republic in particular. Some economists challenged the inclusion of social cohesion, environmental goals and the sustainable development concept as such. Even scholars, who in principle agreed with the structure of the Lisbon Strategy goals and the usefulness of such a programmatic effort, have found it quite difficult to see it as a realistic document. They question its ambitious endeavour to make the EU the most competitive and dynamic knowledge-based economy in the world by 2010.

Social Policy Agenda

No comprehensive Czech national policy has been inspired by the new EU Social Policy Agenda. Nevertheless, piecemeal progress on the majority of its issues is apparent:

- The government has established a cross-party task force to simulate the consequences of alternative pension reform options and thus contribute to a rational discussion among representatives of different ideological views.
- The government prepared a new Labour Code Act, approved by Parliament in 2006. This implements all the traditional core principles of ensuring the balance of power between employees and employers.

- The tripartite body has matured and gained legitimacy and its relatively smooth functioning has resulted in minimal strikes and other forms of open protest.
- The government has discussed gender equality and taken new approaches to close the gender gap in job opportunities, wages and other living conditions.
- The government formulated a new Conception of Family Policy with the aim of strengthening the position of families, especially those with children, and encouraging young people to become parents (Ministry of Labour and Social Affairs, 2005b).
- Other partial agendas (for example, the broad issue of social inclusion) were considered and realised (as mentioned through this chapter).

Open method of coordination

The Ministry of Labour and Social Affairs answered the questionnaire about the open method of coordination (OMC) in June 2005 (Ministry of Labour and Social Affairs, 2005c). It saw the added value of its application to social protection in the increased visibility of this issue among interested actors, that is, non-governmental organisations (NGOs) involved in the delivery of care and advocacy. Nonetheless, the general public was not familiar with the OMC.

In terms of technique and procedure, the Czech Republic has had no problems applying the OMC. The government used it several times when preparing National Action Plans for employment, the first National Action Plan for social inclusion, and so on. The serious problem lies not with formal application but with the administrative and political context in which it is being applied. To cut a long story short:

- the Czech public administration does not possess specific organisational structures with the capacity to deal with strategic issues;
- Czech civil servants are not trained and experienced in dealing with strategic issues in their professional lives;
- Czech politicians in general do not appreciate the importance of strategic thinking and decision making for the realisation of their political missions.

As a result, the real impact of the OMC in national governance has fallen dramatically short of its potential influence. In other words, operative and tactical tasks, short-term interests, lack of time and professional blindness severely limit OMC effects. At the same time, clear positive effects are observable in the raising of the level of civil servants' general awareness about the OMC.

Demographic change

The National Programme on preparation for ageing for 2003–07 was approved by the Czech government as early as May 2002. The Green Paper on *Confronting demographic change: A new solidarity between the generations* (European Commission, 2005c) is very topical for the Czech Republic, which has one of the lowest birth rates in Europe and a rapidly ageing population. The Minister of Labour and Social Affairs, Zdeněk Škromach, welcomed it at the conference 'Confronting Demographic Change: A New Solidarity between the Generations' (Brussels, 11–12 July 2005), pointing out that the Czech government sees the family as a legitimate subject of public interest.

The contribution of the Czech Republic to this document was prepared by the Ministry of Labour and Social Affairs and the Ministry of Health, submitted for public discussion, and finally approved by the Committee for the EU (Výbor pro EU)[3] and sent to the European Commission by the end of 2005. The upper chamber of the Czech Parliament, the Senate, held a public hearing on the EU Green Paper on demographic change on 29 June 2005 and passed a resolution on 6 October 2005. Composed mostly of right-wing political parties, the Senate condemned the OMC and all other non-legislative procedures that the EU applies in the Member States, and rejected any state intervention in the privacy of family life (for example, the division of household chores). The Green Paper positively influenced the preparation and approval of the Conception of Family Policy and the activities of the task force for pension reform.

Services of general interest

The position of the Czech government towards the White Paper on services of general interest (SGI) was prepared by the Ministry of Labour and Social Affairs (2004c). It stressed the specific relevance of this category in social and health care. These types of services call for a separated regulatory framework. Thus, the Czech position does not favour the idea of approving the framework directive on SGI. Instead, the government wants attention paid to the issue of mutual compatibility of EU policies given different conditions in individual

Member States. This position favours the independent solution in the sphere of social and health SGI.

The Ministry of Labour and Social Affairs (nd) has also answered the EU questionnaire on social SGI. This response casts doubt on the concept of SGI arguing that different interpretations of its meaning exist in several EU official documents. The document suggests that as a prerequisite of substantive policy debate, a further discussion be held on the concept and purposes of its application. It concludes that the prevailing majority of social services are non-economic. Meanwhile, new legislation (the Social Services Act, the Act on Assistance in Material Need, the Act on the Subsistence and Existential Minimum) substantially updated the regulatory framework of delivering social services in the country, to make their legal environment compatible with the profound economic and political changes occurring from the beginning of the transition up to 2006.

The transformation of social services should continue through increasing their quality, prioritising services, enabling clients to stay in their natural environment, matching demand and supply, continuously educating social workers, supporting the services delivered by NGOs, and strengthening the partnership of regions, municipalities and NGOs in regional and communal planning and policy implementation. Equal access to public finances should be guaranteed to all suppliers that follow approved standards of social services delivery.

Proposal on the Services Directive

This regulation has been the focus of attention for the Czech authorities. The unit responsible for this agenda is the Ministry of Trade and Industry. The Czech official position is much closer to the original proposal of the European Commission, and quite critical of the amended and changed version that the European Parliament approved on 16 February 2006.

The Czech government's position on the parliamentary version is a preference for:

- the broadest spectrum of services;
- the broadest and clearest definition of conditions for cross-border provision of services in Article 16;
- the easing of the administrative burden associated with a cross-border movement of workers (Ministry of Industry and Trade, 2006).

Social partners expressed their views in letters to the Czech Prime Minister: the Association of Industry and Trade supported the original version of the Commission, whereas the Bohemian-Moravian Chamber of Trade Unions endorsed the amended version of the European Parliament.

According to the Deputy Minister of Trade and Industry, Martin Tlapa, the Czech Republic (along with the Netherlands) headed a group of 15 or 16 governments that did not see the version approved by the European Parliament as inevitably final and that were trying to change the path of development at the March 2006 Vienna Summit. They failed, however, as the European Council in Vienna, with the final approval of the then Czech Prime Minister Jiří Paroubek, endorsed the version approved by the European Parliament.

European Economic and Monetary Union

The Czech government approved the joint paper prepared by the Ministries of Finance and Industry and Trade, and the Czech National Bank (2005) on the progress towards joining the Economic and Monetary Union (EMU) on 23 November 2005. According to the paper, the Czech Republic had no problem following the criteria of price stability, national currency stability and stability of long-term interest rates. Nevertheless, the sensitive issue of public finance sustainability persisted. General government debt was below the upper ceiling of 60%, and fluctuated at about 30% in 2003-05 (30.5% of GDP [gross domestic product] in 2005). According to the government, debt should be kept below 40%. In 2004 and 2005, the public budget deficit remained slightly below the 3% threshold (2.86% in 2004, 2.59% in 2005). The Czech government declared its determination to be able to join the Eurozone by 2010.[4] In view of positive economic developments, the target seems realistic.

Nevertheless, social scientists are debating as to whether this move will be productive, as some nationally sensitive and effective economic and social policy instruments will be lost by a country that has not yet fully recovered from its communist legacy.

Not surprisingly, Václav Klaus belongs to the camp of sceptics. He formulated, in a series of questions, his own set of Klaus' (or českolipská) criteria:

• Have the European countries within the Eurozone profited from its introduction?

- Is the level of the convergence of the Czech economy with the Eurozone economy sufficient in terms of various economic parameters, namely prices and salaries?
- Do we wish to have the monetary union as the pushing factor (or even an accelerator) of further European integration processes (Klaus, 2006)?

Václav Klaus is certain that the Eurozone project is primarily political – with the purpose of pushing Europe nearer to tax, fiscal and political union (Klaus, 2003). Thus, the Czech Republic should first answer the question of whether it would be in its interest to participate in this absolutist unification project, to help create the European superstate, or whether it would be better to co-conceptualise it as the community of states freely collaborating on the basis of intergovernmentalism.

Enlargement

The Czech authorities are generally well aware of the positive impact of the implementation of the core EU principles (and goals) of enlargement on the socio-economic development of a country which is extremely dependent on foreign trade and foreign investment, technology, and experience, and neighboured exclusively by Member States. Thus the Czech government often encounters delays from some older Member States in the full application of these principles, typically in the free movement of labour. This reaction is paradoxical, as the Czech Republic has for several years been a net importer of labour from other Member States. Even Czech politicians who are genuine supporters of Europeanisation have found it difficult to sell this paradox at home.

Conclusions

The institutions of the enlarged EU have the potential to become the main, if not the only, institutional umbrella preventing further widening of the gap between those who work and those who are unemployed, those who have and those who have not, those included and those excluded in the Member States. The social dimension of the Lisbon Strategy 2000 is the blueprint – even if it is somewhat virtual – for the future.

The time delay between the setting of the Copenhagen criteria in 1993 (with their clear priority for economic, political and legal conditions of accession) and the Lisbon Strategy (as presented to the accession countries in 2002, and becoming effective as they joined the EU in 2004, with an apparent shift of priorities towards employment, education and social cohesion as the necessary preconditions of economic success) created a sharp socio-political tension. The new Member States entered the EU with their health, social and employment policies not well enough developed to cope with the legitimate demands of this strategic policy document. The need to solve this discrepancy is urgent.

Nevertheless, the OMC proved to be too weak an instrument when confronted with the enormous public tasks of maintaining high employment, capacity building in health and social services, alleviation of poverty and strengthening social cohesion in the new Member States. In addition, the new Lisbon Strategy 2005-08 de facto considerably weakened the social pillar of the original 2000 Lisbon Strategy.

National initiatives within the new Member States would be an added value to this EU-centred effort. A document called 'The social doctrine of the Czech Republic' (2002), developed for this purpose by a group of scholars in the Czech Republic, might inspire other countries, even though it failed to directly influence social policy making in the country.

Thorough analytical studies of the threats, opportunities and developmental potentials of the EU and its Member States are needed for assisting strategic political decisions on the structural developmental priorities for the entire EU. The development of the ESM as an instrument of improving human and social conditions should be an integral part of that effort.

Notes

[1] I would like to express my thanks to Helena Čornejová, Martin Fassmann, Kateřina Hejdová, Milena Jabůrková, Ondřej Jukl, Ondřej Mátl, Vladimír Matoušek, Kateřina Příhodová, Olga Rozsívalová, Jitka Rychtaříková and Zuzana Zarajošová for the valuable insights they shared with me in the course of the preparation of this chapter. I also thank Jiří Král and Čestmír Sajda for their critical evaluation of the draft.

[2] Klaus had already voiced these opinions in the article 'Why Europe must reject centralisation' in the *Financial Times*, 29 August 2005.

[3] Výbor pro EU was the main coordinative body of the Czech public administration towards the EU until general elections in June 2006. Its chair was the Minister of Foreign Affairs.

[4] As the Czech economy has been booming, the public budgets deficit dropped below 3% in 2005. The forecast of the Czech National Bank speaks of about 2.8% in 2007.

NINE

Finland: towards more proactive policies

Juho Saari and Olli Kangas

The Finnish attitude to the European Union (EU) and to Europeanisation is a mixture of a number of contradictory elements. Every political party has its own opinions of the EU, and the political colour of the cabinet has an impact on the government's official stances on the issue. The official opinion is formed in Parliament, where the Grand Committee, representing all parties, formulates the parliamentary will that does not necessarily need to coincide with the government's standpoints. Usually the Left Alliance and the Centre Party have been quite critical towards the EU, while the Social Democrats and the Conservatives have been more in favour. However, a great deal of political pragmatism rather than political puritanism characterises Finnish policy making (Kangas, 2007). A good example of this pragmatism is that the most EU-critical Centre Party was the leading party in the government (1991–95) that prepared the Finnish membership application.

In addition to these political factors, a few institutional factors affect Finnish attitudes to the EU. Traditionally, there has been a strong emphasis on public delivery of services and income maintenance in Finnish social policy. Since the underpinning motivation has been universalism, institutionalised solutions and equality, the role of various private individual or labour market-based solutions (like second pillar occupational benefits) has been marginal. However, we also find contradictory elements: although all major social benefits are legislated, they are not necessarily run by the public authorities or agencies, a situation in some cases resulting in some definitional problems in the EU context.

The European social model versus the Finnish model

Chronologically speaking, Finland has been a latecomer in the field of social policy (see, for example, Kangas and Palme, 2005). However, the extensive coverage of those reforms that established universal 'national' insurance schemes compensated for the chronological gap.

The explanation for this late-but-extensive developmental pattern lies in the peculiar interaction of structural factors (a huge rural population), political factors (a strong agrarian party and divided political Left) and a peculiar form of parliamentarianism in which a minority of one third could postpone the adoption of governmental bills in the next elections (Lane and Ersson, 2002). These strong minority rights provide the opponents of social reforms effective means of vetoing bills on social protection if these contradict their interests.

In Finland, the political Left was divided into two competing parties: the Social Democrats (SDP) and the Communists. Due to late industrialisation the proportion of the agrarian population, and consequently the importance of the agrarian party in Finnish politics, was strong, and the SDP never attained such a hegemonic position as its sister party in Sweden (Jäntti et al, 2006; Kangas, 2007). Social policy priorities were divergent between the agrarians and the SDP. The agrarians vehemently supported flat-rate universalism (the basic security model, or 'people's insurance'), whereas the SDP and Conservatives were more inclined towards introducing earnings-related benefits. Up to the late 1950s the agrarians had the upper hand in Finnish politics and priorities in social policy reflected that situation. Since the early 1960s, the emphasis has shifted towards industrial workers' interests (or, more generally, employees' interests), and in the 1960s income-graduated benefits were in focus. Comprehensive sickness (1963), employment-related pension (1961) and unemployment (1959) insurance schemes were implemented (Niemelä and Salminen, 2006).

The political dualism is reflected in the institutional set-up of the Finnish income transfer system. Because there were political problems in implementing legislated earnings-related programmes through Parliament, important parts of those programmes were carried through labour markets. Thus, the Finnish institutional design contains a great deal of corporatist elements (see also Salminen, 1993). Since the 1970s, to ensure female labour force participation, the state and municipalities have invested heavily in child and elderly care facilities (Saari, 2001). Again, the controversies between agrarian-bourgeois vis-à-vis social democratic-Left orientations came into play. In contrast to many other Member States, the need for child day care bifurcated into municipal day care centres (what the political Left demanded) and home care allowances (what the bourgeois parties demanded), a kind of cash compensation for families that do not use public day care but either take care of children themselves or use private providers (Hiilamo, 2002). In addition, the Finnish health care system has mainly relied on public services, supplemented by sickness insurance that subsidises private health care. This two-channel system of health care also reflects political tensions between those who prefer private services and the freedom of choice, and those who emphasise broad coverage and the responsibilities of municipalities to organise and provide it.

In the 1990s, the Finnish national economy fell into the deepest recession in the country's history. Due to economic and fiscal difficulties, most social policy schemes became targeted by retrenchment and downward adjustments (Saari, 2001; Heikkilä and Kautto, 2004). The welfare state muddled through the survival test of the turbulent period, acting as a buffer against the most harmful effects of the crisis. Surprisingly, poverty rates did not rise dramatically during the darkest year of the recession (see also Heikkilä and Kautto, 2004). However, the impacts of the crisis are gradual, as now, a decade later, income inequalities have expanded to the same level as in the early 1970s. Poverty levels, too, are higher than they have been for decades. In fact since mid-1995 poverty rates have increased more rapidly in Finland than in most other Organisation for Economic Co-operation and Development (OECD) countries (Luxembourg Income Study, 2007). The main reason is long-term unemployment and cuts in basic security benefits that are more and more lagging behind the general income development. Although the Finnish welfare state is leaner and meaner it has retained some of its basic elements. Following Saari (2005a) these can be defined as:

- Close *links to social risks:* social policy programmes are designated to respond to specific social risks, such as unemployment, old age and work disability, not to specifically respond to poverty or social exclusion.
- *Individuality:* social insurance benefits and taxation are based solely on the individual's work history, payments and income. Only in calculating widows' and orphans' pensions (and in some tax allowances) does the family situation play a role.
- *Independency:* this also encompasses dependencies between adult generations. Adult siblings have no formal obligations to take care of their parents, and parents have no formal obligations to take care of their adult children.
- *Collectivity:* in principle all citizens are covered by the same schemes, and the institutional set-up of the services and income transfers received by the claimant depends on the social risk, not on the insurance policies the individual has signed.
- *Coordination:* individuals can move from one municipality to another or from one working place to another without losing their social rights.

- *Legislated benefits:* almost without exception Finnish social security is based on laws and statutes, and the role of occupational or individual social protection is negligible, although expanding. The expansion of private service and insurance markets has been rapid, but again the focus is on legally regulated benefits with different forms of tax incentives.
- *Residence-based benefits and services:* the first criterion for receiving services and transfers is residence, not employment. Thus, social insurance coverage is wider than in other Member States, except for the other Nordic countries and the Netherlands. The same applies to services.
- *Emphasis on income transfers and social services:* with very few exceptions, assets have no impact on rights to social transfers or services. The most important exceptions are various social assistance-related benefits.

European integration in some cases has had important ramifications for the institutional characteristics of the Finnish welfare state (Kattelus and Saari, 2006; Saari and Kari, 2006). Joining the European Economic Area (EEA) in 1992 and the EU[1] in 1995 accentuated a clearer demarcation between social insurance and non-contributory benefits (including social and medical assistance of different kinds, and some forms of social services). The former is governed by the coordination regulation (1408/17), whereas the latter is left outside. Even in the EEA negotiations the central issue was the principle of symmetry, indicating that Finland tried to avoid a situation in which it would pay a benefit to a country where such a benefit does not exist or where those benefits were clearly lower, thereby discouraging welfare tourism and avoiding some public costs. This principle has formed a more or less explicit starting point for Finland's EU policy.

Finland had several flat-rate benefits that did not fall clearly under either social insurance or social assistance, including child allowance, national pension, basic unemployment allowance and labour market support. In the membership negotiations Finland was prepared to change the institutional structure of these benefits in such a way that their characteristics – either social insurance or social assistance – would be fortified in the spirit of the symmetry principle. The main issue was if and to what extent these benefits are included in the scope of Regulation 1408/71. After EU membership, national pensions are regarded as belonging to the realm of the coordination regulation. However, the entitlement rules have been changed. Previously, the right to full national pension was given after residence of five years in the country. Since 1996 the amount of national pension is linked to the number of years lived in Finland: to get the full national pension, the pensioner must have lived in Finland for 40 years. If the period is shorter, the benefit will be reduced in proportion to the missing years of residence. The sharpening of qualification regulations may lead to situations where the pension is lower than social assistance. In such cases the gap will be filled by social assistance.

Child allowance is also regarded as a family benefit for inclusion under Regulation 1408/71. The reason is the practice followed in many other Member States, where child allowance is (or was earlier) paid to the father in the form of increased wage or salary. The basic unemployment daily allowance (flat-rate unemployment benefit) was classified as insurance, whereas labour market support (a means-tested flat-rate unemployment benefit) was defined to be social assistance and, consequently, it is not included in the scope of the coordination regulation. A Finnish family policy peculiarity is the child homecare allowance. In principle, the homecare allowance was part of the social services system; consequently it was seen as compensation for families that do not use public day care facilities and as such should not fall within the scope of Regulation 1408/71. However, the European Court of Justice (ECJ) ruled in the case *Maaheimo* (C-333/00) that the homecare allowance should be included in the coordination regulation. Therefore, since 2002 homecare allowance has been within the scope of the regulation.

In addition to the coordination regulation, the public–private mix in certain employment-related benefits has resulted in some definitional and conceptual problems. The key issue has been to what extent insurance directives dictated by internal market principles (the four freedoms) should be applied to Finnish private sector employment-related pensions (TEL) or work accident insurance. Although totally legislated and mandatory, these schemes are run by private or semi-private insurance companies, resulting in some confusion over the correct classification. When it comes to the free movement of capital, and services and legislation on competition, the Finnish semi-private earnings-related pensions do not easily fit the three-pillar (public–occupational–private) typology that the EU applies. TEL pensions are partly organised through private for-profit insurance companies, which could, in some cases, be interpreted as occupational pensions, so that the companies running TEL pensions should be subject to certain insurance directives. On the other hand, according to the Finnish interpretation, the main objective of the TEL system is to safeguard basic social security and maintain social solidarity: therefore, these pensions should not fall within the scope of these directives. Thus the TEL scheme has some traits of several pillars, leading to confusion in certain cases. To avoid any confusion and legal uncertainty, when Finland applied for EU membership it successfully negotiated a special clause against demands set by life insurance directives.

In work accident insurance Finland has revised its institutional structures. Again, according to the Finnish interpretation, work accident insurance is without a doubt part of social security and should therefore be left outside the non-life insurance directive (Council Directive 73/239/EEC). However, the ECJ took the opposite stand in a case applicable to the Finnish situation (*The Kingdom of Belgium*, C-206/98). Consequently, the Commission demanded that the relevant directive be fully applied, since private insurance companies carry the insurance. The national position was revised in 1996 when it became possible for EU-based companies to be insurance carriers in Finland.

In addition to direct social policy impacts, there are indirect impacts that in the long run may have important consequences for social policy. Alcohol policy and the national monopoly of the Slot Machine Association (RAY) are two such cases. In the Nordic countries (with the exception of Denmark) alcohol policy has been regulative, with health and other social policy aspects emphasised. The state has collected a substantial amount of tax revenues through its alcohol monopoly. In contrast, in the EU alcohol policy belongs to the realm of agricultural policy. In its entry negotiations Finland won the right to limit the amount of imported alcohol per traveller coming from abroad. Although the exception was extended to the end of 2003, from the beginning of 2004 both Finland and Sweden abolished (or were forced to abolish) the import restrictions. The big issue deals with the alcohol monopoly, whose position remains unchallenged. The few cases on the issue have not questioned the present monopoly situation.

Similarly, lottery and (socio-politically more significantly) gambling have been national monopolies. From its profits the RAY used to subsidise various social policy organisations in the third sector, and these have been heavily dependent on the RAY subsidies. So far, ECJ rulings have been positive for the monopoly. However, according to EU competition laws the RAY subsidies are seen as distorting conditions for competition among various service producers and this may have harmful consequences for the third sector, non-profit-oriented producers of services, as their ability to adjust to a new, more competitive environment is often quite limited. Thus, although the EU has not taken direct measures against the RAY, indirect measures may be significant in the field of social services delivery for some specific population groups.

Main principles in national reforms

Six main challenges for social policy penetrate all Finnish policy making (Saari, 2006). These challenges are:

- balancing the public budget
- maintaining competitiveness
- increasing employment
- adapting to markets
- improving the position of the consumer/client
- adapting to the greying population.

Balancing the public budget has been the underpinning rationale in social policy measures aimed at dampening the growth of social spending. The budget balance of various public actors – the state, municipalities and social security funds – has varied considerably since the late 1980s. The general picture in the early 1990s was that social security funds have been strongly in surplus, the municipal sector more or less in balance and the state budget in deficit. Thus the government targeted the recalibration measures mainly at state welfare spending. One major measure to balance the state budget was the reform of the state subsidy to municipalities. Previously, the state had subsidised municipalities via earmarked contributions. But with the 1993 and 1996 reforms subsidies have been paid on a lump-sum basis, that is, the state partially solved its budget problems by transferring them to the municipalities. To fortify the financial basis of pension funds, Finland has allowed investments abroad since 1997 (Kangas, 2006). Before that pension funds were obliged to invest solely in Finland.

The most important social policy measure for improving *national competitiveness* was the agreement on re-sharing social security contributions between the employers and employees. The process was initiated during the first recession years of the early 1990s, when the employees' pension and unemployment insurance contributions were introduced. Taken together, these reforms shifted greater financial responsibility to employees and the insured.

Employment-enhancing measures fall into four categories. First, to increase the employment rate, the government has introduced various incentives. Benefits are more closely related to contributions, and streamlining the social security system has abolished poverty/income traps – but ironically enough, also increased poverty! Second, by shortening periods in education and sick leave, by better reconciling family and work life and by screening the pension system, Finland has increased its labour supply. Third, there have been attempts to create partial or sheltered employment for disabled people, to better match their qualifications and skills demanded in work. Fourth, corporate incentives have been changed in such a way that it is no longer easy for enterprises to 'externalise' the surplus labour into the public social policy programmes. Enterprises now have to pay more of the costs for redundancy, early retirement and unemployment.

The adaptation to market principles has been accentuated in many ways. The 1993 Reform of Municipality Act gave municipalities more scope for producing and organising social, health and education services. However, once the municipality decides to open its service production to competition and rely on private service providers, it must fully follow competition legislation. A growing number of municipalities have used this option (for example, in childcare, services for disabled and elderly people, and health services). Yet there are attempts to improve competition within the TEL system. As previously explained, although the TEL is a part of social security, it is organised by private companies that to a limited extent compete with each other for customers (employers). The key – and still partly open – issue is how to satisfactorily unify the endeavour for pension security, uniform pension contributions, collective responsibility and competition.

The position of the consumer has been emphasised since the early 1990s as part of a more general phenomenon called consumerism. Citizens are getting the possibility to choose services freely from a wider set of providers. At the beginning of the 1990s new laws on claimants' and patients' rights in social and health services were introduced. A number of subjective rights were also implemented: the most important claim rights were guaranteed to disabled people and children. Finally, in health and elder care services customers' rights to choose among service providers have been increased.

One common denominator for most western countries is the *growing proportion of elderly people*. In Finland a number of proactive measures have been taken to tackle the challenges of ageing. The early 1990s saw a gradual reform of the existing pension schemes, culminating in the 'big' 2005 pension reform (Ministry of Social Affairs and Health, 2006a; Kangas, 2007). The objective was to create incentives to lengthen work careers, fortify actuarial principles and make the pension system more resilient to demographic pressures. In service systems there is a shift from institutional care towards more open forms of (non- or semi-institutional) care, municipal homecare services and homecare allowances payable to those who perform care by themselves. However, the shift from institutional care to open or non-institutional care has not been problem-free. A significant proportion of municipalities badly fail to invest as much as needed in community or non-institutionalised services. The problem will be accentuated by the pace of the population ageing and the municipalities will be obliged to further invest in such services.

National responses to the EU initiatives

Since the early 1990s, the Finnish government has on several occasions debated the various social policy implications of EU membership. It took its first explicit stance in 1990 during the EEA negotiations, which emphasised possible problems of symmetry and demanded that the Finnish system meet certain related demands. The conclusion was that the central characteristics of the Finnish social policy system should be maintained in the future. The Parliament's Social and Health Affairs Committee gave a similar report in 1992 when the EEA was established and in 1994 when the country was about to join the EU. In 1995 the government clarified its position by declaring that 'Finland supports the development of the social dimension in working life and social security in such a way that common minimum standards are jointly agreed and Member States can if they will exceed these minimums but the ways of action should be preserved under the national decision-making' (Finnish Government, 1995). The central role of the Member States in social protection systems was the underpinning rationale of the Finnish stances. In 2001 the government report to Parliament emphasised that the EU should be developed as a community of independent Member States, taking care of dynamic economic growth and social and ecological responsibilities.

These Finnish positions strongly express the wish or a political consensus to preserve the present institutional model of social policy rather than to launch a new European social model (ESM) and change the present one accordingly (on the early debate see Saari, 2002). In sum, the Finnish responses and attitudes have been rather reserved, especially in the coordination or merging of internal markets and social security, particularly health services. In recent years, a number of ECJ decisions have fortified the market (or functional) principles, for example, in the health sector; sometimes these rulings have not been fully compatible with the policy objectives of the Finnish government (Grand Committee, 2003).

Lisbon Strategy and reformed Lisbon Strategy 2005

The Finnish attitude to the Lisbon Strategy was from the start of the 2000s very positive, although some key politicians were doubtful as to whether some other Member States could really keep and implement their promises. From the Finnish point of view the Strategy's strengths were the coordination between separate EU-initiated processes and the overall clarification of the European approach in social protection. Finland welcomed the initiative, particularly as Broad Economic Policy Guidelines (BEPGs) and employment policies (European Employment Strategy, EES) were already under way, whereas no similar progress was visible in social issues.

The reformed Lisbon Strategy (the Growth and Jobs Strategy, 2005) was also received positively. Behind the positive attitude was an attempt to further promote the efficacy of EU policies that clearly needed some revision if they were to implement promised reforms. Furthermore, the emphasis on economic growth and maintaining economic competitiveness – traditionally with a strong foothold in the Finnish public policy priorities (Kosonen, 1987) – was welcomed: 'By concentrating on economic growth and employment the economic competitiveness of the EU can be safeguarded – which is necessary for the guaranteeing of the other elements of sustainable growth. The government agrees with the Commission's view that concentrating now on growth and employment is in concordance with promoting social and environmental objectives' (Governmental EU-Secretary, 2004).

In its response to the reform proposals, the Finnish Parliament (Grand Committee, 2005a) blamed the initial strategy for having too many pillars and sub-objectives or targets, and said that the administration of the process was too dispersed and heavy. Therefore, in general Finland welcomed the reform. However, there was also some criticism. The Lisbon Agenda drafted by the Commission set a number of concrete objectives for Member States in 10 core policy areas. From the Finnish standpoint, the programme was too wide, including inconsistent and partially overlapping recommendations. Thus, they felt that the renewed Lisbon Strategy should not be accepted as such but be re-discussed and redrafted (Social and Health Committee, 2004a), and that was what happened with the revised Strategy in 2005.

The main philosophy in the reformed Lisbon Strategy was a clear concentration on growth and employment (and some structural reforms). This meant pushing social protection cooperation at least partially outside the realm (or the core) of the Strategy. In some Member States the ministries of social affairs regarded this change as undesirable and presented their criticism in, for example, the Social Protection Committee (SPC). In addition, many national and international grass-roots organisations and globalisation-critical action groups saw these changes as indications of EU policies gliding towards neoliberalism, a position in conflict with the objectives of sustainable development.

Despite the critical remarks the Finnish government was in agreement to the reformed Lisbon Strategy and adopted a more proactive approach, emphasising that social protection issues needed fortification within the strategy. The motivation for this stance was that many of the integrated guidelines dealt de facto with social issues (albeit from the perspective of balancing the public economy and creating stronger incentives). This attitude was condensed in the opinion of the parliamentary Grand Committee: 'The committee agrees with the Commission and the government in that the future emphasis should be in growth and employment. However, the other aspects of the strategy must not be neglected, since sustainable growth can be achieved only if simultaneously there is a strong commitment in the social dimension and sustainable environmental development. Sustainable growth and an environmental approach and the fortification of the ESM are those basic solutions which the concrete actions of the Lisbon Strategy should be based on' (Grand Committee, 2005a).

The Finnish National Reform Programme was written in such a way that it balanced different approaches, including those of the Ministry of Social Affairs and Health, which had representatives in the working group that drafted the Programme. The Programme contains no new and innovative ideas but rather the guidelines relied on in previously accepted documents. In negotiations on the EU Constitution Finland welcomed the idea of including the Lisbon Strategy as part of the Constitution, as this inclusion would strengthen coordination and synergy among different policy areas.

Social Policy Agenda

The Finnish government was satisfied with the Social Policy Agenda 2000-05 because it paid satisfactory attention to the dynamic interplay between economic, employment and social policies. The Parliament, however, was more reserved, worrying about the division of competencies at different levels (Grand Committee, 2000). The Social Policy Agenda 2005-10 also received a positive response in Finland (Grand Committee, 2005b). The national response, again prepared jointly by the Ministries of Social Affairs and Health, and Labour, regarded the Social Policy Agenda as successful and underlined the central objectives of the Lisbon Strategy. In addition, Finland strongly supported the life-cycle perspective.

However, the government also underlined that it saw no need to start any new EU-level (sub-)processes. Rather, all focus and energy should be devoted to implementing and streamlining existing policies and processes. As to the adjustment policies, the Finnish government agreed on the issue but also repeatedly emphasised respect for the independence of labour market partners and third sector organisations. This attitude mirrors the continuous debate on the proper balance of competencies between the EU and the national levels. To what extent can the EU give tasks to Member State social partners and non-governmental organisations (NGOs)? It is likewise unclear the extent to which agreements made at the EU level may constrain national activities and agreements between social partners. Finland has stressed the competencies of the individual Member States and their social partners and NGOs in these issues.

The government was satisfied with the inclusion of the external or global dimension of social and employment policies in the Social Policy Agenda. Furthermore, Finland agreed with the Agenda on the promotion of decent work, just as the Commission had proposed, and regarded corporate social responsibility as essential. Finland criticised the Posting of Workers Directive for having stagnated in the Council. Despite the fate of the Directive, Finland argued, the Commission could consider proper measures for controlling and regulating private enterprises hiring and selling labour over state boundaries. Such measures would also benefit the legal and controlled labour force migration from non-EU countries to the EU.

The Social Affairs and Health Committee expressed its more critical attitudes and dissatisfaction. According to the Committee, the Finnish approach in EU social and health policy issues had been too vague and passive. Consequently, it strongly endorsed more active measures: 'According to the committee Finland should be more active in emphasizing the role of strong social and health policy when preparing EU initiatives. According to information the committee has received the quality and content of the governmental stances are very often affected by the tight timetable set for the preparation of these stances. Tight time schedules also affect possibilities to hear various organisations in the process of preparation. The committee regards it important that the government tries to affect the timetables in order to give enough time to get in the issues before the national responses are formulated' (Social Affairs and Health Committee, 2005). The differences of the parliamentary Committee's position in 2000 (when it emphasised the principles of subsidiarity and proportionality, and underlined the key role of the Member States in social protection) and 2005 (when it demanded a proactive approach) indicate that the EU has attained an important role in Finnish social policy discourse.

Open method of coordination

During its EU membership Finland has prioritised the Community method over the open method of coordination (OMC) in social, economic and employment policies. Consequently, it has demanded several times that the preparations and decision making, especially including the OMC, taking place outside the Community method should be abandoned altogether (Grand Committee, 2002, p 5). Thus it is not surprising that when preparing for the second EU Council follow-up Lisbon meeting (March 2002), Finland was frustrated with the OMC, not seeing it as a useful tool. Preliminary experiences indicated that the efforts that the OMC demanded were considerable, further straining the very heavy workloads of a small number of national experts.

Consequently, before the Barcelona Summit in March 2002 the Finnish Cabinet Committee on EU Affairs demanded that measures created for the OMC should be as light as possible. Strengthening the Lisbon Strategy called for limiting the overlapping of different measures and jettisoning the preparation processes. Instead of the full-scale OMC, less heavy methods would be more cost-effective. Finland expressed the same attitude during the Greek and Italian presidencies in 2003 (Saari, 2003).

In 2002, the government delivered its report to Parliament, summarising its view on the OMC, with a few issues falling on the positive side. The government saw the OMC as a good means of promoting systematic exchanges of information on different policy solutions between Member States, as well as helping to promote the social objectives in the Lisbon Strategy. However, there were also negative aspects, and to eliminate these problems the government defined a number of unmet conditions:

- the OMC should have a concrete goal
- the OMC should be the most relevant measure for achieving the goal
- the OMC should be as light as possible
- the use of the OMC should not change the institutional division of competencies
- Parliament should have a say on EU issues.

In recent years signs of more positive attitudes towards the OMC are re-emerging. In the context of the mid-term review of the Lisbon Strategy in 2004 the Finnish government admitted that Finland was previously quite reserved about the OMC. However, since it has become an integral and permanent part of the Lisbon Strategy, its usefulness and national positions need re-evaluation. Furthermore, the government stated that a more proactive approach would improve Finland's possibilities for affecting how and to what purposes the OMC is applied (Finnish Government, 2004). The government suggested that the OMC should concentrate more on finding best practice and benchmarking. It is hard to say in which way the more positive views of the OMC will manifest in Finnish policy definitions.

Several reasons explain Finland's lukewarm attitude towards the OMC. First, it was seen as going against the national priority of emphasising the traditional Community method over the new mode of governance, that is, a question of competencies. Second, Finland feared too rigid and bureaucratic an application of National Action Plans on social inclusion, pensions and health care, which reflected the basic difference and discrepancy between the Finnish and EU way of looking at social policy issues (see Saari, 2005b). In the Finnish tradition social policy responds to various social risks, such as childhood, sickness and ageing, or deficiencies in education or housing, lack of employment, or problems in the reconciliation of work and family life, and so on. Within this framework, poverty or social inclusion/exclusion is not a separate social risk but rather a consequence of inadequate socio-political combating of social risks. Consequently, if a Member State has proper social policy measures against social risks, separate poverty measures (or action plans against poverty and social exclusion) are strictly speaking unnecessary and may often be harmful, as they generate unnecessary social divisions in the institutional structures of social protection systems. So, in the initial phases of the OMC the nomination of best practice to combat poverty in particular was considered problematic (and Finland actually decided not to name or nominate individual projects). From the Finnish perspective this approach was inadequate, as the existence of such best practice reflects the failure of social policy aimed at combating social risks.

A third problem deals with policy cycles. In Finnish political culture major social policy reforms and objectives are defined after elections in cabinet negotiations, not in separate strategy papers. For example, the report on social protection and social exclusion that was delivered in September 2006 could not include new openings or policies from the Finnish side, as new strategic lines were not drawn up before the

2007 parliamentary elections and cabinet negotiations. Fourth, there was some aversion to the EU Commission's behaviour of sometimes drawing its own conclusions before proper SPC discussions. After criticism from several Member States the Commission changed its procedure, influencing the Finnish attitude in a more positive direction.

Demographic change

The ageing population is a common problem for all Member States. Most Member States have initiated national activities to meet this demographic challenge. The Finnish government has invested significantly in evaluating the magnitude and scale of the problem, and related social and economic costs (Prime Minister's Office, 2004). All agree that the challenge is quite formidable, that policies must be proactive and that producing maximum added value calls for coordination among the ministries. However, it has been somewhat unclear what EU-level actions would be required and what the value-added contribution of possible new EU measures would be in comparison to existing national social protection reports, programmes and strategies. These issues are visible in the Finnish responses to the Green Paper on demographic change (Grand Committee, 2005c).

Finland's answers were often quite general, thereby leaving much scope for interpretations and further policy making. Some questions, such as that on the VAT policies, were left unanswered. On the other hand, Finland's answer also indicated that the (perhaps) needed measures (for example, flexible retirement ages, investment on the quality of work life, and better reconciliation of work and family life) are well in line with the existing Finnish model. More broadly, a main frame of reference is global, with the 2002 United Nations' (UN) decision on the ageing of the population as its starting point.

The Finnish emphasis was that the main responsibility and competence lies with individual Member States, which must find their own solutions. Nonetheless, dialogue with the EU may help Member States to learn from each other. In the EU, the demographic issue should be part of European economic policy making, employment and social protection strategies. Consequently, Finland underlined that separate EU-level actions or new processes were not needed. Demographic considerations could also be included in European Social Fund (ESF) policies. Typically, Finland also emphasised that demographic change should be considered an opportunity and that measures should be proactive (aimed at adjusting existing institutions to changing circumstances) rather than defensive (aimed at maintaining the status quo) (Finnish Government, 2005a).

Services of general interest

Services of general interest (SGI) is a wide area, and stances have been formed in discussions led by the Ministry of Trade and Industry, with various partners. Finland has been an active participant in discussions on this issue, expressing concerns about the extension of the concept from gas, electricity, post and telephone services to social and health services (including social insurance and housing). In short, Finland believes that the concept of SGI is too vague and unspecified and that its implications for health and social services are not properly spelled out.

The Finnish opinion is that it is up to the individual Member State to define what services must be guaranteed to everyone and on what terms. The ESM allows national decision makers to define what services should be solely under the public domain and what could be opened to profit-making competition. According to Finland, 'for the reasons of justice and the functioning of the systems it is important that legislated, obligatory social security schemes including income maintenance programmes and public social and health services are in the future left out of the economic sphere and are not subject to regulation on economic issues. General directives on other than economic services of general interests should be avoided' (Social Affairs and Health Committee, 2004b).

In its 2004 memorandum the parliamentary Social Affairs and Health Committee concluded that the concept of SGI was not clearly defined in Finland. Finnish legislation did not clearly distinguish between SGI and other services. The Committee deemed it important to clarify relations between national and EU competencies, particularly the role of the Services Directive on the internal market, state subsidies and competition (when discussing social and health services). Doing so was seen as necessary because solving these issues at a more general level than case-by-case before the ECJ was preferable. The Finnish government believed that it was necessary to establish the criteria that described national institutional differences in service production, and to define those principles; Member States could then decide how to organise their social and health services.

Proposal on the Services Directive

Preparations on the Services Directive in Finland lie with the Ministry of Trade and Industry. The Ministry of Social Affairs and Health has been involved in issues dealing with social and health services, pharmacies, the gambling monopoly (one of the main financers of the third sector) and alcohol policy. In principle, the ministries have agreed on all issues and on the scope of the Services Directive: which services should be included and which should be left out. The common starting point was that although the scope should be as wide as possible, covering social and health services, guaranteeing the rights of patients and the quality of services called for not applying the country-of-origin principle in social and health issues.

Parliament's Grand Committee that delivered its report on the Services Directive in 2004 regarded the Directive as necessary for realising the Lisbon Strategy in general and for maintaining European competitiveness (Grand Committee, 2004). The Committee also had more national reasons: it thought that the Directive might open new possibilities for Finnish enterprises to enter European (Central European) services markets.

As to the interplay between the Services Directive and health services (and certain other socio-politically motivated themes), the tone was less enthusiastic. The report strongly stressed that the Directive must not violate a Member State's right to decide on the structure of education, and the production and financing of social services. More concretely, there were demands that issues such as the alcohol and gambling monopolies should fall outside the scope of the Services Directive. Pharmacies, too, should be left out unless equal access to medicine in all parts of the country could be safeguarded. Neither must the Directive be applied when a municipality bought services from a health service district or from other municipalities. In particular, in health and social services the country-of-origin principle should not be applied, and all services providers regardless of origin should cover risks through patient insurance that fully corresponded to Finnish standards. In short, the rationale in the Finnish discussion on the Services Directive has been that the scope of the Directive should be defined as widely as possible for commercial services, with more reservations in social policy questions and demands for preserving and strengthening the national characteristics of service provision.

European Economic and Monetary Union

When joining the EU in 1995, Finland had no reservations on membership and never seriously considered opting out of the third stage of the European Economic and Monetary Union (EMU). In this respect the Finnish approach was different from the Danish and especially Swedish decisions to keep their currencies. However, in the mid- and late 1990s came heated discussions on the fate of social policy under possible EMU membership (after the third stage).

The 1997 government report stated: 'The adaptation to changes in national economy may change indirectly preconditions for social policy. When making social policy decisions demands of economic efficiency and social justice must be coordinated. The government emphasises that it is necessary to map social and economic consequences of the monetary union and other forms of integration' (Finnish Government, 1997). Both the government and various interest organisations provided such 'mappings'; the results varied, depending somewhat on the colour of the 'mapper'. The governmental conclusion was that the EMU would not cause such severe problems that the country should not join. 'In the short run the EMU impact upon social needs can be considered neutral.... In a longer run the EMU, if successful, can enchant economic growth and facilitate the development of social policy' (Finnish Government, 1997, part 5.2). In its report to Parliament in February 1998, the government further asserted that its aim was to maintain the Nordic model of welfare state under the EMU criteria (Finnish Government, 1998).

However, the common currency was seen as a problem under certain conditions. The previous way of improving competitiveness through repeated devaluations would be excluded, and there was a danger that during a recession wages would have to be adapted through 'internal devaluation', that is, by decreasing wages, leading to detrimental effects on the demand side. To solve this problem and a number of other problems, the government implemented buffer funds. The idea was quite simple: during an economic upturn buffer funds would accumulate for use in the next recession, to cover the costs of increased unemployment. The buffer covered annual costs (resulting from unemployment) of 3.6%. The buffer fund reached its maturity in 2002.

The fulfilment of the EMU's Stability and Growth Pact (SGP) (1997) has not resulted in significant problems for the Finnish public economy. At present the ERM95 budget balance is strongly positive and is likely to remain so, and public debt is among the lowest in the

EU hemisphere and decreasing. However, the Finnish government has sometimes become quite frustrated because some Member States have not met the SGP requirements. While their not doing so has not increased interest rates, excessive deficits and the lack of budgetary disciplines are nevertheless considered a major risk for Finnish and European economies. Consequently, the government welcomed the renewed SGP in 2005, hoping that the new rules of the game would increase the commitment of all Member States to the common EMU objectives, and that these objectives in the long run would improve EU economic performance and thus fortify the sustainability of social policies.

Enlargement

The EU enlargement in 2004 did not arouse strong sentiments in Finland, mainly due to the country's position in the North Eastern corner of the EU. Furthermore, Finland already had bilateral agreements with the new Member State Estonia, so enlargement did not dramatically change the prevailing situation. However, mainly by following the demands of trade unions, Finland introduced transitional regulations similar to those of many other Member States.

Finland applied a transition period of two years in the free movement of labour from the new Member States, excluding Cyprus and Malta (Finnish Government, 2005b). In certain cases the free movement of labour has been disguised as free movement of services resulting in some problems in 2005/06. In spring 2006 all transitory regulations were terminated as unnecessary. However, simultaneously, efforts to control labour movement were made more effective. The government viewed this surveillance as necessary to prevent (further) violations against labour conditions, the negligence of employers' social responsibilities and biased or distorted competition between enterprises and entrepreneurs. As to the possible membership of Romania and Bulgaria, Finland considers no additional regulations necessary.

In the context of social and health services the main question attached to the recent enlargement dealt with residence-based social protection. Immigrants from other Member States got residence-based rights if their stay was regarded as 'permanent'. The government listed some factors that might increase the demand for social and health services. One such factor was the poorer quality of health and health services in neighbouring countries, possibly increasing the demand for intensive care of certain diseases (for example, HIV, tuberculosis) previously not prevalent in Finland. However, the government decided that limitations targeted to immigrants coming from the new Member States were not only unnecessary but also discriminating and unfair.

Conclusions

Finnish responses to the European social dimension have fluctuated. They can be divided into two periods or modes of thinking. In the early 1990s, when Finland was negotiating membership, it took a very defensive stance of safeguarding the institutional structures of national social policy as much as possible. Although its basic approaches and attitudes to EU membership were positive, dubious voices pinpointed possible detrimental social and political consequences of membership and the coordination (regulation) of social policy systems. These attitudes were linked not only to somewhat unrealistic ideas of the excellence of Finnish social policy but also to the limited possibilities of affecting EU decisions. By the turn of the millennium, however, a slight reorientation had taken place. Although the underlying trend was as positive as before, the convention and intergovernmental congresses particularly emphasised social policy issues.

Recently, a clear reorientation has occurred. The main idea or new point of view is that the EU impact on Finnish social policy has been recently mediated through so many channels – such as economic and employment policies, competition law and structural policies, and the four freedoms – that the earlier, mainly defensive approach based on the emphasis on subsidiarity and proportionality, and the reliance on the Community method, is no longer fruitful and may actually be counterproductive in the long run. Consequently, Finland sees a stronger need for an EU-level social policy based on different emergency brakes, transition rules or horizontal principles aimed at balancing the internal markets vis-à-vis policies aimed at modernising social protection systems. In this respect, Finland wants a stronger social Europe to make Member States' social policies possible. The draft Constitution contains some elements of this proactive thinking. This new approach was also included in the strategy of the Ministry of Social Affairs and Health: 'From Finland's perspective it is important to actively influence political processes and legislation initiatives in the European Union in order to secure preconditions for our social welfare and its development potential' (Ministry of Social Affairs and Health, 2006b, p 29).

Finland is not willing to define some policy areas or issues as belonging solely to the realm of national decision making or competence, something that would be unsuccessful, anyway, at the current stage of integration. But neither is the country prepared to sacrifice central institutional elements of its own social policy model. This dual emphasis is also visible in discussions of the relative roles of economic and social issues. Despite a strong emphasis on opening up internal markets and prioritising economic growth, Finland does not want this to happen at the expense of social security (protection), health, labour protection or the environment. The dual approach, as discordant as it might appear, tries to balance the two major objectives and accurately describes Finnish attitudes and responses to European integration.

Note
[1] In the Finnish 1994 October election on joining the EU 56.1% voted 'Yes', and 43.1% 'No'.

TEN

The Netherlands: social and economic normalisation in an era of European Union controversy

Anton Hemerijck and Peter Sleegers

In recent years the European integration project has become increasingly controversial in the polarised political landscape of the Netherlands. The legitimacy of engaging in further deepening and broadening of European Union (EU) integration, in the further enlargement of the EU, and in a sensitive constitutional discourse on the EU has become challenged in Dutch society, which has traditionally been supportive of the EU.

Three days after the French rejected the proposal for a Treaty establishing a Constitution for the EU, Dutch voters did the same. How this message should be interpreted is still unclear. Although general support for European integration is still high (although a bit lower than a decade ago), dissatisfaction with the fast pace of enlargement and with the lack of democracy in the EU has increased strongly: in 2004 no EU citizens were more dissatisfied with European democracy than the Dutch (Aarts and van der Kolk, 2005).

The Dutch 'Nee' seems to differ from the French 'Non'. Unlike the French, the Dutch debate on the Constitutional Treaty was less fuelled by a cleavage between protagonists and opponents of competing social models. The Dutch 'Nee' seems to express a lack of acceptance of EU policies beyond the specific content of the Treaty or of a concept such as the European social model (ESM). The Dutch 'Nee' results from the transformation of the EU (the deepening and broadening of EU integration, enlargement) and of changes in the relationship between Dutch citizens and the democratic political system in general.

Unlike in France, the Netherlands does not see much controversy over current EU socio-economic policies and initiatives as these are clearly not at the centre of the Dutch political debate.[1] The Dutch political elite failed to communicate the European dimension of socio-economic policies.

Furthermore, the changing character of the Dutch welfare state in the 1990s, from Continental laggard in the 1980s to 'Dutch Miracle' in the 1990s (Visser and Hemerijck, 1997), and to a normal European country by the beginning of the 21st century, has inspired the EU socio-economic reform agenda, which in turn reinforced the direction of the Dutch welfare state in the 1990s: this explains the current lack of controversy in the Netherlands over EU socio-economic policies.

Generally speaking, the EU influences national socio-economic policy making through four channels: the European Economic and Monetary Union (EMU) and the Stability and Growth Pact (SGP), European law, European Court of Justice (ECJ) case law, and the agenda setting and innovations of the open method of coordination (OMC). Apart from downloading from the EU to national policy-making arenas, Member States simultaneously upload to the EU agenda as well (Börzel, 2005).

The parallel and mutually reinforcing character of interactions between the EU's and the Netherlands' socio-economic policy making makes it impossible to draw conclusions about causal relations in these interactions.

The European social model versus the Dutch model

Academics have defined and analysed the ESM (and politicians have used it) as a particular set of *institutions*, common *values*, a particular way of dealing with common *problems* (policy paradigms and legitimating rhetoric), and in terms of *outcomes* (different levels of social performance) (Canoy et al, 2005). Its taken-for-granted nature and ambiguous meaning is characteristic of the use of the model. According to Jepsen and Serrano Pascual (2005), the ESM is used in three ways: as an entity, as an ideal type and as a European instrument for social cohesion. They label the ESM as a politically constructed project, a way to legitimise European social policy. Thus, the ESM is rather based on common problems and policy paradigms than on common values.

It should be stressed that debates about models tend to be ideological discussions, depicting the welfare state as a static phenomenon and suggesting high degrees of uniformity and coherence. This way, welfare state arrangements are too easily qualified as export commodities. Problems with the transportability of institutional solutions between different welfare states are ignored (Hemerijck and Berghman, 2004).

Given this background, the term 'European socio-economic discourse' describes the specific convergent set of policy directions on the European level better. Convergence in policy challenges and a certain similarity in policy paradigm can be deduced from the different national debates and from the European debate, although national cultural diversities and institutional differences point out the hybridisation of welfare states. Contrary to the term 'social model', the term 'European socio-economic discourse' captures hybridisation in institutional solutions to common challenges.

In spite of the difficulties in applying a specific notion of the ESM, a specific set of characteristics can be extracted from the socio-economic discourse in the EU and from individual Member State developments. The European social discourse is a set of common challenges and an agenda of policy directions.

All European Member States are challenged by demographic ageing, by the ongoing internationalisation of the economy and by the monetary and budgetary constraints on national political economies stemming from the EMU and the SGP. As a result of a change in the configuration of households and work careers, women's participation in the labour market has increased (which has triggered a rise in demand for high-quality childcare services), and workers change jobs more often.

The European agenda sets four policy directions. First, it sees activation and labour market participation as a vehicle for social inclusion and economic growth. Second, it regards social policy as a productive factor; the European Community's latest social agenda goes further and emphasises the cost of a lack of social policy. Third, it promotes emancipation on the labour market, gender equality, anti-discrimination of minority groups, and strategies to combat social exclusion. Fourth, it promotes the consultation of social partners in the social dialogue, and, in general, strong involvement of non-governmental organisations (NGOs) in policy making.

The specific characteristics of the Dutch social model were formed in the 1980s and 1990s, in tandem with the European socio-economic discourse, and departed from the traditional belief that full employment could come about only by redistributing existing jobs. As a result, the most followed strategy was one of compulsory reduction of working hours.

Social partners played a pivotal role in Dutch social policy reform. The 1982 Wassenaar tripartite accord was a turning point. In order to fight rising unemployment, high public debts, inflation and interest rates, and to revive the economy, social partners agreed to wage moderation and reducing working hours. Wassenaar paid off: profits grew, real wages and working hours declined. Simultaneously, moderate monetarism replaced the Keynesian approach: the Wassenaar accord was accompanied by the pegging of the Dutch guilder to the Deutschmark in 1983.

Moreover, with Wassenaar, the character of social pacts changed from hard bargaining over wages and hours towards more qualitative agreements, containing multiple choices for the needs and preferences of individual workers at the workplace level.

The activation of inactive people via participation in the labour market has been a leading goal in Dutch welfare reform since the 1990s. Since then the Dutch policy consensus favoured voluntary work-sharing through the expansion of part-time work. The Dutch economy developed into the first 'part-time economy', and its success is largely due to the part-time participation of women in the labour market.

Recent history has seen the rise and fall of a number of national success models. Central to the success of these models was their ability to adapt to changing conditions while continuing to provide effective social protection (Visser and Hemerijck, 1997). The Dutch model of tripartite bargaining, wage restraint and the promotion of part-time work – resulting in a substantial growth in service jobs – has attracted much attention from abroad since the mid-1990s. The socio-economic model, soon coined the Polder Model, was presented as a third way, an alternative to neoliberal deregulation and to traditional social democracy.

As a result of changes (in the past 15 years) in both methods and substance of EU socio-economic policy, European welfare states have transformed into semi-sovereign welfare states.

Further economic integration and enlargement inspired the European Council to seek new methods of European cooperation, beyond the traditional juridical route. As a result, the mechanisms by which the EU influences Member State welfare state policies have changed considerably, since the second half of the 1990s.

The leeway of national governments has been limited by the monetary and budgetary integration via EMU, the SGP and the introduction of the euro: monetary instruments and the government budget can no longer be used for safeguarding welfare state expenditure.

Next to the instruments for European monetary and budgetary integration, experimentalist governance methods functioning as new agenda-setting mechanisms have emerged, creating a new environment in which now semi-sovereign welfare states operate.

The OMC is of great importance in this new environment for socio-economic policy making. It came into being when the European Council expanded the method it used for the Broad Economic Policy Guidelines (BEPGs) (the 'Luxembourg method') to cover other policy areas: employment policy, pensions and social inclusion. Later it was labelled the open method of coordination. 'Open' reflects its desired nature, that is (1) the emphasis on policy learning by means of peer reviews, and (2) the involvement of state and non-state actors in the preparation of national policy reports on the basis of commonly agreed objectives. 'Coordination' reflects its non-binding character, along with the need to develop common understandings of common problems of Member States' welfare states (Zeitlin et al, 2005).

Main principles in national reforms

Partly as a result of tightening labour supply in the 1980s, the Dutch welfare state in the early 1990s faced typical 'Continental' problems: high payroll taxes meant high labour costs (preventing growth in employment ratios), high levels of unemployment, high numbers of inactive people in the workforce, and low female labour market participation. As a result of economic restructuring in the 1980s and the early 1990s, many redundant workers ended up on disability pensions.

The main principles in the reforms implemented to tackle the 'Continental' problems consisted of increasing labour supply, ensuring fiscal austerity and involving the social partners in the process. As a result, access to disability benefits and to early retirement was restricted; part-time work was promoted by the introduction of 'flexicurity' (WRR, 1990, 2000); health care was privatised; and social assistance decentralised. In this process, social pacts and the 'jobs, jobs, jobs' reports prepared by Wim Kok proved important.

Following strong political pressure in 1993, the employers and trade unions in the Social and Economic Council signed a multi-annual agreement, 'A New Course', on wage moderation and further decentralisation of wage setting paired with work-time reduction (more flexible working arrangements and further expansion of part-time work). The 'New Course' was followed by the 'werk, werk, werk' approach (that is, 'jobs, jobs, jobs') of the 1994 government led by Wim Kok. It emphasised social inclusion by increasing labour participation, stimulating economic growth by increasing the labour force, and increasing women's labour market participation. The approach fed the EU social discourse of the 1990s, when the interaction between the Netherlands and the EU socio-economic policy agendas culminated in the preparation of the 'European' Kok report, in which Wim Kok repeated the message 'jobs, jobs, jobs', signalling a European consensus on policy direction for Continental welfare states (European Task Force Employment, 2003).

The dissemination of the concept of flexicurity followed a pattern of uploading from the Dutch to the EU level and subsequent downloading to other Member States. The Dutch embraced flexicurity when it was included on the Dutch agenda for collective bargaining in 1996. It was an attempt to balance flexibility and security by lowering the dismissal protection of existing workers alongside enhanced employment and social security for atypical workers in temporary work agencies (Wilthagen, 1998). In 2000 the Working Hours Act normalised part-time work. The Act gave part-timers access to arrangements in social security, pensions, training and education, care provision and holiday pay. The 2003 'European' Kok report embraced flexicurity and showed how Dutch and Danish flexicurity measures had inspired other Member States to implement reforms in the same direction (European Task Force Employment, 2003, pp 28-9).

Furthermore, the Kok report dealt with the problem of high and rising disability claimant figures and the gender pay gap in the Netherlands. EU pressure for reforms in these policy fields contributed to the political legitimisation of reforms, as interviews with senior civil servants show (interview, Dutch civil servant, 2005). The EU acted as an *amplifier* of three Dutch reforms: on disability/incapacity pensions, on equal treatment and on a policy (*Sluitende Aanpak*) directed at the prevention of long-term unemployment by means of activation (Ministry of Social Affairs and Employment, 2004).

Traditional pledges for fiscal austerity in Dutch politics were reinforced by the SGP, while the government changed the direction of its macroeconomic policies from anti-cyclical to pro-cyclical. The introduction of the EMU and the SGP in the 1990s 'increased mutual dependency' among the Member States (interview, Dutch civil servant, 2005). The criteria laid down in the SGP (Dutch Finance Minister Zalm was an architect of the SGP) reinforced the fiscal austerity tradition in the Netherlands. In order to legitimise welfare state retrenchment efforts, Dutch politicians no longer needed to refer to a national tradition of fiscal austerity that pre-dated EMU and the SGP, but could use EMU and SGP criteria as a scapegoat instead. The emphasis of the government on fiscal austerity contrasts with its pro-cyclical macroeconomic policies, which contributed to an overheated economy in the late 1990s. Higher inflation rates, the result of these pro-cyclical policies, were perceived by the Dutch public as a consequence of the EMU and the introduction of the euro, feeding existing eurosceptic trends in Dutch society.

The Balkenende Centre-Right government's defensive reform efforts, emphasising fiscal austerity and traditional retrenchment, contrasted sharply with the offensive approach of the Kok governments in the 1990s (which combined retrenchment efforts with new innovative policies, reflecting the emphasis on flexicurity). The 2003 government implemented a reduction in collective 'first-pillar' provisions (analogous to the three-pillar configuration of pensions systems), the introduction and expansion of semi-collective second-pillar provisions, and the introduction of third-pillar individual private insurance. This three-pillar philosophy was extended to include old-age pensions, disability pensions, unemployment insurance, social assistance, health insurance, life course arrangements and the curtailment of poverty traps.

Reforms in pension policy were confined to the rise of contribution rates and changes in indexation rules. A reserve fund was built to ensure the continuation of the basic public pension system, under conditions of demographic ageing. Part of the November 2004 Social Pact restricted possibilities for early retirement. Fiscal incentives for early retirement were abolished, with a 'life course' arrangement enabling workers to save up to 12% of their annual income, to spend during their lifetime for parental care or sabbatical leave. This programme claimed that it enabled people to shape their own life course: to take time off for raising children or for investing in one's own education. However, focused as it was on the mid- or late-career group with a higher income, this programme had little to offer the young. Ironically, for elderly workers, the life course arrangement enabled early retirement (age 62) at a 70% income rate. In the drawing up of the life course arrangement, the interests of the baby-boom members (the vast majority of union members) were well represented, so much so that it sparked fierce union debates and the creation of a new union, the AVV (Alternative for Union). The AVV represents the interests of young workers, flexi-workers and other 'vulnerable' groups.

At the beginning of the 1990s, about 900,000 people were disability pension claimants – more than 10% of the labour force. The reform in disability pensions resulted from a primarily national political process (interview, Dutch civil servant, 2005). However, EU recommendations for limiting disability pensions helped legitimise the reform, leading to the adoption of the Employment and Income According to Capacity to Work Act (WIA) (interview, Dutch civil servant, 2005). The Kok report explicitly dealt with the problem of disability pensions in the Netherlands:

> The disincentives for inactive people to take up a relatively low-paid job are also serious issues in several Member States, usually due to the loss of income-dependent social assistance

> benefits combined with other obstacles to participation. Inactivity traps for beneficiaries of disability/sickness benefits are particularly serious in some Member States such as the UK with 2.7 million recipients, the Netherlands with 985,000 people and, to a lesser extent, Sweden with 320,000 people on long-term sick leave, and Luxembourg. (European Task Force Employment, 2003, p 34)

Although in the 1990s it was extremely difficult to reform the disability law (WAO) the adoption of the WIA (the reform of WAO) by Parliament in 2005 did not entail the political opposition that earlier attempts at WAO reform had triggered. This lack of opposition is remarkable, as the effects of the law are far-reaching. First, instead of passive compensation for disability risks, the law emphasises the capacity of disabled people to work. Second, the WIA represents a classic form of retrenchment, tightening eligibility criteria and lowering the number of claimants. A probable explanation for the relatively easy adoption of this law is that it came into being during a weaker economy, a condition that makes legitimising reforms easier.

A reform of social assistance in January 2004 shifted responsibility to local government. Municipalities received strong incentives, full financial responsibility and more room to manoeuvre, in reintegrating people on social assistance into the labour market. Apart from the reform of social assistance, the new Social Support Act (Wet Maatschappelijke Ondersteuning, WMO), which took effect in January 2007, is a second sign of further decentralisation of social policies. The Act put an end to scattered laws and regulations directed at support for elderly people and people with disabilities.[2]

In 2006 a controversial Health Care Act was passed, eliminating the difference between public and private health care insurance. Essentially, the reform resulted in a private health care system, constrained by public guarantees and compensation systems. People who used to benefit from relatively low-cost public insurance now have access to tax benefits that enable them to pay the higher insurance bills. Health insurance companies are now at the centre of the health care system, competing on a basic health care insurance package. Since the insured populations of health insurance companies differ, companies with insured populations characterised by higher-than-average health risks get compensation from a fund. The insurance company Azivo has filed a complaint at the ECJ, arguing that the compensation system is not adequate and in fact functions as illegal state aid to health insurance companies with healthier insured populations (*NRC Handelsblad*, 23 May 2006, p 1).

Via the rules of the internal market, competition, non-discrimination and EU citizenship, the ECJ interferes in the working of national welfare state arrangements (van de Brink, 2005). Given the historical role of the ECJ in European integration, ECJ case law could accelerate integration in socio-economic fields. National welfare state arrangements are increasingly subject to EU law and EU decision making.

National responses to the EU initiatives

Most EU initiatives on socio-economic policies do not differ substantially from the Dutch socio-economic policy consensus. Given more commonalities than differences, the EU–Dutch link is politically not much of an issue. This section briefly summarises the main recent EU documents and initiatives and indicates the Dutch national political and policy-making responses.

Lisbon Strategy and Social Policy Agenda

The initial Lisbon Strategy of 2000, after the Kok report of 2004, was transformed in the renewed Lisbon Strategy for growth and employment. The Kok report was directed at evaluating the relevance of the Lisbon Strategy, to determine ways of using EU potential and improving the Strategy's execution and implementation. In the report of the European Employment Task Force of November 2003, Wim Kok repeated the policy diagnosis and policy directions that formed the basis for his governments in the 1990s arguing for reform, activation and flexicurity. 'Werk, werk, werk' was translated into 'Jobs, jobs, jobs'. This development indicates both the changing socio-economic discourse in the Netherlands in the 1990s and the emerging policy consensus in the EU at the end of the 1990s and beginning of the 21st century.

Key to the Lisbon Strategy is that it considers the welfare state as a 'productive factor'. This idea was put forward by the Dutch presidency of the EU in 1997, when the EU launched its common employment policy (Hemerijck, 1998). Increasing economic growth was necessary for guaranteeing a prosperous, social and sustainable society.

Because the Lisbon Strategy and the Dutch socio-economic discourse developed hand in hand, it is no surprise that the Dutch government supported the new approach in the renewed Lisbon Strategy, arguing that sustainable economic growth and employment was central to it. Clearly establishing the responsibility of actors on the EU and Member

State levels was key to the success of the new strategy. In it, Member States prepare (every third year) a National Reform Programme, setting out the policy measures taken in the framework of the Lisbon Strategy. Apart from the Reform reports, the Member States send a yearly implementation report to the Commission, reporting on actual implementation. These reports are combined with the Lisbon Strategy setting out the EU measures. The Commission annually evaluates the execution of the Lisbon policies and examines the progress of the Strategy. The European Council decides on the adjustment of guidelines and advises both the Member States and the EU on how to achieve the Lisbon goals (Ministry of Economic Affairs, 2005a).

In a letter to the Dutch Parliament, the Dutch government embraced the Kok report and its recommendations. In short, the government underlined the need to reform the Lisbon Strategy: to decrease the number of goals in the OMCs, to do more naming and shaming, to improve the governance of the Lisbon Strategy (the OMC), streamline the OMCs, and introduce one integral (streamlined) National Action Plan. Special attention should go to the 'knowledge economy', the completion of the internal market, the stimulation of entrepreneurship, the better functioning of labour markets and environmental issues (Ministry of Foreign Affairs, 2004).

The new Social Policy Agenda is framed within the Lisbon Strategy. It emphasises the positive interplay between economic, social and employment policies; the promotion of quality (of employment and social policy and industrial relations) to improve human and social capital; and the need to modernise social protection systems, on the basis of solidarity and by strengthening their role as a productive factor. The Dutch Parliament, after receiving the government's reaction, has not debated the Social Policy Agenda in detail. The Dutch government has argued that most of its wishes have been absorbed in the new agenda, linking it directly to the Dutch 2004 EU presidency ambitions, but added that more attention should go to the positive effects of labour market participation on the social integration of immigrants. The fears among many European Parliament delegations were that the economic competitiveness objectives of the Lisbon Agenda would overshadow the social goals it envisioned. In its new Social Policy Agenda, the EU goes beyond social policy as a productive factor by paying attention to the cost of the lack of social policy. The strategy is twofold.

First, the confidence of citizens needs strengthening. It is important to take an intergenerational approach (chances for young people, intergenerational partnership, contribution to the European Initiative for Youth), to establish partnerships for change (role of social partners) and to seize opportunities offered by globalisation (social dimension of globalisation): 'Decent work for all should be a world objective at all levels' (European Commission, 2005a, p 5).

Second, the Agenda promotes measures on employment and equal opportunities and inclusion. Combining the prosperity and the solidarity objective is of key importance.

The Agenda hints at two forces that make change necessary in the ESM: first, increased competition in a global context and, second, technological development and population ageing. It argues that challenges remain: low rate of employment, unemployment, poverty, inequality and discrimination. The Commission reports that the link between the European Social Fund (ESF) and the Social Policy Agenda would be strengthened. Further, an integrated approach was envisioned (building on the proposed Constitutional Treaty) in the impact assessment tool. All EU policies should take social and employment dimensions into account. The Social Policy Agenda thus has four instruments at its disposal: legislation, the social dialogue, financial instruments like the ESF, and the OMC.

Open method of coordination

The Dutch government has supported recent initiatives in the framework of the streamlining of the different OMCs. It welcomes the new streamlined OMC procedures, and argues that the current involvement of the Council reflects a more politicised OMC. Nevertheless, the Netherlands has in recent years promoted simplified OMC procedures, with fewer goals and more coherence. Thus it would have welcomed the inclusion of the social OMCs as sub-goals in the EES (European Employment Strategy). However, the current streamlining and parallel reporting procedures are a significant improvement, compared to the old OMC procedures that reflected a more bureaucratic approach to EU coordination. The Dutch generally believe that the comparison of best practice in the European arena contributes to reform efforts in welfare state arrangements. Although there are prospects for policy learning via the OMC, two observations stand out: first, the presentation of Dutch best practice to others receives a lot of attention in Dutch ministries, while best practice from other Member States might also be very relevant to Dutch welfare state issues (interview, Dutch civil servant, 2006). Second, participants in the OMC from the EU15 think the OMC is more beneficial to the EU10 than to the EU15, while participants from the EU10 generally do not have high expectations on policy learning via best practice (Sleegers, 2005).

The Dutch approach to reforms in the OMC has traditionally centred around four recommendations. First, the reporting process in the OMC (including social inclusion, pensions and health care) could be revised further, with fewer reports and page limits. Second, the OMC on social inclusion should focus on a concise set of five concrete topics relevant to most EU countries. The renewed focus in the Lisbon Strategy should also clarify how social inclusion could contribute to growth and employment. Third, the peer review process for social inclusion and pensions should be revised, as the current peer reviews are not possible with 25 Member States. Fourth, pension reform should be included in the National Reform Programmes, as they will be greatly important in the Lisbon process. The integrated guidelines on growth and employment allow for this inclusion in the National Reform Programme (interview, Dutch delegation to Social Protection Committee, 2005).

Proposal on the Services Directive

The European Parliament in 2001 and 2003 adopted resolutions giving the completion of the internal market top priority. In 2004, the European Commission brought a Services Directive proposal before the European Parliament. Largely the codification of existing EU legislation, this Directive would make freedom of services (already formally established in the Treaty of Rome) a reality.

In December 2004, the Dutch government asked the Social and Economic Council for advice on the Services Directive. In its official reaction to the advice, the Dutch government supported the idea of a genuine single market in services, as a necessary step to completing the internal market, and as a part of the Lisbon Strategy, promoting a more dynamic EU economy (Ministry of Economic Affairs, 2005b).

The Dutch consensus is that a genuine single market in services would enhance the EU economy and lead to economic growth and welfare gains, since more than 70% of all production is located in the services sector. The unions and Dutch government alike are committed to the recommendation of the Social and Economic Council (2005).

The Dutch government has reported that, although it wanted more, it supports the EU consensus around the renewed proposal for the Services Directive. The government favours a more liberal approach to the Directive, for example, for services of general interest (SGI) like health care.

Demographic change

The European Commission's Green Paper *Confronting demographic change: A new solidarity between the generations* covers three characteristics of demographic ageing: increase in life expectancy, low birth rates and the baby-boom generation (European Commission, 2005c). The increase in life expectancy reflects a well-developed welfare state with high living standards, a population in relatively good health, and developed professional health care systems. The Green Paper argued for new forms of solidarity between generations and the development of human capital among both the young and the old. The Dutch Cabinet underlined the need for action and placed the challenges of demographic ageing in the framework of the Lisbon Strategy (Ministry of Social Affairs and Employment, 2005, pp 1-3).

To prevent future generations from having to bear the costs of demographic ageing, the Dutch Cabinet sought to: (1) increase the legitimacy of collective services; (2) adjust collective arrangements; and (3) lower the national debt. Old people in the Netherlands are richer than their predecessors, as a result of generous first-pillar pensions, well-developed second-pillar pensions and a very friendly tax system. Furthermore, most old people in the Netherlands have built up large capital reserves (for example, mortgage-free houses). Dutch women have fewer children than desired; the 1.7 fertility rate is low but, compared to other Continental welfare states, not dramatically low.

The Dutch position on policies for demographic ageing was to handle such problems via BEPGs and the EES and to use existing institutional structures such as the Economic Policy Committee (EPC) and the Social Protection Committee (SPC) instead of developing new specific policies. In the Netherlands, the baby-boom generation is expected to bear more of the rising costs associated with demographic ageing. One way they could contribute is by participating in the labour market. The Dutch government therefore underlined its ambition to increase the participation rate of elderly workers (55-64 years) to 50% by 2010. The Dutch government saw an important EU role in monitoring life expectancy rates and the desired number of children (Ministry of Social Affairs and Employment, 2005, pp 1-3). Furthermore, from this monitoring, the EU could indicate causes of life expectancy changes, and changes in the desired number of children (the Dutch experience shows that this number follows the economic cycle) and publish a comparison of Member State policy results. Thus, according to the government, the Commission should take an integrated approach to problems of demographic ageing and facilitate the comparison of best practice. The EU should integrate the monitoring procedures and comparison of best practice into the processes of the already existing BEPGs and employment guidelines, guaranteeing involvement of both the Employment Committee and the SPC. Developing new institutional structures for activities on this policy field was not necessary (Ministry of Social Affairs and Employment, 2005).

In recent reforms, the Dutch Cabinet has introduced life course arrangements, which should make it easier to combine care for children with participation in the labour market. As argued earlier, such life course arrangements are not attractive for young parents; they are directed only at enabling early retirement. Childcare facilities have been improved recently in the Netherlands (although further reform, in terms of both quality and costs, is still necessary) (Esping-Andersen, 2005). Nevertheless, of all women active in the labour market before having a child, 90% return to the labour market after the birth of their child(ren).

To combat age discrimination in the labour market, the EU should use its legal anti-discrimination framework. In the Netherlands, an effort to mainstream anti-discrimination policy on labour market issues is under way. Furthermore, the government supports initiatives for comparing best practice for the integration of young people into the labour market, more specifically, for dual trajectories of combining work and study. The Dutch government does not consider immigration as contributing to solving problems associated with demographic ageing.

Services of general interest

In its 2003 Green Paper on SGI, the Commission covered issues connected to the development of SGI: 'Given their weight in the economy and their importance for the production of other goods and services, the efficiency and quality of these services is a factor for competitiveness and greater cohesion, in particular in terms of attracting investment in less-favoured regions' (European Commission, 2003f, p 4). The Dutch government welcomed the Green Paper and set out the Dutch position in an official government reply (Ministry of Economic Affairs, 2004). Although the Green Paper built on European traditions for social services, it connected the right to non-discriminatory and efficient access to SGI to the concept of EU citizenship. The Commission's Green Paper underlined the importance of SGI to the functioning of the internal market: the increase in employment and downward pressure on costs, as a result of the privatisation of network industries, were relevant for social goals. The increase in employment and downward pressure on costs should benefit not only society as a whole, but low-income citizens in particular.

For social services, education and health care, the Commission emphasised that it respected the national varieties of organisational and institutional make-up. The Green Paper covered issues connected to subsidiarity in these fields. It argued that the function of welfare and social protection had a recognised role in promoting cooperation and coordination in these areas. The Commission stressed that a particular concern was the promotion of Member States' cooperation in the modernisation of social protection systems. The Commission had legal powers insofar as they were linked to anti-discrimination and to the freedom of workers in the EU.

The Dutch government position on the scope of the competences of the EU and the Member States is clear: the current system functions well with regard to subsidiarity as laid down in Article 86 of the Treaty. Changes in the Treaty were not necessary, according to the Dutch government, although the concept of economic activity could be defined more precisely. As to the desirability of an EU regulator, the Dutch government is sceptical, proposing a case-by-case approach. The necessity and added value of a network of regulators or an EU regulator should be evaluated by sector and market. An EU regulator per se was not desirable.

For various reasons, the Dutch government strongly opposes a horizontal approach to SGI. First, the Dutch approach is to evaluate and define SGI by sector. Second, Member States have very different definitions of SGI. Third, the proposed framework directive would have to be general, given the diversity between sectors and Member States. Framework directives of such a general nature can hardly be effective. Moreover, the current framework in the Treaty would be so altered by the framework directive that the authority for defining SGI would go to the EU. While the Netherlands would oppose such a development, it would welcome a benchmarking approach to SGI, by comparing best practice in the EU.

European Economic and Monetary Union

The budget of the Dutch Ministry of Finance clearly and explicitly states that the EMU, the SGP and the Lisbon Strategy determine the framework for Dutch socio-economic and budgetary policies (Ministry of Finance, 2005). This is peculiar, since the Dutch emphasis on fiscal austerity pre-dated the EMU and SGP. The Netherlands has a tradition of budgetary and fiscal austerity, and has always promoted the importance of EU budgetary restraint on the road to the EMU. The Dutch government has been a forerunner of fiscal austerity in the EU (notably Finance Minister Zalm, one of the architects of the SGP), leading to political clashes with other Member States. The Dutch hard line in the EU was accompanied by an even more austere national budgetary policy. Not only did the Dutch want to comply with the EMU and SGP criteria, but they also surpassed them (that is, the budget deficit in 2005, after an economic downturn, is only 0.3%). This attitude has had great consequences for the development of the Dutch welfare state. Since joining the EMU, and especially after joining the SGP (even though the Dutch emphasis on fiscal austerity pre-dated the SGP), the Dutch government has used SGP criteria for political purposes. The Centre-Right Balkenende government could now legitimise far-reaching welfare retrenchment efforts by referring to strict EU austerity criteria. This position represents a classic form of blame avoidance and of using the EU as a scapegoat for legitimising national reforms. As such, it is a specific manner of downloading EU policy into the national political domain.

Enlargement and the free movement of workers

The High Level Group (2004a) on enlargement wrote a report on the future of social policy in an *enlarged* EU. The High Level Group argued that seeking a renewed balance between economic integration (always on the forefront of EU integration) and the social dimension was important. The EU should therefore deal with three major challenges in the next decade: enlargement, population ageing and globalisation. Five major policy orientations needed defining, for a new intergenerational pact.[3] The High Level Group identified a gap between the broad and integrated approach to social policies in the Lisbon Strategy and the narrowly defined understanding of social policies in the accession process. New Member States had only to implement the acquis communautaire, which does not yet reflect the ambitions of the Lisbon Strategy, leaving some catching up to do.

One very important difference between the older Member States and new Member States is their level of social dialogue. Unions and employer organisations in the new Member States are less well organised and play a less important role in fostering change in their social protection systems. Furthermore, the neoliberal approach in the new Member States during the transition period led some of them to neglect social policies. In some cases this neglect resulted in their vulnerable position on the capital market and the involvement of the World Bank in promoting and coaching change in social protection systems (Sleegers, 2005).

The High Level Group findings indicate yet again that the populations of many new Member States have strong egalitarian expectations that contrast sharply with socio-economic realities. The findings also reveal an insufficiently transposed and implemented social acquis in the new Member States, mainly in health and safety at work and equal treatment.

The Accession Treaty regulates the free movement of workers. Regulation 1612/68 on the free movement of workers will apply in all Member States seven years after the enlargement and perhaps in most Member States after two or five years. Only workers can be restricted from free movement; other citizens are free to move from day one. In January 2004, the Netherlands reversed its original 2001 policy (under the Kok II government). The change was a result (mainly) of fears of a deterioration of the Dutch labour market. The Dutch also justified their move by referring to other Member States that had changed their restriction on labour since December 2002 (Kvist, 2004). Thus, the Netherlands has continued its practice of requiring work permits for nationals from the eight Central and Eastern European countries, and imposed a quota of 22,000 employees until May 2006. After pressure from the opposition, the government agreed to review the Dutch labour market sector by sector and allow migrant workers only in sectors in need of labour (Kvist, 2004). In 2005, 30,000 work permits were issued (80% to Polish migrant workers).

Recently, the Secretary of Social Affairs and Employment pledged to open the Dutch labour market for migrant workers from the new Member States. However, Parliament insisted on further research into the expected number of migrant workers, and postponed the decision about opening the labour market to the autumn of 2006, and made it conditional on efforts to fight illegal labour. Until at least January 2007, migrant workers from the new Member States had to apply for a work permit before they could enter the Dutch labour market. Opening the labour market for migrant workers from the new Member States will be evaluated by sector in dialogue with social partners.

Conclusions

In terms of its macro- and socio-economic policies and performance, the Netherlands transformed from a laggard Continental welfare state in the 1980s to a European forerunner in the 1990s. After the 'Dutch

Miracle' of the 1990s, the Netherlands became a *normal* EU Member State at the beginning of the 21st century. During this development, the Netherlands was transformed from a Continental welfare state into a hybrid, containing occupational welfare and pensions, a relatively generous universal first pillar in pensions, decentralised social assistance and a privatised health care system.

This chapter has shown that interaction between Member States and the EU takes place through four channels: the EMU and the SGP, EU law, ECJ case law, and agenda-setting mechanisms such as the OMC. Interaction takes place in two directions: downloading and uploading. The Dutch social model and the policy directions promoted by the European socio-economic discourse are similar, as a result of parallel development and the sometimes mutually reinforcing interactions of the Netherlands' and EU's socio-economic policy agendas in the 1990s.

Dutch politicians fail to communicate European policies to their public. Consequently, little political controversy on EU socio-economic policy occurs in the Netherlands. While the Dutch socio-economic policy directions of the 1990s have fed the European socio-economic discourse, to which the Kok reports and the Lisbon Strategy testify, the European socio-economic policy agenda has reinforced national reforms in the Netherlands. In recent years, three social policy reforms in the Netherlands were amplified by the EU: the reform of disability pensions, the equal treatment dossier and the prevention of long-term unemployment.

The Dutch welfare state reform efforts of the 1990s and the beginning of the 21st century have, in line with the EU socio-economic discourse, emphasised decreasing the number of inactive people in society by promoting and stimulating activation and participation in the labour market, and decentralising socio-economic policies. In contrast to the traditional Continental solution of decreasing labour supply, reforms in unemployment schemes, disability pensions and social assistance have all been directed at activation and participation in the labour market – to increase labour supply. The involvement of municipalities in the execution of social policies has intensified, through the decentralisation of social assistance and the adoption of the new Social Support Act.

The strict interpretation by Dutch politicians of the concept of fiscal austerity, reinforced by the SGP, forms an important influence on Dutch socio-economic policy making, and has led to serious retrenchment in recent years. Dutch public expenditure on social policy has thus decreased drastically, whereas eligibility criteria for disability pensions and unemployment benefits have tightened. Community law, apart from labour conditions and equal treatment, has not influenced Dutch socio-economic policy making to a great extent. However, discussions about the Services Directive and the free movement of migrant workers have been highly topical.

Strategic behaviour in the EU, combined with political opposition, led to change in the initial Dutch position on opening the borders for migrant workers from the new Member States. ECJ case law could, in the near future, accelerate integration in socio-economic fields.

The Dutch government has embraced the Lisbon Strategy and (on the basis of the second Kok report) the renewed Lisbon Strategy. The government has also supported the streamlining of the EES and the social OMCs. It has promoted simplified OMC procedures, fewer goals and guidelines, and more coherence between economic and social goals. Furthermore, the government thinks that the comparison of best practice and other benchmarking systems in the socio-economic policy fields is a good instrument for further coordinating social policies.

As to demographic ageing, the Dutch government welcomes European Community-led monitoring of life expectancy and the desired number of children, and comparison of national policy results in the EU. However, the Dutch government believes that the EU should not strive to develop a new specific policy on demographic changes but use existing institutional structures instead. For SGI, the government sees no need to change the Treaty. The single most important EU influence on welfare state policy making in the Netherlands is the result of the narrow interpretation by Dutch politicians of the EMU and SGP criteria. This interpretation has led to serious, far-reaching retrenchment in the Dutch welfare state in recent years.

Multi-level Europe depends on democratic legitimacy derived from and mediated through national legislatures, which remain the primary focal point of political identity in Europe and the cornerstone for further policy integration. Less binding and legal-pluralist modes of governance such as social dialogue and the OMC should therefore be viewed not as alternatives to the Community method but as necessary or indispensable complements. It is a sign of good health that 50 years of European integration have developed such a wide range of modes of governance for European cooperation (Best, 2003).

The Dutch government has retained a one-dimensional, defensive position towards proportionality and subsidiarity issues, whereas a more constructive attitude – taking into account the recent enlargement of the EU – would be more appropriate.

Notes

[1] Since 2001, the European dimension of social policies has been visible in yearly reports of the Ministry of Social Affairs and Employment in The Hague. While politicians fail to communicate European policies, three annual reports have mentioned, on the sideline, the European dimension of social policies, signalling increasing attention to the European dimension of social policies in Dutch policy makers' circles as witnessed by the annual Social Report of the Ministry of Social Affairs and Employment.

[2] The WMO encompasses the Services for the Disabled Act (WVG), the Social Welfare Act and parts of the Exceptional Medical Expenses Act (AWBZ).

[3] The five policy orientations were: (1) focusing the EES on three objectives: to extend working life, by increasing the employment rate of both the old and the young, to implement lifelong learning and to address economic restructuring; (2) reforming the social protection systems; (3) fostering social inclusion and investing in children and young people; (4) allowing European couples to have the number of children they desire (increased emphasis on family policies); (5) developing a European immigration policy, in order to arrive at more selective and better integrated immigration.

ELEVEN

Denmark: from foot dragging to pace setting in European Union social policy

Jon Kvist

The relationship between national social policy and the European Union (EU) is a recurrent theme in public debates throughout Europe. These debates are typically sparked by EU referenda, irrespective of their official theme, with Dutch and French polls on the European Constitution as vivid illustrations. Both entailed heated discussions of the impact of EU enlargement and European integration on national social policy. And both polls resulted in rejections of ratifying the Constitution.

In this context, changing Danish government responses to European integration in social policy may be of more general interest for at least two reasons. First, Danes have a reputation for being eurosceptics. Denmark holds the world record for the most EU referenda. In two out of six elections, Danish EU scepticism had the upper hand: in 1992 when 50.7% of the electorate voted against ratification of the Maastricht Treaty, and in 2000 when 53.2% rejected Denmark adopting the euro.[1] The relationship between the Danish welfare system and a further deepening or widening of EU collaboration figured high in public debates surrounding all six referenda. Second, Denmark has a welfare model that in the late 1990s received praise from the European Commission and the Organisation for Economic Co-operation and Development (OECD) for its active labour market policies and extensive social care schemes. Most recently, the model has been praised for the way it combines lax employment protection legislation (providing flexibility in the labour market) with generous social protection and active employment policies (providing social security). In a word, this combination has become known as 'flexicurity'.

Changing Danish governments have aimed at calming a belief about potential negative consequences for national social policy stemming from EU collaboration, a belief particularly dominant on the Left side of the political spectrum. When Denmark joined the EU in 1973, together with Ireland and the United Kingdom, little EU social policy existed besides the coordination on migrant workers' social rights. During its first 25 years in the EU, Denmark backed the line supporting national sovereignty in social policy, perhaps most notably spearheaded by the UK. Denmark was thus generally against an expansion of EU social policy initiatives, a behaviour that we may see as 'foot dragging' with respect to further European integration.[2] In Edinburgh in 1992, when Denmark was exempt from participating in four areas of European collaboration, it also became a 'fence-sitting' nation.

Against this background, it is perhaps not surprising that the Social Democrats in government from 1993 to 2001 were active in not only trying to promote Danish policies with other Member States and the European Commission but also attempting to persuade Danish eurosceptics that EU collaboration had a social dimension. That social dimension was said to consist of the European Employment Strategy (EES) and the Structural Funds, especially, the European Social Fund (ESF). The adoption of the Lisbon Strategy and the open method of coordination (OMC) in 2000, however, was decisive. The Lisbon Strategy placed more and better employment, as well as the combating of poverty, high on the political agenda, while the OMC allowed individual Member States to decide how to achieve these goals. Both were grist to the Danish mill. Since then, as we shall see, Danish governments have been pace setting in the EU arena of social policy.

The European social model versus the Danish model

International events have historically influenced the design of the Danish welfare system. Today's main principles, for example, universalism and tax financing, were introduced when large corn imports in the 1870s from Russian and North American markets made European corn prices fall. Many farmers in agrarian Denmark intensified their production, and unemployed workers moved from farms to the cities. Farmers tried to stop this move by advocating for social reforms through their influential party in Parliament. This advocacy resulted in a decision against social insurance and for people's insurance, in explicit contrast to the situation in Germany. Thus entitlement based on need and residence (rather than on record of work) and financing entitlement shifted from taxes on corn to central state subsidies. In this way farmers' pressure laid the foundation for the principles of universalism and tax financing that many years later became hallmarks of the Danish welfare model (Petersen, 1985). Being a small country with an open economy has continued to have important ramifications for the choices made in Danish social policy.

Denmark introduced its social security schemes early. In 1891, two years after the German introduction of the first national old-age pension in the form of social insurance for workers, the Danes implemented a tax-financed pension for all citizens above a certain age. Sickness insurance was introduced in 1892 followed by industrial accident insurance in 1898. Unemployment insurance came relatively late, in 1907. The Social Reform of 1933 merged 55 separate social policy laws into four 'people insurance' laws. Although the laws for disability and for old age had nothing to do with (social) insurance, 'insurance' had a nice ring to it at the time. The Social Reform was part of a larger political package that meant a stop for liberal governance and a green light for state intervention in the economy.

After the Second World War the ideas of Keynes and others legitimised economic intervention. The 1960s and early 1970s in particular saw the consolidation of the modern Danish welfare state. Social security schemes were expanded to new groups such as students, disabled people and housewives, and new schemes such as child family benefits were introduced. Perhaps most importantly, care and services became the second leg of the Danish welfare system, a leg that later became the most distinctive part of the Scandinavian welfare model. Often these benefits in kind are anchored in the local authorities – that is, health care in the regions and social care for elderly people and children in the municipalities – and the services enjoy some subsidies from the central level.

International events had their say in social policies once again when the oil crises of the 1970s and 1980s stopped the marked expansion of the Danish welfare state, even though high and stagnant rates of unemployment caused social expenditures to rise. It took Denmark two decades of dealing mainly with economic problems before welfare reforms again became the centrepiece of national policies.

Characteristics of the Danish welfare state

Denmark belongs to a group of Member States that, to a larger or lesser extent, share a Scandinavian welfare model (Kautto et al, 2001). Specifically, the Danish welfare state is characterised by:

- *Individualism:* rights are based mostly on the individual (the main exceptions are family benefits and social assistance).
- *Universalism:* the right to basic social security benefits (in cash and in kind) covers a wide range of social contingencies and life situations.

- *Comprehensiveness:* the scope of public policy is broad; the state has a larger and more active role vis-à-vis the market and civil society than do most other countries.
- *Full employment:* policies are aimed at creating full (that is, more) employment and/or preventing unemployment, particularly long-term unemployment.
- *Equality:* policies are aimed at contributing to equality between groups based on gender, age, class, family situation, ethnicity, religion, region and so on.
- *High-quality benefit:* services, provided by welfare professionals, are considered high quality.
- *Generous benefits:* cash benefits are generous for low-income groups, as these are most likely to be exposed to social risks and as the aim is to allow for a 'normally' accepted standard of living (but benefits for middle- and high-income groups are not as high as those in Finland and many Continental European countries).
- *Decentralised:* the administration and delivery of benefits is decentralised to the regions (health) and municipalities (care for children and elderly people, and active labour market policies).
- *Tax financing:* taxes accrued at the municipal and state level finance the majority of benefits (a so-called labour market contribution of 8% of gross income is merely a gross tax, as it gives no rights to any benefit).

Although these traits are generally shared by the Nordic countries, the heavy reliance on taxation in financing the welfare state is particular to Denmark. This reliance shows that what differentiates welfare state models is not the mode of financing.

Services for sick, young, old and unemployed people: what makes the Danish – or, more generally, the Scandinavian – welfare model distinct in a European context is its emphasis on benefits in kind. It is 'heavy on services'. For many years public health care made up the bulk of services. In the 1960s the public schemes of care for children and elderly people emerged, and they have been expanded through to today. More recently, however, the expansion and reformulation of active labour market policies has changed the nature of the Danish welfare state model. From securing the labour supply of women, the emphasis in service provision shifted towards combating unemployment, and in the light of ageing populations is now turning back to increasing the labour supply, this time of minority ethnic groups and groups with reduced work capacity.

Flexicurity: in an international context, the combination of good social security with a flexible labour market has perhaps received the most recent attention (Madsen, 1999; Beskæftigelsesministeriet, 2005). Known as 'flexicurity', this combination is seen as offering something good from two worlds. One is that lax employment protection legislation contributes to high turnover in the labour market and therefore to flexible labour markets that are important in a global age. The other is that the social security system takes care of those made redundant, in part by operating widely accessible schemes with benefits that allow a certain standard of living for some time, and in part by emphasising vocational training and other measures directed at getting unemployed people back to work.

The early impact of the EU

It is doubtful whether the EU has had a large impact on the Danish welfare state. As already demonstrated, Denmark has managed some 30 years of EU membership without leaving the group of countries with a Scandinavian welfare state model (just like Finland and Sweden, albeit for shorter periods).

This observation is not to belittle the changes. Indeed, before entering the EU in 1973, Denmark made changes to its national old-age pension. Previously, eligibility had been based on citizenship and residence, but in 1972 a full pension became dependent on 40 years of residence between the ages of 15 and 65, with proportional cuts for periods of non-residence. In addition, three years of residence became a threshold for eligibility. (Sweden and Finland took similar measures when they became EU members about 20 years later.)

Basing the pension size on the number of years of residence made the scheme more compatible with the *pro rate temporis* principle in European Community Coordination Regulation 1408/71. More importantly, the change dealt with the fear of social tourism. The concern was of becoming a welfare magnet for scores of Europeans south of the Danish border; they would, it was argued, particularly by the no-to-the-EU side, come to Denmark for the universal, tax-financed pension. Although the Danish welfare system has not spurred social tourism, fears of this pop up from time to time, especially in connection with EU referenda.

Main principles in national reforms

Danish welfare in the 1990s had a bad start but a happy end. In the early 1990s, Denmark still suffered from its economic crisis of the 1980s. Unemployment was high, and budget and trade deficits large. From 1994 onwards the situation improved markedly. Trade surpluses were followed by budget surpluses so that unemployment was the main problem on the political agenda. Moreover, the problem of unemployment gradually made a U-turn, so that lack of labour is now perhaps the most pertinent challenge on the political agenda. The favourable economic climate was partly facilitating welfare reform and partly the result of fundamental changes to Danish welfare policies. From 1993 to 2001, shifting coalition governments, all led by Prime Minister Poul Nyrup Rasmussen, made welfare policies undergo silent revolutions in at least four respects.

First, the scope of services for children and elderly people was extended significantly. Second, increased activation and orientation towards labour market participation characterised the transformation of labour market policies and the social security system, perhaps most notably activation policies for unemployed people, but also for sick and disabled people (Kvist, 2002). Third, decentralisation marked the decade: the expansion of social services took place at the municipality level and increased activation efforts were largely planned and implemented on the regional level in collaboration with the social partners, municipalities and the labour market exchange. Fourth, these reforms reflected higher political ambitions, a greater emphasis on securing everybody a place in society. In Danish political life this 'place' has become nearly synonymous with a place in the labour market, along with providing a decent standard of living for those unable to work.

A fifth silent revolution took place in the labour market. Social partners negotiated a significant expansion in the scope of benefits to supplement the relatively basic benefits from the state schemes. From 1990 onwards more supplementary coverage through collective agreements was introduced, especially for disability and old age (Kvist, 1997). In the 2000s a growing number of collective agreements introduced supplementary unemployment insurance, topping up benefits from the conventional unemployment insurance and health insurance, providing among other things faster access to private hospitals for treatment of some diseases.

Benefit levels have not been directly cut, except for young unemployed people, but benefit generosity for large groups of claimants has gradually eroded (Hansen, 2002). This erosion has primarily resulted from indexation mechanisms and changes to the tax system, most notably the introduction and expansion of labour market contributions, a de facto gross tax that is also levied on income from most social security benefits. Looking in the rear-view mirror, however, one can see that the generosity of social security remained high for events that were difficult to predict and for people who were unlikely to create enough savings. Thus, generosity for disability and for unemployed low-income groups remained high.

Thus in the 1990s the guiding idea was not so much to cut benefits to save money or increase work incentives but rather to target benefits to the needy and to invest in equality-promoting policies (for example, childcare, education and active labour market and social policies), now known as employment policies.

The activation line in employment policies constituted a big expansion in activation measures and a greater emphasis on the obligation of social security claimants to accept work and activation offers (Madsen, 1999; Kvist, 2002). The aim was not only to deter the able-bodied (including the unemployed low-income groups with generous benefits) from drawing social security but also to enhance the qualifications of claimants so that they could get back to work and become self-supporting. In subsequent revisions, activation measures were offered still earlier in the unemployment spell, and a lot of energy went into making individual action plans.

Rather than material poverty, non-monetary deprivation framed in terms of social exclusion and marginalisation from the labour market has been high on the political agenda. People with mental ill health, the homeless and drug addicts have been perceived as the most vulnerable groups. For most other groups the goal of self-support has been salient.

However, the one exception to this rule is voluntary early exit from the labour market. The early retirement benefit (*efterløn*) was originally intended to allow a dignified exit possibility for unskilled workers worn out from hard and monotonous work. However, the *efterløn* has become a popular way of leaving the labour market at the age of 60, rather than at the official retirement age at 67, for all social groups, even the privileged. It is the social security scheme with the biggest participant increase in the 1990s, so that today there are more early retirees than unemployed people. Despite the costs and a shortage of labour, politicians have so far refrained from undertaking major reforms or abolishing the scheme.

The current coalition government between Liberals and Conservatives took office in late 2001. The Liberal Party won a huge victory in the

November 2001 elections, not least by pledging to preserve welfare and stop tax increases. The Liberals made more or less the same promises during the last election (February 2005), again with a massive victory. The promises of neither reducing welfare for anybody nor increasing taxes set limits on the range of possible welfare reforms. By and large, the government has continued the social policy line set in the 1990s.

Nevertheless, in three areas the current government has put a special emphasis that to some extent deviates from the previous government:

- *Consumerism:* a great emphasis exists, especially in rhetoric, on consumers' choice among different providers. These choices include, for example, the choice of home help for elderly people, for parents to choose childcare institutions (and, to a lesser extent, schools within and between municipal districts), and for patients to choose treatment in different regions and for certain diseases across the Danish borders.
- *Special treatment of special groups:* in tandem with falling unemployment and the rising labour shortage, there has been renewed interest in activating people from groups characterised by low labour market participation rates, that is people from minority ethnic groups and people with disabilities. Young people will also probably soon face increased incentives to start and finish education earlier than today.
- *Reorganisation:* the Structural Reform took effect in January 2007, reducing the number of regions from 13 to 5 and the number of municipalities from 273 to 98. The idea was to achieve increased efficiency through economies of scale, and greater effectiveness by having larger units capable of meeting more specialised needs.

In addition, Denmark gives special treatment for people (Danes as well as non-Danes) coming to Denmark in the sense that they will get a reduced social assistance benefit, called Start Help, during their first seven years of residing in Denmark.

In sum, Danish policy developments are largely driven by economic considerations. Denmark expanded its policies to get as many people as possible to work, first to fight unemployment and more recently to meet the rising demand for labour. In other words, welfare reform was driven neither by the ideas of international agencies such as the EU or the OECD nor by economic crises related to globalisation or other factors. All Danish governments believe that economic growth and welfare are not adversaries but can go hand in hand.

National responses to the EU initiatives

In general, Danes have an ambivalent attitude to the EU and social policy. On the one hand, they share a strong belief that the fate of the welfare state is closely intertwined with that of the nation state. On the other, they love their welfare state and want others to be able to develop similar paradises for themselves. As a consequence, while Danes generally favour social policy initiatives on the supranational level, they do not want such initiatives to be binding for Member States or to get in the way of national social policy in any other way. This attitude may help explain the apparent Danish contradiction of embracing European social policy initiatives while simultaneously arguing against their institutionalisation at the EU level.

Lisbon Strategy: then and now

Denmark embraced the Lisbon Strategy from its very start in 2000. For example, Prime Minister Poul Nyrup Rasmussen (Social Democrat) argued in the Danish 2001 euro election campaign that for the first time the Lisbon Strategy gave the EU a social dimension and that it was to be credited to the collaboration of European Social Democrats. For the Danish government the Lisbon Strategy was a 'commitment to full employment and welfare societies in collaboration between sovereign states'.

The change of government in November 2001 did not alter the official Danish views. However, year by year it became clear that the process of the Strategy was becoming more cumbersome and that the chances of meeting the 2010 targets were becoming slimmer. On various occasions the Danish government expressed doubts about the increasing number of targets and increased complexity of the process: 'Too many goals, targets and means have been agreed upon. We must prioritise, rationalise, ensure consistency, and focus the Strategy towards knowledge-based growth and the creation of more and better jobs', was, for example, the objection and objective expressed in a non-paper by the Danish government in the autumn of 2004 (Danish Government, 2004).

Together with the UK and the Netherlands (among others), Denmark worked for a revision of the Lisbon Strategy. Not surprisingly Denmark therefore endorsed the suggestions for a refocused and simplified Strategy made first by the High Level Group chaired by Wim Kok in its mid-term review of the Lisbon process, and later by the Commission in its proposal for the Council meeting of 22-23 March 2005 (see, respectively, High Level Group, 2004b; European Commission, 2005g). At that meeting, the Council decided on a number of measures for revitalising a revised Lisbon Strategy. The Danish government endorsed the refocusing on growth and employment and the new form of governance.

Active social and labour market policies were among Denmark's chief inputs to European employment and social inclusion strategies during the 1990s. The same ingredients are still promoted, now under the umbrella of flexicurity, where activation policies combine with lax employment protection and generous social security. Most recently, Denmark included the improvement of the situation of children for promoting social mobility and social cohesion, or, in the words of the Presidency conclusion from the Spring Summit 2006, 'to reduce child poverty, giving all children equal opportunities, regardless of their social background'.

Open method of coordination

The OMC is popular in Denmark, as it meets the needs of Danish ambivalence towards the EU and social policy. More specifically, it allows for a non-binding integration in social policy.

However, a certain amount of hesitation has been observed among some of the actors involved in the national process of making National Action Plans, for example, interest organisations, the social partners and civil servants from various ministries. Many of them have carried a large workload where efforts may not always have matched outputs. Before the revision of the Lisbon Strategy, many actors thought that an annual action plan for employment, social inclusion and pensions was a little too much, since annual changes hardly justified a whole new document.

The revision of the Lisbon Strategy resolved the latter problem by the creation of a three-year policy cycle. However, a new problem may then arise in the form of little connection between the policy cycle set by the OMC and the national policy cycle, thereby rendering some OMC exercises less valuable.

Social Policy Agenda

Part of the new Lisbon Strategy has been a streamlining and integration of various strategies and activities. Importantly, the Broad Economic Policy Guidelines (BEPGs) for Member States have been merged with the guidelines for employment policies under the EES into a set of integrated guidelines. The integrated guidelines are now part of the new Lisbon Strategy focus on growth and jobs, as decided by the Council in late March 2005.

As stated earlier, Denmark supports the new Lisbon Strategy. National governments prepare a National Reform Programme at the start of the new three-year policy cycle outlining the country's reform strategies within the Lisbon Strategy. This three-year cycle runs parallel with that of the integrated guidelines adopted at EU level, and contains a number of recommendations for Member States to use in preparation for the National Reform initiatives. In October 2005, Denmark submitted its first National Reform Programme as part of this process (Danish Government, 2005a).

The Reform Programme lists a number of ongoing activities but does not announce new initiatives, although many are soon expected. The reason is simple. The government does not want to signal its policy to the opposition or the public before negotiations between the government and the opposition are complete. Reaching a compromise with the opposition, especially the Social Democrats, is sacrosanct for the government, as it wants neither to claim credit for nor blame welfare reforms alone.

The Secretary of State for Social Affairs formulated the Danish position neatly when he said, 'We put national social policy into the framework of the OMC, but we do not frame the policies to fit the OMC' (Børner, 2005).

Early in 2006, the Commission made its first recommendation to the spring Council meeting in the first annual progress report on the new Lisbon Strategy (European Commission, 2006j). From the Danish perspective, the recommendations were very much in line with current political priorities and strategies. For example, the Danish Ministry of Foreign Affairs noted that the Commission was recommending flexicurity as best practice (Udenrigsministeriet, 2006). Therefore, it is no surprise that the Danish government welcomed the Commission progress report and its recommendations.

Demographic change

Greater longevity, larger proportions of elderly people in the labour market and persistently low birth rates are central trends, according to the Green Paper on demographic change in Europe. According to the Commission, demographic challenges face all Member States (European Commission, 2005c). The Danish government welcomed the Green Paper but did not think demographic aspects called for new initiatives:

> ... it seems unlikely that the area needs an actual framework in addition to existing structures. The actual managing of the impact of demographic trends is a question of national competencies and a matter of national agreements between the social partners. However, demographic aspects should be integrated into the European activities aimed at employment, growth and social inclusion. (Danish Government, 2005b, p 1)

Thus policies confronting demographic challenges are best handled at the national level. The European level may be used for discussion and exchange of ideas and experiences.

Substantively, the Danish government did not agree with the Commission's suggestion of increased immigration as a solution to the lack of labour supply caused by an ageing population:

> ... the solution to the labour shortage is not large scale immigration, but rather a managed migration model, which first and foremost provide better integration of immigrants already residing in Denmark with a view to ensure their labour market participation, and secondly, facilitates highly skilled immigration into certain specific sectors where there is a shortage of labour. (Danish Government, 2005b, p 6)

The Danish government therefore found it 'essential that any measures adopted allow the individual Member States to determine the number of third country nationals into its territory to work' (Danish Government, 2005b, p 6).

Services of general interest

The big issue here concerns state subsidies. Are there social services of such general interest (SGI) that they qualify for state subsidies? By implication this question raises the politically sensitive question of which services are not of such a general interest that they qualify for state subsidies. This issue is particularly thorny in a country with a welfare model that is 'heavy on services'. The Danish public service sector is indeed large by international standards, with most of the social services either free or state-subsidised, locally or centrally, making user fees much lower than market prices would otherwise suggest.

The Danish government supports the Commission initiative of starting a consultative process that aims to clarify the social SGI concept and their interaction with the principles of free competition in the Treaty (Socialministeriet and Beskæftigelsesministeriet, 2006). This support has to be seen in the light of the increased Danish use of contracting out of public services to private providers. The current Danish government endorses this development because it wants to keep services from becoming either 100% public or private. However, as a result, boundaries between public and private services are becoming increasingly blurred. The government also sees the need for clarification in light of its emphasis on consumerism.

Social SGI may for these reasons turn out to become a political minefield, especially in Denmark with its huge public sector. Strong trade unions for public sector employees and various interest organisations have expressed their interests and points of view in connection with the hearing process.

Proposal on the Services Directive

From a Danish perspective the two main issues on the Services Directive concern, first, what counts as welfare services and, second, whether the principle of host country or the country-of-origin principle needs applying. The fear of Danish trade unions and some social interest organisations is that the Services Directive in the first version (2004) by the Commission may lead to social dumping and a hollowing out of the public sector.

The European Parliament had the same concerns when it markedly changed the draft Directive. The Parliament totally exempted the welfare area from the Directive and chose the principle of host country. Furthermore, charities and the public sector at large were exempted, as were revenue-making vehicles such as the lottery. As is probably well known, first the Commission and then the Council adopted more or less the same text as that suggested by the European Parliament.

The Danish Prime Minister, Andersen Fogh Rasmussen (Liberal), and Vice Prime Minister, Bent Bendtsen (Conservative), stated that they were pleased with the decisions of the European Parliament.

European Economic and Monetary Union

Danish kroner, not euros, are the currency of Denmark. On 28 September 2000, 53.2% of Danish voters rejected Danish participation in the third phase of the European Economic and Monetary Union (EMU), that is, rejected the euro as currency. The referendum campaign was characterised more by general discussions on the EU and welfare than by the particular issues of European economic and monetary collaboration. With a turnout rate of 87.3%, political participation was level with or higher than that of national parliamentary elections (87.1% in 2001 and 84.5% in 2005).

Denmark remains a member of the second phase of the EMU, the ERM II, meaning that the Danish National Central Bank (Nationalbanken) employs a policy of stable currency towards the euro. Moreover, the Nationalbank is part of the European System of Central Banks, that consists of the European Central Bank and the central banks from 25 Member States.

It is not easy to guess when another referendum on the euro will take place. Even though opinion polls in 2005 and 2006 show that a majority of the population favours the euro, neither the government nor the opposition are pushing the issue. Moreover, the French and Dutch 'No' votes on the Constitution, as well as the UK postponement of the euro vote, have not promoted the idea of having a Danish euro election in the short term.

Enlargement

In general, Denmark supports the EU taking on new members as long as they fulfil the Copenhagen criteria (1993):

- *Political:* stable institutions guaranteeing democracy, the rule of law, human rights and respect for minority groups.
- *Economic:* a functioning market economy.
- *Incorporation of the Community acquis:* adherence to the various political, economic and monetary aims of the EU.

Indeed, the present and previous Danish governments strongly advocated the recent EU enlargement towards Central and Eastern European countries. Historical links with Baltic countries meant that Denmark argued for a large extension of the EU, with 10 countries rather than fewer becoming members over several rounds. In Denmark, the slogan 'From Copenhagen to Copenhagen' symbolised that accession talks started (1993) and ended (2002) in Copenhagen. Prime Minister Anders Fogh Rasmussen was proud when, as EU President, he declared that the Eastern enlargement was 'a great moment for Europe. 75 million people will be welcomed a new citizens of the EU. Our common wish is to make Europe a continent of democracy, freedom, peace and prosperity. Our aim is One Europe' (Rasmussen, 2002).

At the same time, however, a group of civil servants in the Ministry of Employment was busy writing a report on the potential negative unintended effects of enlargement (Beskæftigelsesministeriet, 2003a). In particular, their concern was the possibility of social tourism and social dumping. Their thinking benefited from the works of colleagues in Sweden and from estimates on migration from a study prepared for the Commission (see Boeri and Brücker 2003; Rollén, 2003).

Fears of social tourism and social dumping led a coalition of political parties in the Parliament to agree on a set of measures that regulated work permits and conditions for migrant workers from the eight new Member States from Central and Eastern Europe and to curb their social rights for a transitional period. The coalition was unusually broad. Only two political parties on the very Left (Enhedslisten) and Right (Dansk Folkeparti) did not join in (Beskæftigelsesministeriet, 2003b). The agreement stipulated that workers from the new Member States in Central and Eastern Europe could get permission to stay in Denmark only if they had jobs meeting regular standards of work relating to wage and working conditions (Beskæftigelsesministeriet, 2003b). If the migrant worker lost his or her job, the residence permit would be withdrawn, and the only economic support would be a subsidy to travel back to the country of origin; no social security would be available.

The Danish Minister of Employment announced the transitional measures by saying that:

> Danish employees can now sleep safely. EU enlargement will not result in undue pressure on wages. Firms can be happy that they will get access to labour from the new EU Member States. And we can all be happy that we have put a fence around the Danish welfare schemes. (Frederiksen, 2003)

The first transitional period of two years ended on 1 May 2006. The political parties behind the first agreement decided to make it easier for firms to hire workers from the new Member States through a system of prior approval.

Conclusions

The nature of Danish reactions to EU initiatives has changed over the past 20 years. When the Commission originally tried to get Member States to agree on harmonisation through the adoption of legal acts, Denmark was generally against it, foot dragging. Social policy was – and still is – seen by Danish governments as an area of competence primarily for the Member States.

European collaboration changed after the 1992 project on a 'social dimension' achieved only a single directive on maternity. Rather than seeking harmonisation through legislation, Member States began to collaborate in non-binding ways by setting up common goals and guidelines for policies, and forums for discussion and exchange of experience. Danish governments have supported this line of non-binding European collaboration in social policy. They also endorsed it when it became an official EU policy with the adoption of the Lisbon Strategy and the OMC, and (perhaps even more pronounced) with the new Lisbon Strategy, which Denmark also supported.

Denmark is likely to remain one of the pace-setting Member States in discussing social issues and setting the Social Policy Agenda to the extent that European collaboration on such matters can provide concrete results for EU citizens or tackle cross-border issues. Moreover, Denmark will most likely support the continued use of the OMC in meeting these social issues, so that responsibility for social policy starts and ends at the national level.

Notes
[1] The referendum on the Maastricht Treaty was held on 2 June 1992. The Edinburgh European Council (12/1992) gave Denmark exemption from collaboration in four areas: Union citizenship, the third phase of the Economic and Monetary Union (EMU), military collaboration and supranational collaboration on justice and home affairs. On 18 May 1993, 56.7% of the Danes voted 'Yes' to ratification of the Maastricht Treaty plus the Edinburgh agreement. The euro referendum on 28 September 2000 prevented Denmark from entering the third phase of the European EMU. Denmark still needs a new referendum on this matter before it can adopt the euro. In the meantime, Denmark remains a member of the second phase of the EMU.

[2] This term was coined by Tanja Börzel (2002) in an article called 'Pace-setting, foot-dragging, and fence-sitting: Member State responses to Europeanization'.

TWELVE

Greece: the quest for national welfare expansion through more social Europe

Theodoros Sakellaropoulos

This chapter aims to analyse and explain Greece's official response to the European Union's (EU's) evolving social policy. Understanding this response entails considering four important factors influencing the overall Greek attitude towards the European integration project: the country's economic underdevelopment in relation to other EU countries; the late and inadequate development of social structures and the welfare state; the wide consensus among the major political parties on European integration, based on the predominance of political criteria; and the underdevelopment of civil society and the ineffectiveness of public administration.

The first two factors significantly influence Greece's goals towards European integration: the country's principal priority is a catch-up effort with other Member States in terms of salaries, incomes and social protection levels. Additionally, the underdevelopment of the welfare state further enhances the demand for welfare state expansion, while constraining the efforts for rationalisation and adjustment (as evidenced in mature European welfare states). Therefore, Greece perceives the aspiration for a European social policy, either explicitly as in the past or implicitly as in the present, as a harmonisation and convergence project. This strategy – pursued, albeit in varying degrees, over the past two decades – has been strengthened by the common strategic approach of the three major political parties (PASOK, ND and Synaspismos) towards European integration and EU social policy in particular. Finally, the state-centred society and the bad public administration significantly constrain the economic and social modernisation processes, toughen problem solving, restrict initiatives and negatively affect policy effectiveness overall.

The European social model versus the Greek model

In contrast to most Member States, whose citizens are proud of their own welfare reality, Greece has not developed a distinct type of welfare state. Until recently, the country lacked adequate state-supported social structures and social protection. Social protection expenditure was low compared to the EU average, focusing almost exclusively on a Bismarckian-type pension system with a corporatist base, operating on a clientelistic basis. Social services were inadequate, while the transfer of resources was limited. Social needs and risks were covered to a great extent by the family.

The Socialists, in power from 1981 to 2004 (with a brief interruption from 1989 to 1993), inaugurated an era of social modernisation. They established Beveridge-type institutions of universal coverage like the national health system, amended family law, expanded social insurance to new groups and geographical areas, established the freedom of collective bargaining, inaugurated social dialogue, reduced social inequalities and increased the share of salaries and pensions on GDP (gross domestic product). Nonetheless, significant gaps in the social protection system remain. As public opinion polls demonstrate, factors such as high unemployment rates, low pensions and salaries, the inadequacy of basic social structures and social services institutions, the failure of effective active labour market policies, and the gradual undermining of the public health and educational systems diminish citizen trust in the national welfare state and increase the role of the family.

With these characteristics, the Greek welfare state is classified in the literature as either the conservative-Bismarckian welfare regime or the Mediterranean/Latin one (Ferrera, 1996 ; Matsaganis, 2002; Katrougalos and Lazaridis, 2003, p 3). However, Greek citizens do not have a feeling or consciousness of experiencing a special social protection reality, as do citizens of advanced welfare states (see Chapter Four on France, this volume). It is thus difficult to compare the Greek model to other European welfare models or to an ESM, as evidenced in other EU countries (see Chapter Two on Germany, this volume). Thus, Greeks appear as strong supporters of a rather vague ESM and of social policies emanating from Brussels.

From the very beginning of discussions on Europe's future Greece has displayed a strong commitment to a European social state. The memoranda on regional cohesion (Greek Government, 1982) and social Europe (Ministry of Foreign Affairs, 1988), submitted by the Socialist governments of Andreas Papandreou, have until now defined the positions of Greece on EU developmental and social issues. The same policy line was followed during the 1996 Intergovernmental Conference.[1] The Greek proposal for the social dimension included: (1) a greater degree of coordination in the EU's social actions and the formulation of a more active employment policy than those currently in existence; (2) a special chapter on employment and the establishment of an employment committee; (3) the strengthening of social protection policy through the incorporation of the Social Chapter and the Social Protocol; and (4) the support of the goal of sustainable development and the promotion of environmental Research and Development (R&D). These same positions appeared once more during the debate on the Constitutional Treaty, where the Greek parties supported the idea of a politically united federal and social Europe (European Parliament, Greek Office, 2003; Karamanlis, 2005a).

Public opinion, the government and the trade unions favour EU initiatives aimed at filling the social deficits in Greece and expanding social protection. Greeks associate the ESM with a high level of social protection, higher salaries and pensions and a social safety net, expecting EU funds to be a significant contributor. Greece views the content of the ESM as equal to the parameters of a social market economy, a high level of solidarity and income redistribution, along with the protection of labour and social rights.

In the public debate taking place in Greece the Socialists constantly refer to the virtues of the Scandinavian model, that is, social protection and flexibility. The majority of the Centre-Right party members and part of its leadership seem to favour Bismarckian welfare principles, while the economic ministers of the Centre-Right government seem to promote the values of an 'Irish-type' model, that is, growth and employment. For labour unions and Socialists the upward convergence of salaries and pensions towards the EU average constitutes the utmost imperative. Therefore, the public debate in Greece is focusing on the search for a social model worth adopting. Not surprisingly, therefore, the ESM is a constant point of reference for political leaders and citizens. According to the most recent opinion polls – including Eurobarometer measurements – Greeks are in favour of further EU interventions on issues of employment, social inclusion, health and pensions, and of delegating the decision-making authority to the EU bodies. In contrast, Greece views coordination policies implemented after 2000 as neoliberal policies, jeopardising social protection systems and ultimately undermining the ESM.

Within this context the principle of subsidiarity, whether advocated openly or not, never had ardent supporters in Greece. The national goals of harmonisation (1980s and 1990s) prevailed over subsidiarity and national decision-making approaches. The fear about a race to the bottom and cutbacks in labour and social rights as expressed by the trade unions is constantly present in the public debate. Even before 1989 (that is, before the emergence of cheap labour from Eastern European countries) Greece did not seek to benefit seriously from a comparative and developmental advantage such as its cheap labour. Only business people and industrialists supported subsidiarity, arguing for growth but opposing the harmonisation of national social policies (see Association of the Greek Industries, 1991). Their views did not appeal to the public. The strategy of the convergence of wages, incomes and pensions, currently followed by trade unions and welcomed by public opinion, reconfirms the persistence of Greek political attitudes on EU norms and initiatives.

Therefore, the common social denominators of EU social policy should not only be about the great challenges facing European societies (ageing population, new family patterns, unemployment, globalisation, and so on) but also about common policies and institutions contributing to overcoming such challenges and expanding welfare provisions at the EU level. Ultimately, for Greeks the European integration project requires more legitimacy, along with the status of a European social citizenship for all EU citizens. Greek EU representatives always welcome projects strengthening social cohesion in Europe. For example, on the way to the Lisbon conference (2000), Greek Prime Minister K. Simitis suggested a common initiative for combating youth unemployment in Europe (Simitis, 2000a). Another field of common European action could be disabled people or children (Sakellaropoulos, 2004, p 58).

Main principles in national reforms

The deficits of the social protection system in Greece led to major social reforms, implemented from 1990 through to the present, responding mainly to domestic priorities and needs. The EU influence became gradually apparent from the mid-1990s. The basic principles underlying these changes were expansion of coverage, safeguarding of the system's ability to respond to population ageing, rationalisation of services and institutions, active labour market policies, budget consolidation, adjustment to globalisation and economic competitiveness.

The 1990s were characterised by a further expansion of the welfare state through the establishment of new institutions and policies, while retrenchment was limited. The rise in social expenditure as a share of GDP brought Greece closer to the rest of the Member States. Major reforms were attributed predominantly to domestic factors. The 1990–92 pension reforms aimed at fiscal consolidation and at securing the viability of the social security system by raising the retirement age, by reducing expenses by separating recipients into two categories, and by reducing entitlements (Tinios, 2005). Furthermore, the reforms introduced state contributions for new labour market entrants. Through a blame-avoidance strategy, the existing Bismarckian system was maintained and reinforced. In 1996-97 domestic political factors and the Socialists' programme led to the expansion of social insurance to farmers (contributions based) and to low-income pensioners at risk of poverty (targeted, means-tested complementary assistance benefit) following the opening of the single market to international competition.

By contrast, the reforms of 2001–02 took place within a radically different environment. The EMU and the Stability and Growth Pact (SGP) required – and still require – fiscal discipline, while social insurance deficits now form part of the general deficit. Recommendations or pressures from international organisations also contributed to strengthening the case for further government initiatives (Featherstone et al, 2001; Featherstone, 2005). The reform was based on a study by the British Actuaries Department. The first reform attempt of 2001 led to a series of unprecedented strikes and mobilisations. It ultimately failed, mainly because, in an egalitarian way, it significantly reduced the replacement rate for both low-income pensioners and high earners in the public or semi-public sector. The second attempt succeeded because it focused on private sector pensions, entailed provisions for unifying primary and supplementary pension funds, and introduced occupational pensions. The government covered the Social Security Institute's (IKA's) annual deficit by granting 1% of GDP, and the reform did not alter the system's basis. Nonetheless, the introduction of a funded pillar constitutes a step towards the establishment of a multi-pillar system similar to those of other Member States (Sotiropoulos, 2004).

The field of health has been constituted since the 1980s as a privileged domain of national social policy. The new Socialist government views the establishment of the national health system in 1983 as the height of its socio-political programme, as it provides state-financed universal health services. The Greek social model, based until then on Bismarckian principles, acquired mixed characteristics through the introduction of a second pillar based on the principles of Beveridge. The reform attempts of the 1990s reflected the internal ideological and political conflicts. In 1992 the Conservative government attempted to change these principles by introducing elements of private economy and individual responsibility. However, in 1994 the Socialists brought the national health system back to its original principles, and the 1997 reform attempted to deal with the chronic and structural problems: health organisation and management, hospital management and financing, and the restructuring of primary care.

Yet once again the government never implemented the innovative elements of the new law, as the government lacked clear orientation on its goals and domestic interest groups pressured for the withdrawal of the reform. The EU impact starts mainly from the mid-1990s, through to the modernisation of existing hospitals and the creation of new ones, especially in the periphery of the country, financed by European funds. However, as the structural and operational deficiencies of the national health system multiplied, the government undertook a new reform in the early 2000s, focusing on decentralisation, the rationalisation of expenses and the management and improvement of the quality and effectiveness of health services (Economou, 2004, pp 207-10; Davaki and Mossialos, 2006, pp 310-18).

Over the past 20 years no major reforms in social care have taken place. Its provision is still based on a complex system of cash benefits comprising minimum threshold pensions, various pension-type benefits for elderly people, and provisions for targeted groups in poverty, for example, disabled people, children and single mothers. But social services and benefits in kind are less developed. Progress in recent years has occurred mainly under the influence of the EU strategy for social inclusion and EU funds. New instruments, institutions and approaches have been developed in parallel with focused interventions in specific fields (for example, psychiatry). Yet social care is still lagging behind. The unemployment rate is among the highest in Europe, the percentage of people characterised as poor was 20% in 2001 (compared to an EU average of 15%), while the transfer of resources has not significantly affected poverty.

In the field of social protection, we can view social care as the most explicit example of the intense confrontation between Europeanisation and domestic resistance. However, until the 2004 elections this resistance stemmed mainly from the government. Despite the two Community recommendations on sufficient resources, published during the Greek presidency in 1992, successive Greek governments, while displaying a pro-European and reformist orientation, have been unwilling to adopt them, citing fiscal problems, their inability to control benefit provision and so on (Ministry of Labour and Social Security, 2003). Along with Italy and Hungary, Greece has not therefore adopted the core of the ESM, that is, a coherent and generalised system of minimum income guarantee protecting its citizens from the risk of poverty in terms of equal access and guarantee of sufficient resources. This contradiction between Greece's pro-European attitude and its unwillingness to adopt a significant component of the ESM constitutes a Greek paradox in the Europeanisation of social protection. It is only recently that both the government and major political parties suggested the introduction of minimum income guarantee schemes.

The 1990s also prepared the ground for radical changes in industrial relations and employment policies. In 1990, under pressure from trade unions, the government replaced the state-corporatist system of collective bargaining and industrial conflict resolution with a European-type neo-corporatist system of open and free collective bargaining between social partners. Although a series of mechanisms and instruments supporting the new system were created, the introduction of a tripartite social dialogue (Confidence Pact for Growth, Employment and Competitiveness, 1997), based on the model adopted by other Member States, proved unsuccessful. Pacts and dialogues on the way to EMU membership and on the building up of social alliances for implementing restrictive fiscal policies and labour market changes remained on paper.

More substantive and coherent labour market and employment policies emerged after 1997 with the preparation of the first National Action Plan for employment in the framework of the European Employment Strategy (EES). The reforms, while reflecting the Greek peculiarities, were integrated in the framework of the Lisbon Strategy. Greece set the following goals for 2010: 65.8% total participation in the labour force and 57% female participation. Research has shown that unemployment in Greece is mainly a problem of unsuccessful labour market entrance from: (1) lack of previous professional experience, especially among young people and women; (2) a mismatch between the demand and supply of skills and training; and (3) a lack of knowledge acquisition after a certain age. Even though these traits require targeted interventions, such interventions have not happened in most cases.

To facilitate the entrance of young people and women without professional experience into the labour market, the government created incentives for expanding part-time work in the public sector, lowering social insurance contributions for unskilled workers and subsidising the employment of young people. The government also used EU funds for establishing organisations and institutions to monitor labour market policies and developments (Ministry of Labour and Social Security, 2003; Ministry of Employment and Social Protection, 2004). Vocational training represents one of the most important forms of active labour market policies. In Greece vocational training developed mainly through EU funds, programmes and orientations since the 1980s. In the late 1990s more than a third of those not eligible for unemployment benefit took part in active labour market policies, while 53%-58% of them are annually integrated in vocational training programmes (Dimoulas, 2005, p 227).

To sum up, from the mid-1990s the EU has significantly influenced employment policies. Measures of flexibility and active labour market policies were implemented through the National Action Plan for employment as part of the EES. However, the implementation of flexibility measures (in working hours, pay, employment contracts and dismissal limits) was hindered by pressures from trade unions, employers and even the government itself (Sakellaropoulos and Angelaki, 2007).

The major reforms of this period responded to the need for welfare expansion covering structural and historical social deficits. The EU influence is discerned in three domains: (1) the direct introduction and financing of new instruments, institutions and focused interventions for specific population groups; (2) the indirect yet clear instigation and recommendation of policies in the framework of the OMC; and (3) the indirect influence of the EMU and the SGP in financing social policies and the formulation of employment policies. In the latter case the policies of radical reform of social relations have failed, as depicted in the 2000-01 attempts at reforming the labour market and the social security system. By contrast, EU-inspired and funded reforms for expanding social protection and its institutions were positively received.

National responses to the EU initiatives

During the same period, Greece's aspirations for a supranational, pan-European social policy were accompanied by a moderate participation – and often absence – in the evolving European social policy. National distinctive traits, the ideology of the political party in power, casual problems and insufficient public awareness have negatively influenced the Greek attitude towards various EU initiatives.

Lisbon and the renewed Lisbon Strategy

Greece's reaction to the Lisbon Strategy and the policy triangle of growth, employment and social cohesion was positive. To a certain extent Greece viewed the Lisbon goals with relief, given the constant pressures from the trade unions. In the Greek response Prime

Minister Simitis stressed that growth should occur in parallel with the establishment of a climate of security and trust, thereby limiting the risks arising from rapid technological and social changes. Technological and social change should not lead to a 'two thirds society' but rather ensure the social character of the European model of growth. This growth model should aim at reducing the wealth gap among EU regions and preventing an increase in inequalities from increases in GDP (Simitis, 2000a). The Prime Minister pointed out that growth and employment should be linked to the rise of real wages and citizen participation in the profits from GDP increases, to the general and social values shaping the wider social and political framework for every person, and to trust in European integration.

Greece's views in terms of the measures proposed were quite interesting. General recommendations included: (1) better coordination between macroeconomic policies, structural policies and measures and active labour market policies; (2) greater efficiency of active labour market policies and their connection with the production process; and (3) amelioration of the environment to encourage new business and thereby the creation of new and better jobs. In addition, two other recommendations deserve to be mentioned: the first pertains to the development of integrated programmes for the social integration of young people. The second pertains to the inclusion in the benchmarking process (as proposed by the presidency) of all significant factors, that is, benchmarking should not be limited to reporting success or failure in creating new jobs but should also include issues such as the developments in wages, insurance and working rights. Otherwise, given the interaction of various factors not always considered, a simple quantitative approach could lead to inaccurate conclusions (Simitis, 2000a).

Nevertheless, the Socialist Prime Minister did not propose the obligatory Maastricht-type character of the coordination procedure as some Socialist Members of Parliament suggested (Simitis, 2000b). Greece's proposals in Lisbon were mainly dictated by a severe unemployment problem (not confined to Greece but affecting the entire EU), the ideology of the governing Socialist party, and the economic situation (Simitis, 2000a). In 1999 Greece had the highest rate of unemployment increase and the second worst performance in Europe, while youth unemployment was particularly high (GSEE, 2000). Given that Greece had already joined the EMU, the Prime Minister could now set advanced targets (more welfare state, higher employment and redistribution) as top priority issues during his 2000 electoral campaign and in his Lisbon proposals (see, respectively, Simitis, 2000c, 2001a).

The renewed Lisbon Strategy (2005), signifying the weakening of the goal of social cohesion relative to those of growth and employment, was positively accepted by the new Centre-Right government of C. Karamanlis and the Ministry of Finance (Karamanlis, 2005a, 2005b; Louri, 2005). The government considered competitiveness and employment as preconditions for social cohesion (Alogoskoufis, 2005a, 2005b). But the Ministry of the Economy and the Ministry of Employment had different approaches. For example, during the European Council on Employment, 2 June 2002, the Ministry of Employment supported (along with France and Belgium) the need to preserve the link between Lisbon and the goal of social cohesion (Permanent Representation of Greece in the EU, 2005). Although it was within Greece's discretion to include a chapter on social protection, socio-political goals were absent from the Greek Reform Programme prepared by the Ministry of Economy and Finance (2005a). The government perceived social cohesion as merely an aspect of regional cohesion and therefore not linked to employment policies. Furthermore, a strategy on ageing and social security reform was absent.

This approach did not conform to the pre-electoral economic programme of the Centre-Right government. Nonetheless, the positions of Greece were put forward mainly orally at the Ecofin Council, not in a separate document, as the Minister of Finance himself admitted (see Alogoskoufis, 2005a). Employers' organisations supported the reformed Lisbon Strategy on the occasion of the Kok report (ESEE, 2004; SEV, 2004). For Greek industrialists the existence of the ESM was not a separate policy goal. By contrast, the Greek Economic and Social Committee expressed its opposition to the elimination of the goal of social cohesion, pointing out that the revision endangered the ESM (OKE, 2005). The Greek Trades Unions Federation, in accordance with the European trade unions, pointed out that social Europe was a precondition for the success of the Lisbon Strategy and emphasised strengthening lifelong learning, social protection and employee participation in work environments (GSEE, 2005; Polyzogopoulos, 2005).

Open method of coordination

Greece originally viewed the OMC and benchmarking with mistrust and reservation, even at the highest level (Simitis, 2000a). This attitude comes from the inability of a state-centred society to come to terms with decentralised and participative processes, from the absence of a civil society that could claim participation, and from the mistrust of trade unions towards a particularly central state with no intentions of promoting a genuine social dialogue. Both the government and the political forces favoured the old Community method of bringing immediate results and financing through EU funds. Greece has gradually accepted the OMC but without so far having fully developed its potential. For cohesive policies it contributed substantially to the formulation and pursuit of integrated policies in the fields of employment and social protection. It mobilised forces, politicians and funds, contributed to the Europeanisation of policies, and expanded EU legitimacy in Greece (Sotiropoulos, 2004). However, evaluating the OMC's results separately from national procedures is difficult. This difficulty applies not just to Greece but also to all Member States.

The positions of Greece on the OMC can be found in its answer to the European Commission's OMC evaluation questionnaire (Ministry of Employment and Social Protection, 2005). In terms of giving a further impulse to the OMC in the field of social protection Greece pointed out the need to preserve the broad objectives. These objectives should be accompanied in the National Action Plans by priorities for action in specific areas requiring immediate attention. Similarly, Greece emphasised the need to expand EU-level targets in the following areas: decent housing conditions, homelessness, child poverty, social services and accessibility for disabled people. In the field of indicators the government pointed out the inclusion of a broader spectrum of topics.

As the future development of the OMC evolves in a streamlined context, Greece supports the maintenance of the distinct identity of each strand of the social field. It proposes a smaller number of overarching objectives encompassing the different strands, with a second tier of more detailed objectives pertinent to each. It favours a smaller number of indicators requiring the development of main indicators for each strand. It also favours a three-year reporting cycle, with light updates and implementation reports in the intervening years. Greece wants the OMC sustained and further strengthened through a concrete, clear expression of Member State political will, leading to an agreement on setting targets at the EU level, as well as through EU financing, through the substantial involvement of the European Parliament (ensuring transparency and publicity), and through the active engagement of the social partners and non-governmental organisations (NGOs) at the EU level. The Joint Social Protection and Social Inclusion Report should be submitted to the European Council.

Finally, Greece has proposed to add a separate chapter for social protection/inclusion to both the National Reform Programmes and the annual report of the Commission on the Lisbon Strategy implementation. This addition entails incorporating the social protection/inclusion objectives in the integrated guidelines for growth and employment (European Commission, 2005f).

Proposal on the Services Directive and services of general interest

In the case of direct legislative intervention at the EU level (as in the draft Services Directive on the internal market), Greece's reaction was prompt, continuous and expressed at the highest political level. During the Spring Summit (March 2005) Greece aligned itself with the majority of Member States on a full revision of the draft Directive, the inclusion of the values of the ESM and the preservation of workers' and consumers' rights. The positions of Greece, like those of most Member States, centre on the point stating that 'during the general application of the country-of-origin principle, less restrictive legislation should not prevail' (Ministry of Economy and Finance, 2005b).

This position remained unaltered even after the Gebhardt report and the reformulation of the principle of free provision of services (Alogoskoufis, 2005c; Ministry of Economy and Finance, 2005b). Greece has exemptions regarding the professions of tourist guides, legal services, legal functionaries, notaries, the audiovisual and tourist field of gambling, the health sector (along with Austria and the Czech Republic), SGI, private employment offices and temporary employment offices (along with Luxembourg, Belgium and Finland) (Ministry of Economy and Finance, 2005c, 2006a, 2006b).

As to the SGI, the negotiation on the Services Directive offered the opportunity for dealing with issues of the interplay between the provision of SGI in the social and health fields, and further steps regarding EU internal market rules (Ministry of Economy and Finance, 2005d, 2005e). For health services, Greece favours their exemption from the country-of-origin principle and their treatment in a more balanced and appropriate way. For employment services, Greece evaluates positively the foreseen provisions in terms of the licensing procedure. Reservations were expressed about the provision for an implied acceptance of granting of licences in the case of the lapsing of an acceptable period of time, not exceeding a period of six months. For compensation for receiving health services in a Member State other than that of affiliation, Greece supports the incorporation of the related EU jurisprudence in Regulation 1408/71 (883/04) and its total exemption from the body of the Directive.

Finally, as for the Posting of Workers Directive, Greece suggested reframing the draft articles for the non-compulsory provision for a labour representative and securing the necessary conditions for the cooperation of the authorities between country of origin and posting. Greece also favours facilitating attachment of workers from third countries, when satisfying the precondition of having previously worked for a reasonable time (over six months) in the Member State of origin, and the obligation of the original Member State to readmit them after the posting period ends (to avoid abusive forms of posting) (Ministry of Economy and Finance, 2005d, 2005e).

The Greek positions have been defined to a great extent by the social stratification of Greek society. A wide spectrum of social groups saw the Services Directive and the SGI as a threat. The lower independent middle-class professions, dominant in the services sector, and the liberal professions protested strongly against such regulations. In parallel, the same dynamic resistance was displayed by the powerful trade unions fearing the weakening of their positions, the introduction of labour law of variable speeds and social dumping (APE, 2006).

European Economic and Monetary Union

Greece's attitude towards the EMU has been determined mainly by three goals: the pursuit of monetary and fiscal stability, the development and modernisation of the economy and the creation of the conditions necessary for successful employment and social policies (Simitis, 2001b). According to one of the basic economic architects of the 1996-2004 period, Greece viewed the EMU as an external instrument and a vehicle for the country's economic, social and political transformation (Giannitsis, 2004, pp 44-5). Greece's position during both the preparatory phase and that following EMU accession derives from a holistic approach. For Greece, monetary and economic integration require joint examination, along with the process of social and political union. This approach reflected the continual and permanent problems of the Greek economy and the government's inability to solve them by exclusive recourse to national means (Simitis, 2001b).

From a Greek perspective, EU goals in the post-euro period should be about: (1) strengthening redistributive policies so as to achieve real convergence and cohesion in an enlarged Europe; (2) modernising and strengthening the ESM; (3) strengthening macroeconomic management coordination in the framework of the EMU; and (4) increasing the

EU's resources for implementing its policies and goals. According to the Greek government, the EMU in 2001 was characterised by a strong monetary dimension and a weak economic one. Greece therefore considered it unbalanced (in terms of its development), unreliable and incapable of surviving for long, since a common economic and monetary policy cannot operate in the vacuum of other policies. Employment and social policies should also be put at the centre of European integration, and social union should also be a goal, with social solidarity expressed at the EU level in the next Convention for the European Constitution (Simitis, 2001b).

Enlargement

For political reasons Greece was positive about enlargement from the beginning. The Eurobarometer (2004) opinion polls also showed Greece (67%), along with Denmark and Sweden, with the highest rates of acceptance. This attitude results primarily from the accession of Cyprus, the importance given to the region, and the political stability expected to follow from EU enlargement towards the Balkans. This national and political choice could not have been changed by any economic or social reason or implications, such as the exodus of Greek capital to Balkan countries or labour force immigration to Greece. In addition, the Foreign Affairs Minister, Th. Pagalos, supported enlargement in terms of economic benefits entailed for Greek enterprises (Pagalos, 1998, pp 561-3). The social consequences of enlargement in terms of labour force migration, while preoccupying Greece and Spain, were not thought of by labour market economists as having significant consequences (Boeri and Brücker, 2000). Industrialists, too, favoured enlargement (Blavoukos, 2002). The Greek trade union GSEE, however, agreed with the enlargement goal on condition that the European social aquis would be adopted in time to prevent social dumping or putting the ESM at risk. The Greek trade unions reckoned that migratory flows from new countries could not diminish employment (Polyzogopoulos, 2002).

Conclusions

Greece's reactions to EU policies and initiatives on employment and social protection in recent years were neither sufficient nor especially consistent nor clear. This problem is demonstrated by the absence of Greek responses to EU documents, such as the Green Papers on demographic change and SGI, as well as to the Social Policy Agenda

(2006-10). Greek positions on those issues are scattered in documents such as the National Action Plans for employment and inclusion, and speeches or articles by various government ministers. In various European Committees and meetings Greek representatives lack clear instructions, so they usually either express their personal opinions, improvise, or make general statements.[2] The preparation of national positions is usually assigned to a very closed circle of technocrats near the Prime Minister, thereby excluding highly educated public servants from current information, the decision-making process and substantive participation in EU fora. Furthermore, the Greek ministries involved have not always paid the necessary attention to EU matters, especially for soft procedures. On the contrary (as evidenced in the case of the Greek position on the draft Services Directive on the internal market), when specific social interests are at stake and where strong social pressure is exercised, effective interventions at the EU level take place, especially in the framework of the Council of Ministers. Greek reactions are mostly in accord with the Bismarckian model countries and sometimes with the Scandinavian countries (for example, Greece agrees with the positions of Sweden on health services in the SGI discussions). But when social and occupational interests are weak, Greece cannot formulate national positions on European social issues, even in a general way.

The poor performance of the Greek contribution to the evolving EU social policy results from an inherent contradiction concerning the Europeanisation process in Greece – a contradiction between the ambitious goal for a common social European space and the mediocre results of the Europeanisation processes in the national context. Greece's aspiration for a common social Europe is embedded in the overall strategy towards European integration. Economic, social and regional inequalities, insecurities at the level of foreign policy and defence, and the instability of democratic structures in the 1970s have made Greece an ardent supporter of the political-institutional federal model of European integration. A strong, federal and politically united Europe – endowed with a strong economy and social protection system, regional cohesion, a democratic constitution (role of European Parliament), a common foreign and defence policy, and a common fiscal policy with its own resources – constitutes a permanent goal of Greek politics. The social dimension constitutes a strong component of this strategy. During the debate on the Constitutional Treaty, Greece again supported forward-looking positions aimed at social convergence and the creation of a single social Europe.[3] Albeit in varying degrees, almost all political parties continued to support the basic arguments first articulated in the social memorandum of 1988 and later during the 1996 Intergovernmental Conference. Many groups aspire to convergence with the rest of Europe on wages, and many social groups aspire to convergence on living standards. For many Greeks, whether citizens or politicians of different ideologies, social Europe is still understood in federal terms of active solidarity and the social identity of the European citizen, requiring common social institutions, unified regulations and EU-level redistribution.

In contrast to this 'centralistic approach', the current EU strategy for a multi-pillar social protection system based on intergovernmental principles, coordination and active subsidiarity (where EU and national policies coexist and influence one another) neither excites nor motivates most politicians, policy makers and the public in Greece. Thus we see the inferior efforts in and the poor results of the Europeanisation of Greek employment and social protection policies. The same inconsistency is observed in the adjustment of Greek practices and policies to common EU goals and initiatives promoted in the framework of the OMC. The impact of the OMC on Greek social policy is very modest, as Greece underestimates its positive contribution to the further development of EU social matters. Important reforms have been dictated mainly by national priorities. Policy reforms under EU 'influence', such as the pension and labour market reform (2000-01), received no public support and ultimately failed. Research has shown, however, that a series of important positions on European social policies have been articulated by civil society or small NGOs like the OKE, the Greek trade union confederation GSEE and some large NGOs. But in most cases the government more or less ignored these positions. The underdevelopment of NGOs and civil society constitutes an important burden in the participative articulation of national discussions on EU social issues.

The conclusion is obvious: the Europeanisation of Greek social policy (from Brussels to Athens and from Athens to Brussels) is not a dynamic process. Although Greek social policy follows the general pace of other Member States, it does so with no particular enthusiasm, faith or inspiration. Greek governments trapped in the quest for pan-European social integration, underestimated and responded unwillingly to 'minor' European social initiatives, such as the OMC, the Green Paper on demographic change and the Social Policy Agenda. Greece needs to adopt a more proactive approach. The government should strengthen the managerial and planning capacities of public administration, while granting more authority to medium-level policy makers. A significant part of the current shortfalls in ideas, policies, proposals and implementation could be filled through the mobilisation of the increasing potential of NGOs, unions and local/regional authorities.

Notes

[1] See, for example, IGC 96 Task Force–European Commission (1996).

[2] This is derived from the writer's extensive interviews with the Greek representatives in the Economic Policy Committee, Social Protection Committee and Employment Policy Committee.

[3] See the contributions of the representatives of all Greek parties during the European Convention in European Parliament (Greek Office) (2003).

THIRTEEN

The Europeanisation of social protection: domestic impacts and national responses

Jon Kvist and Juho Saari

During the past 10 years, the Europeanisation of social protection has undergone a remarkable transformation. Europeanisation of social protection concerns the relationship between the national and EU levels in social protection. Originally, Jean Monnet and other architects of the European Communities (later the European Union, EU) bought into neofunctionalist theories of European integration. According to neofunctionalism, cooperation among European countries in economic areas and technical matters – called 'negative integration' – would gradually spill over into 'positive integration', with countries agreeing on the formulation of common policies at the EU level (see Haas, 1958). Thus defined, positive integration entails a transfer of sovereignty from the national to the supranational level, that of the EU.

Two waves of research have examined the relationship between the EU and social protection. First-wave scholars noted the weak foundation and mandate of EU institutions in social policy. Because the EU had no legal or monetary means of carrying out its own social policies, it resorted to regulatory social policy (Majone, 1993). Typical of many first-wave studies, a study on the impact of membership on British social policy found an impact in only two domains: gender equality and non-discrimination against EU nationals (Baldwin-Edwards and Gough, 1991). Scholars in this period generally shared the view that the EU had little impact on national social protection (for example, Lange, 1992) and that EU social policy was regulatory and symbolic (Majone, 1993).

Parallel with the first wave, the EU also sparked interest for two other groups of researchers. Evaluation researchers studied the poverty programmes that the EU ran from the 1970s to the early 1990s, and legal experts studied European Court of Justice (ECJ) case law, particularly on gender equality and coordination of social security.

These legal experts created the empirical foundation for the second-wave scholars.

Inspired by neofunctionalist arguements, second-wave scholars made an analytical distinction between positive and negative integration. Their starting point was the observation that European integration in social policy was characterised less by positive integration (that is, initiatives of political actors for developing either EU social policies or common social policies across Member States) than by negative integration (that is, spillover from economic markets to social policy). Their argument was that the ECJ and markets drove the process of negative integration, leading to both adjustments of national welfare states to market requirements (see Leibfried and Pierson, 2000) and an erosion of national competence over social policy. At the same time, second-wave scholars – in agreement with first-wave scholars – found that the positive integration of social policy was limited, not making up for losses made nationally (Streeck, 1995; Scharpf, 1999). Thus they depict a development towards a multi-tiered social policy system in Europe, with fragmented EU social policy and semi-sovereign welfare states (Leibfried and Pierson, 1995).

These important observations are still valid today. However, what could not be known 10 years ago were the changes that have since unfolded, with implications for social protection. This book has centred on four such developments: new policy processes, the internal market, the European Economic and Monetary Union (EMU) and EU enlargement. Whereas some of these developments have accelerated the pace or changed the nature of negative and positive integration processes, others constitute new dynamics in the relationship between the national and the EU levels.

The first set of developments, the new policy processes, is most spectacularly presented by the Lisbon Strategy and the open method of coordination (OMC). They exemplify positive integration. But unlike 'old positive integration' that leads to more policy making at the EU level, the 'new positive integration' mainly provides input to policy making at the national level. Although the EU acts as a forum or arena for the discussion of policy objectives and the exchange of knowledge on policies, decisions on social protection nonetheless occur at the national level. As the country chapters in this volume have shown, most Member States support this type of non-binding EU social policy collaboration over traditional binding legal EU social policy. Within social protection, new positive integration takes place chiefly in the areas of social inclusion, pensions, long-term care for elderly people and child family policies.

The second development, the extended realisation of the internal market (especially in the field of services), is well captured by second-wave scholars. In essence, they argue that the ECJ in particular has been instrumental in deciding on market-adjusting measures that directly influence national social policies, and that this process was 'low politics' (Leibfried and Pierson, 2000). Things have changed over the past 10 years, especially in the 2000s. As the country chapters make evident in discussions on the Services Directive, the interplay between the internal market and social protection has become 'high politics'. European and national politicians and interest organisations had weighty discussions on whether the Services Directive should include social and health services, and whether the country-of-origin principle should determine the applicable law. Various ECJ decisions have sparked similar debates.

The third development, on the EMU, highlights how certain policy initiatives at the EU level spill over into other fields like that of social protection. The EMU constrains Member States from carrying out certain traditional policies, for example, monetary policy, that were hitherto national matters. This depletion of the politicians' toolbox in itself makes social protection relatively more important at the national level. But the EMU also sets the agenda for national social protection in other ways. Through the accompanying Stability and Growth Pact (SGP), a Member State taking part in the EMU must adhere to a certain budgetary discipline. Member States must not run budget deficits of more than 3% of GDP (gross domestic product), and the ratio of public debt to GDP must not be more than 60%. Although a March 2005 revision, based on the first five years of SGP experience, left these levels unchanged, it introduced greater flexibility for exceeding the deficit threshold in hard economic times or for financing investment in structural improvements to the economy. The revision also gave Member States more time to reverse their excessive deficits. Ultimately, if a Member State does not bring its economy back into line, the EMU can impose corrective measures or fines. Because social expenditures make up the bulk of public budgets, social protection comes under scrutiny when Member States have difficulties meeting SGP requirements.

Importantly, however, no direct relationship exists between the EMU and the SGP on the one hand, and welfare reform on the other. Indeed necessary public savings might as well be carried out in fields other than social protection, such as the military or infrastructure. But as certain country chapters show, national governments often use the EMU to justify cost-containment measures. Stefano Sacchi (Chapter

Five) describes how different Italian governments have used the EMU to legitimise pension reform, sometimes making the EMU a scapegoat. Even governments in the Netherlands with no problems in meeting the SGP criteria, as Anton Hemerijck and Peter Sleegers (Chapter Ten) show, have used them in a blame-avoidance strategy for cutting costs.

Finally, this book examines the relation between social protection and EU enlargement. Evidently, a potential for Europeanisation develops when new countries join the EU. To become a new Member State, each country must live up to the Copenhagen criteria and bring its legislation in line with the body of European law built up over the years. Accepting the acquis communautaire is thus a prerequisite for entry into the EU. In practice, the acquis was divided into 31 chapters to negotiate between the EU and the candidate Member States for the Eastern EU enlargement. To the extent that the EU requires specific types of social protection, such requirements could constitute a Europeanisation of social protection. However, as the chapters on Poland and the Czech Republic show (see Chapters Six and Eight, respectively), this was not the case. Besides limited EU legislation in social policy, the EU was also passive compared to either other international organisations, such as the International Monetary Fund (IMF) and the World Bank, or individual Member States. Both Irena Wóycicka and Maciej Grabowski for Poland and Martin Potůček for the Czech Republic note that, parallel with accession negotiations, the World Bank and the IMF had a considerable impact on pension reform in particular – hardly a sign of Europeanisation (see also Ferge, 2001).

Enlargements may also influence social protection in the old Member States. Debates in these Member States on the potential negative effects of enlargement in the form of spurring social tourism and social dumping flourished immediately before the 2004 enlargement (see Kvist, 2004). The country chapters describe how all these Member States officially supported the recent Eastern enlargement of the EU while simultaneously opting for transitional measures regulating the mobility of workers and/or certain restrictions on access to national social protection. In response, Poland adopted similar measures.

These developments are among the factors that have transformed the relationship between the national and EU levels since the mid-1990s. These developments also stimulate the emergence of a new third wave of studies on the relationship between the EU and social policy. Forming a subset of the exponentially growing Europeanisation literature, the interest of third-wave scholars is in the ways in which Europe matters for social policy (see Falkner et al, 2005). We contribute to this literature by this study on the relationship between national and

EU levels in social protection. This relationship – transformed markedly over the past 10 years – is best described as the 'Europeanisation of social protection'.

What does the Europeanisation of social protection actually mean? We find that EU social policy is indeed driven by negative integration, or by courts and markets, as elegantly phrased by second-wave scholars (for example, Leibfried and Pierson, 2000). However, we also find significant developments at the EU level, including developments driven by politics (that is, not by courts or markets) that amount to more than 'fragmented EU social policy'. The point here is that positive integration in social protection is no longer geared towards a transfer of sovereignty from the national to the EU level, but rather to facilitate collaboration among sovereign Member States. Collaboration is primarily achieved by the establishment of an EU-level arena and procedures for exchanging knowledge, monitoring developments, collecting statistics and information, and much more. We also find that EU-level developments like the EMU, internal market extensions and EU enlargement have a significant potential influence on national social policy.

The rest of this chapter proceeds as follows: acknowledging that Europeanisation is a complex process, we first discuss a series of adaptational pressures and mediating aspects that may be important for understanding the different impacts that we expect across countries. This next section also describes how these country-specific pressures and aspects have been used as criteria in selecting 11 countries for case studies, so that they not only mirror the existing diversity between Member States but also allow the testing of different hypotheses on why the European impact differs across countries. Second, we set out a simple model that depicts the Europeanisation of social protection as a downloading process and examine whether the model helps us understand recent welfare reforms and government responses. Since the simple model ignores uploading from the national level to the supranational level, as well as level-specific processes at both the EU and national levels, the dynamics of Europeanisation are not captured. Therefore, and thirdly, we propose a more complex model of Europeanisation, one that better describes the increased interweaving of the national and the EU levels, even in perhaps the least likely areas where the EU has little competence, such as social protection. Finally, we conclude with some perspectives for the evolving relationship between the EU and the national level in social protection.

What determines the scope of Europeanisation at the national level?

Scholars generally expect the EU to play a different role across countries. The Europeanisation of social protection is thus likely to differ across countries. The general starting point is that before something can become 'Europeanised' there needs to be a difference between the national situation and what the EU level requires, demands or seeks for that particular situation. The larger the difference or misfit, the greater the adaptational pressure and thus scope for Europeanisation. However, many scholars also see Europeanisation as being filtered, mediated or transformed by a number of other national aspects. A major part of their research exercise consists of unravelling which factors – or, in social science jargon, 'intervening variables' – are important in this regard. The lion's share of Europeanisation studies focus on differences in national political systems.

Our approach is different. We have instead identified five sets of intervening variables of broad political, economic and historical significance. We used these intervening variables to strategically choose 11 Member States for testing different hypotheses about the Europeanisation of social protection. First, the *size* of the Member States may have a bearing on the economic and political importance of certain Member States. The large Member States with big populations, many votes in the Council, and significant economic and human resources may have a stronger say over EU-level developments than Member States lacking such resources. Therefore, large Member States may be more positive towards developments at the EU level as these developments largely mirror their own policies. At the same time, however, smaller Member States may be more positive towards Europeanisation because the EU acts as insurance for small countries against them being bulldozed by large Member States. To reflect on the potential importance of size, our study included the 'Big Four' (Germany, France, Italy and the UK), two medium-sized Member States (Poland and Spain), and five smaller Member States (the Czech Republic, Denmark, Finland, Greece and the Netherlands).

Second, we considered different *welfare regimes*. Since Esping-Andersen (1990) introduced 'the three worlds of welfare capitalism', we have become accustomed to grouping countries by welfare state types or welfare regimes. When it comes to the number of welfare regimes within the EU27, the jury is still out – and will probably be for some time. However, one can argue that the post-Socialist Member States share some institutional characteristics that are *not* typical of other regimes.

Table 13.1: Selection of case studies according to intervening variables

Intervening variable	Category	DE	FR	UK	IT	PL	ES	CZ	FI	DK	NL	EL	Sum
Size	Small							X	X	X	X	X	5
	Medium					X	X						2
	Large	X	X	X	X								4
Welfare regime	Anglo-Saxon			X									1
	Central and Eastern					X		X					2
	Continental	X	X								X		3
	Southern				X		X					X	3
	Scandinavian								X	X			2
EU entry	1957-69	X	X		X						X		4
	1970-79			X						X			2
	1980-89						X					X	2
	1990-99								X				1
	2000-					X		X					2
Political legacy	Non-authoritative		X	X					X	X	X		5
	Authoritative	X			X	X	X	X				X	6
Global competitiveness ranking (0-50)	0-10	X		X					X	X	X		5
	11-30		X			X		X					3
	31-50				X		X					X	3

Notes: DE = Germany; FR = France; UK = United Kingdom; IT = Italy; PL = Poland; ES = Spain; CZ = the Czech Republic; FI = Finland; DK = Denmark; NL = the Netherlands; EL = Greece

While they may or may not form a single group, they nevertheless belong outside the three regimes. Furthermore, within the EU15 and Cyprus and Malta, one may argue that Southern Member States from Portugal to Greece share some common geographical, institutional and cultural characteristics, none of which are typical for any other regime. Consequently, our study comprises nine case studies from four well-established welfare regimes (Anglo-Saxon/Liberal, Continental European/Corporative Conservative, Scandinavian/Social Democratic and Southern European/Catholic) and two case studies from the group of new Member States (Central and Eastern European/post-Socialist). The fit or misfit between a country's welfare regime and the result of the EU pressure – direct or indirect, economic or normative – may have a decisive impact on explaining policy responses. Thus Member States with extensive social protection systems may have a different approach to the EU, and perhaps even consider the EU a threat, while those Member States with more fragmented systems might consider their membership as an opportunity to improve those systems.

Third, the study includes Member States with different *membership histories and legacies*. These differences allow us to investigate different attitudes and policy responses in Member States that have joined at different stages. Basically, those Member States with a long membership history (including France, Germany, Italy and the Netherlands, which have been members since 1957) should have had good opportunities to influence European policies. In contrast, Member States with shorter periods of EU membership (especially Finland from 1995, and the Czech Republic and Poland from 2004) may feel more uneasy about adjusting to the rules of a game in which they feel no ownership.

Fourth, the *political legacy* of countries prior to EU membership differs. Six of the 11 countries had authoritative political systems 15 years or less before entering the EU. This goes for two of the founding members, Germany and Italy, and for countries that were part of the Southern enlargement (Greece and Spain) or the Eastern enlargement (the Czech Republic and Poland). Countries with an authoritarian past may view the EU and Europeanisation as welcome alternatives and a desired 'return to Europe'. Countries with an authoritarian past prior to EU membership may thus be more favourable towards the EU, be more receptive to a Europeanisation of social protection and take on a more active role in the process than countries without such a history.

Finally, government responses to Europeanisation and its domestic impact may differ according to a country's economic situation. Most simply, there may be a link between the impact of and attitudes towards the EU on the one hand, and the economic relationship of the country to the EU on the other. Countries that are net recipients of EU funds may be more positive towards the EU and Europeanisation than countries that are net contributors. Before Ireland became the Celtic tiger economy of the EU, large EU subsidies to Ireland were commonly used as explanations for the Irish being more EU-positive than their British neighbours. But this 'bribery argument' may be too simple. For example, Ana Guillén (Chapter Seven) notes that positive Spanish attitudes towards the EU are unlikely to wane despite significant cuts of EU subsidies to the country in 2007. In any case, our interest here is on the possible link between country competitiveness and Europeanisation. The Lisbon Strategy is essentially the master plan of the EU. Many EU efforts aim to make the EU the world's most competitive economy, with higher growth and more and better jobs. Accordingly, we may expect that the worse the competitiveness of a country, the greater the adaptational pressure and potential for Europeanisation. Given the World Economic Forum Global Competitiveness Index, we thus distinguish between three groups of countries: five countries are in the global top 10 of best-performing countries; three medium-performing countries are ranked between 11 and 30; and the remaining three are ranked between 31 and 50.

Our selection of countries not only allows testing of the Europeanisation thesis but also reflects Member State diversity. This country selection enables informed assessments of what policy action is likely, preferred and commendable (see Chapter Fourteen, this volume).

Europeanisation effects on the national level

Europeanisation can be narrowed down to its domestic impacts. According to this view, developments in EU-level institutions and policies may change Member State social protection policies, polities and politics (Börzel and Risse, 2000). Some scholars have already investigated the Europeanisation of social protection in detailed studies on how decisions in various ECJ cases have led to changes in national social legislation or how the EU has changed the national politics of social protection (for good examples, see, respectively, Martinsen, 2004; Ferrera and Sacchi, 2005). Typically, such studies cover one to four countries, as any one or two researchers are basically unable to have more in-depth case knowledge.

Moreover, there is a trade-off between the number of countries and policy areas covered and the degree of detail. Here we adopt a broad perspective on the possible impact of the EU on social protection by investigating the situation of 11 countries. The broad perspective is illustrated in Figure 13.1, which depicts a simple model of the Europeanisation of social protection. Figure 13.1 shows how we investigate the impact of four types of EU-level developments – new policy processes, internal markets, EMU and EU enlargements – on national social protection, that is, welfare reform and governments' responses to the various EU-level developments, assuming that country size, welfare regime, membership record, political legacy and competitiveness act as intervening variables.

We examine the impact on welfare reform by looking at whether national welfare reform was inspired by the European social model (ESM) and if the reform agenda was influenced by the EU. Findings are based on the first half of the preceding 11 country chapters. The chapter authors were asked to focus on the perception(s) of the ESM in their country rather than on some common definition shared by all authors or an official definition given by, for example, the European Council. Authors similarly had relatively free hands in setting out recent national welfare reforms and assessing the roles of the ESM and the EU. The underlying rationale was to best grasp the dynamics of national welfare reform with regard to the role of the EU: has the ESM worked as a blueprint for welfare reform? Have EU developments facilitated or pressured Member States to specific reforms of social protection systems?

The European social model and national welfare reform

Member States do not share a common understanding of the ESM, which means different things to different countries. This observation

Figure 13.1: A simple model of the Europeanisation of social protection

EU-level developments	**Intervening variables**	**Member State level reactions and change**
Policy processes	Country size	Welfare reforms:
Internal market	Welfare regime	- European social
EMU	EU membership	model as a blueprint
Enlargement	history	- Reform agenda
	Political legacy	Government
	Competitiveness	responses to EU
		developments

is perhaps the most striking. Not only is there general agreement that Europe has different social models, the dominating perception is that these models more or less reflect the welfare regimes described earlier (see also Esping-Andersen, 1999; Alber, 2006).

At a more abstract level, however, most countries acknowledge that there may be a common ESM in the sense of certain common values and a commitment to social objectives, thus making Europe stand apart from other regions of the world (for more on this, see Chapter Fourteen, this volume). One such shared understanding is that the ESM is a normative device for collaboration in the EU, as when the 2000 Nice European Council concluded that 'the European social model can be characterised in particular by systems that offer a high level of social protection, by the importance of social dialogue and by services of general interest covering activities vital for social cohesion, is today based, beyond the diversity of the Member States' social systems, on a common core of values'. This definition is generally accepted by national governments.

In practice, however, many national politicians and social policy debates stick with stereotypes or even enemy images of the ESM – particularly in three of the studies covering the 'Big Four'. In Chapter Three, Julian Le Grand, Elias Mossialos and Morgan Long note that many 'opinion formers in the UK have a perception that only one kind of ESM exists – one close to their understanding of the Continental model', that 'many decision makers in the rest of Europe have a perception of the UK model that is almost the mirror perception of the UK perception of the Continental model' and that in the UK 'key policy makers are not impressed by what they interpret to be the ESM'. In Germany (Chapter Two), Milena Büchs and Karl Hinrichs note the perception that the ESM is different from the German social model (Sozialstaat), although the latter has moved closer to the ESM in recent years. The French believe, according to Bruno Palier and Luana Petrescu (Chapter Four), that the ESM should be like the French social model, perceived as high-quality jobs offering a high minimum wage, high employment protection and high social protection. When this is not the case, the ESM or a given EU policy initiative is, by French definition, not French and thereby not social, and therefore, following French logic, might be considered a possible threat to the French social model.

Post-authoritarian countries have a more favourable view of the ESM, one largely matching the Nice definition. For some of these countries the ESM works as a beacon, a signpost of an ideal, whereas others see it as a potential threat. In particular, Greece, as Theodoros

Sakellaropoulos notes (Chapter Twelve), uses the ESM as a 'constant point of reference' in national debates over social protection. In sharp contrast Poland is sceptical of attempts at harmonising Member State social protection following the ESM, as Poles fear 'pressure from certain older Member States to increase social spending and labour costs' (Chapter Six). In other words, two countries that presently share a dismal record on competitiveness have different ideas of how the ESM may work to improve their situation: Greece sees the ESM as carrying the promise of catch-up convergence, while Poland fears losing economic competitiveness.

In any case, given different national understandings of what constitutes the ESM and varying opinions on whether the ESM works or should work as a template for national reforms, the ESM has not been a common blueprint for recent European welfare reforms.

Have EU developments influenced national welfare reforms?

Although the ESM may not function as a template for reform, there may be other direct and indirect influences on national social protection. In all countries, anti-discrimination legislation and the coordination of social security for migrant workers have had their impact in adjustments of national social legislation. But here we are interested in the non-legal impacts and the big picture of welfare reform. The Lisbon Strategy, the extension of the internal market, the EMU and EU enlargements may all have had a considerable impact on national welfare reform.

Five of the 11 countries believe that the EU has had an impact on recent social protection reforms through policy processes: the Czech Republic, Greece, Italy, Poland and Spain. This grouping of countries indicates that neither country size nor length of EU membership determines EU influence on national social policy. Instead, the country groupings indicate that national problem perceptions tied to welfare regime and degree of competitiveness are what count for the different impact of Europeanisation across countries.

The EU has contributed to a reorientation of national social protection towards more modern, universal and active policies in the Czech Republic, Greece, Italy, Poland and Spain. The EU has also stimulated institution building and sometimes even the introduction of certain social protection schemes, especially of universal social assistance. Paradoxically, Greece, while perhaps the most pro-EU country, still has not introduced a universal social assistance scheme (see Chapter Twelve). In addition, the EU, especially by facilitating a forum for discussion, has inspired certain policy developments in the other countries, for example, a tax credit in France.

The indirect impact of the EMU on national social protection is clear in some countries. In Italy the need to restructure public financing and cost-containment led to two health reforms and four pension reforms (see Chapter Five). In Spain, the EMU has helped national governments legitimise the rationalisation of social protection (Chapter Seven). But other countries that faced difficulties in meeting the criteria of the SGP, for example, France and Germany, do not report such effects.

Enlargement has so far had little impact on national welfare reform. The old Member States have introduced transitional measures for the free mobility of workers from the new Member States or restrictions on their access to social protection. Fears of the adverse affects of a larger and more heterogeneous EU resulting in regulatory dumping or a race-to-the-bottom in social protection are as yet unfounded. EU enlargements, however, are likely to stay on the national social protection agenda for some time, as transitional measures run out and as more enlargements are discussed.

The influence of the EU on national social protection increased after 2000. The Lisbon Strategy and the wider application of the OMC in the field of social protection and (for the Czech Republic and Poland) the start on accession talks all contributed to more national focus on social protection.

In sum, EU developments have influenced national welfare reform, but in varied ways and to different extents. The EU influence on social protection agenda setting, institution building and policy formation is especially pronounced in countries with Southern or Central and Eastern European welfare regimes and with dismal records of competitiveness. In these countries EU funds have probably helped reform processes. If social protection reforms have led to changes of the national welfare regimes and competitiveness, the result may be some socio–economic catch-up convergence. At the same time, the developments may also reflect parallel trends in policy, but with persistent diversity in social protection systems. It is too early to judge the result of this aspect of the Europeanisation process, the increased influence of the EU on national social protection. For all countries, however, the overall influence of the EU on national social protection appears mediated at the national level and based on voluntary adjustments.

The Europeanisation of social protection: the interweaving of national and EU levels

Member States do not merely receive stimuli from above, that is, from the EU level, as is implicit in the previous section. Member States are actors that also interact at both the national and the EU levels. The Europeanisation of social protection is a multidimensional process where Member States interact with other Member States at the national level, where they upload ideas to the EU level, where actors at the EU level are active, and where initiatives at the EU level download to or impact on the national level. Figure 13.2 shows a model incorporating these elements. In the previous sections, we focused on the impact of the developments at the EU level for national social protection. In this and the following section we focus on Member State perceptions of and opinions about EU-level developments.

First we examined the government responses to EU developments. Are governments embracing or being positive towards the new policy processes as exemplified by the Lisbon Strategy (later the revised Lisbon Strategy) and the OMC, attempts to extend the internal market to social services, the EMU and EU enlargements? Or are national governments either critical of or indifferent to these developments?

Figure 13.2: A complex model of the Europeanisation of social protection

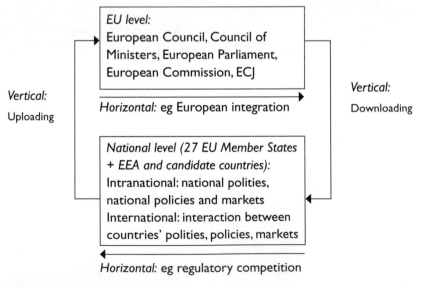

Note: EEA = European Economic Area

No Member State is against the Lisbon Strategy. The original strategy adopted at the 2000 Council Spring Meeting in Lisbon had varying impacts on national social protection debates. Two extremes are observable. In France the adoption of the Strategy was not observed due to internal politics (Chapter Four). In contrast, the Danish Prime Minister heralded the Lisbon Strategy as the coming of a new and more social Europe up to the euro referendum in 2001, albeit with little success (Chapter Eleven). After a few years the Strategy became more complex and heavy, leading to a more streamlined version adopted in 2005. This version made growth and jobs the prime objectives, with social protection no longer officially part of the Strategy. Again, all Member States officially support the revised Strategy. Representative of many countries, the UK and Poland argue that pursuing economic objectives is the best way of ensuring social objectives (Chapters Three and Six).

Most Member States also support the use of the OMC in social protection. In the 1990s the OMC had been applied in economic and employment policy; however, with the Lisbon Strategy in 2000, the OMC also became applicable to social protection. Traditionally considered foot dragging in EU social policy matters, Denmark and the UK have become ardent supporters of the OMC. They believe that the OMC incorporates subsidiarity, autonomy, flexibility and transparency (see, respectively, Chapters Eleven and Three). But Denmark and the UK are not proponents of a stronger or more binding OMC. Meanwhile, Spain and the Netherlands want more country rankings and more naming and shaming, while Italy wants stronger procedures in pensions (see, respectively, Chapters Seven, Ten and Five). Germany directly opposes more naming and shaming, and fears a creeping expansion of EU competence (Chapter Two).

However, the OMC also has its critics, especially Greece and Finland. Both were against the adoption of the OMC, which they think is too weak an instrument. For some years, these two countries preferred the old Community method of social protection (see, respectively, Chapters Twelve and Nine). Over the years, however, they have become lukewarm proponents of the OMC. The two new Member States also politely support the OMC, although Poland is critical of the measure of relative poverty and the social exclusion strategy that it considers of little relevance, and the Czech Republic believes the OMC has little impact on national policies (Chapters Six and Eight). As we can see, the seemingly unanimous support for the OMC masks important national differences in the motivation behind the support, the strength of the support and the perceptions on the use and effectiveness of the

OMC. Similarly, ideas for how to reform the OMC differ, although all countries officially support the streamlined version after the integration of the social inclusion and social protection strategies.

The extension of the internal market to the field of services has become perhaps the most disputed area of social protection in the EU. This is most vividly illustrated through government responses to the recent Services Directive. Two camps are distinct: they differ on their views on the scope of the Services Directive, that is, whether or not to exclude health and social services in particular, and the legislation to be applied for the cross-border service provider, that is, the country-of-origin principle or some amended version, making more of the host country legislation or standards applicable. One camp argues that as many services as possible should be covered and that the country-of-origin principle should apply. Broadly speaking this was also the content of the first proposal of the the Services Directive by the Commission in 2004. The other camp wanted social and health services to be exempt from the Services Directive. These countries also believed that the country-of-origin principle should not be applied, as they feared the adverse impact on service provision standards and guarantees as well as social dumping in the service sector.

As evident from the 11 country chapters, the first camp included the Czech Republic, Italy, the Netherlands and Poland, while the second camp included Denmark, Finland, France, Germany, Greece and, to some extent, the UK. However, the European Parliament was instrumental in brokering a widely supported compromise, receiving so many parliamentary votes that changing the amended Directive became immensely difficult for national governments. On 12 December 2006, the Council passed the Parliament's version of the Services Directive, meaning that social and health services were explicitly exempted and the country-of-origin principle was replaced with a demand that any Member State requirements on service providers must be non-discriminatory, proportional and necessary for securing public order, health or the environment. Indeed, when the market-making process of the EU seriously entered the core fields of social protection, it became high politics.

National government views on the EMU vary, especially on the usefulness of the SGP criteria. Most Member States have full participation as their goal. To enter the third phase of the EMU and adopt the euro, Member States must meet the criteria of the SGP. Originally, the SGP was proposed by German Minister of Finance, Theo Waigel, in the mid-1990s. In 2003 and 2004, however, Germany faced economic problems that meant they could not meet the criteria. The same was true for France. Normally, the result would be an 'excessive deficit' procedure, whereby the country in question could be fined. However, the Council decided in 2004 not to initiate the procedure against France and Germany, a decision that the ECJ deemed unlawful in 2004. Obviously, the EMU is a sensitive issue. Some countries within the Eurozone, for example, Finland and the Netherlands, argued that France and Germany should be ready to take their own medicine. For the old EU15 Member States currently outside the Eurozone – Denmark, Sweden and the UK – this lack of enforcement strengthened their opposition to entry. Even though all three countries meet the SGP criteria, they are unlikely to adopt the euro any day soon.

In any case, the Council decided in March 2005 to relax the rules to respond to the criticism. Although the thresholds of 3% annual budget deficit to GDP and 60% gross public debt to GDP were maintained, Member States were allowed greater flexibility in exceeding the annual deficit threshold and a longer time for reversing their excessive deficits. These changes received broad support, even among critics because, as described by Juho Saari and Olli Kangas in the Finnish study (Chapter Nine), Member States hope that the SGP is now more enforceable.

Eleven EU15 Member States adopted the euro in 1999. Greece was admitted in 2001. Physical coins and banknotes were introduced in 2002. In 2007, Slovenia became the first of the new Member States to enter the Eurozone, which now encompasses 13 countries. Of the EU15 Member States, Denmark, Sweden and the UK have opted to stay outside the Eurozone. Denmark, the Baltic countries, Cyprus, Malta and Slovakia are inside the European Exchange Rate Mechanism (ERM II), meaning that their currency can float within +/– 15% of a central euro rate. The remaining EU27 Member States are outside both the Eurozone and the ERM II, including the Czech Republic and Poland. Both these countries attempt to become members of the Eurozone (Chapters Eight and Six, respectively).

Many current Eurozone countries still experience difficulties meeting the SGP criteria. Six of the 12 old EU15 Member States within the Eurozone did not meet one or two of the criteria for the third year running, as of 2007. The EMU and the SGP criteria are thus likely to remain important means of legitimising cost-containment measures in many national social protection systems in the coming years.

At the same time there is a risk of an EU backlash from the EMU if it is perceived nationally as the catalyst for unpopular social protection reform (see Chapter Two). In France and Italy, the EMU is already associated broadly with a deterioration of purchasing power and thus relative wealth (Chapters Four and Five). To avoid unpopular social protection reforms and EU backlashes, Member States will likely further reform or even cancel the SGP criteria.

Enlargement has figured high on the EU agenda in the 2000s. The Eastern enlargements in 2004 and 2007 have nearly doubled the number of Member States. As evident from the country chapters, enlargement was supported by all national governments, some more strongly than others. However, it is similarly evident that enlargement has caused national debates in the old EU15 Member States over the potential adverse impact on national social protection and labour markets in the form of social tourism and social dumping that may stem from allowing less prosperous countries with smaller benefits and lower earnings to enter the EU. In response to public pressure or to pre-empt xenophobic fears, all old EU15 Member States (except Sweden) restricted access for workers from the Central and Eastern European new Member States either to national labour markets or to national social protection. While these transitional measures may last only for seven years, many Member States used the first occasion in 2006 to ease or cancel them. Almost at the same time, many decided to introduce transitional measures for Bulgaria and Romania (entering in 2007).

For historical and geopolitical reasons some Member States are stronger supporters of EU enlargement than others. Finland, for example, has not been a strong supporter of enlargement whereas Denmark has actively advocated a large Eastern enlargement so as to include the small Baltic countries (Chapters Nine and Eleven). Greece supported the last enlargement, not least to include Cyprus, just as Greece welcomes the inclusion of Balkan countries into the EU so as to obtain stability and growth for its region (Chapter Twelve).

Maybe a certain enlargement fatigue is occurring. As the Dutch and French chapters make clear, EU enlargement constituted a significant part of the debates up to their referenda on the European Constitution. In particular, discussions dealt with the consequences that a more heterogeneous EU is likely to have on social protection, or, more generally, on national welfare states. While these fears have proven unfounded thus far, national governments may react to popular concerns.

Conclusions

The Europeanisation of social protection has taken place over the past 10 years, with a remarkable intensity in the ways in which the national and EU levels have become interwoven in social protection. Without a doubt the competence over social protection rests firmly and primarily at the national level. No strong direct influence from the EU to the national level dictates the form, scope or principles of social protection. However, according to EU legislation, national social protection must not discriminate, and other EU nationals have increasing access to national systems, just as nationals can increasingly receive services in other EU countries at the expense of the national exchequer. But perhaps the most profound impact lies in the way Europe plays a much greater role in how policy makers think about social protection than it did only 10 years ago.

The new policy processes, represented by the Lisbon Strategy and the OMC, show how the Member States turn to the EU for a platform for discussing social protection solutions for common problems such as globalisation, ageing populations and technological change. We view this change as a new form of positive integration, as it does not entail a transfer of sovereignty from the national to the EU level (as was the case in the old Community method and as neofunctionalism described the old form of positive integration). Instead, this new form of positive integration enables a non-binding form of collaboration between Member States, a form that, as the contributors to this volume show, enjoys wide support among national governments.

Over the past ten years, more Member States adopted universal social assistance schemes and introduced universal minimum income guarantees for the elderly. Modernisation of social protection aimed to take better account of changing family and job patterns. Finally, and perhaps most importantly, Member States' social protection systems – from social assistance over unemployment insurance and disability pensions to child care – have became much more oriented towards labour market participation.

Negative integration or market-making measures persist in having their say in social protection. They have been expanded by a series of spectacular ECJ rulings, starting with the *Kohll* and *Decker* cases in 1998. However, market-making in social protection has moved from a low- to a high-politics area, as the debates on the Services Directive testify. Not only national governments but also the European Parliament have taken a much greater interest in social protection than was the case a decade earlier.

In recent years, the EMU and especially the SGP criteria have been seen as having potential negative effects on social protection. When governments have to cut costs they are likely to cut back where expenses are large, that is, in social protection. Indeed, national governments, as many country chapters show, use the EMU to legitimise cost-containment measures in a blame-avoidance strategy. But perhaps this strategy, too, has its limits, and SGP criteria could be further loosened to avoid unpopular retrenchment of social protection and an EU backlash.

The possible adverse effects of EU enlargement on national social protection have also been heavily discussed. Transitional measures regulating the free movement of workers and restricting access to social protection have been put in place and later lifted either in part or completely. Although evidence of social tourism and social dumping is limited and the contribution of workers from the new Member States is considerable, enlargements and social protection are likely to remain on the national and EU agendas for years to come.

The Europeanisation of social protection has so far not led to a convergence of welfare models. The 11 case studies do not indicate common welfare reform patterns pointing towards convergence. There is no sign of the formation of a common ESM in different countries. By the same token, there seems to be an influence on the timing and agenda of reforms. In other words, individual Member States appear occupied with the same range of welfare reforms, namely pensions and care for elderly people, social inclusion and child family policies. However, significant differences remain in the reasons for reform and in the type of reforms made.

As expected, different patterns of Europeanisation of social protection manifest across countries. Those with the biggest adjustment pressures are also the ones that report an EU impact on national social protection. This goes for the countries with the lowest rankings on competitiveness and for countries with welfare regimes of either the Southern European or Central and Eastern European types. In these countries we have seen a certain downloading of ideas. By contrast, one group of countries is happy with the OMC in social protection, perceiving themselves as being perhaps particularly active in the process of uploading ideas – particularly Denmark, the Netherlands and the UK.

However, this last observation is not meant to dichotomise countries as either recipients of EU-level ideas or donors to the EU level of ideas. Indeed, the overall most striking feature of the Europeanisation of social policy is that EU-level developments increasingly interact with social protection in all countries.

FOURTEEN

Seeking a new balance

Juho Saari and Kari Välimäki

European social policy has evolved significantly since the late 1980s, when the idea of a social dimension to the European Union emerged onto European policy agendas. During the early 1990s, the common points of departure for these discussions were the concepts of subsidiarity and proportionality, both of which underlined the limited competence of the European level to proceed in this field. Today, after the introduction of the Lisbon Strategy and the open method of coordination (OMC), systematic attention has been focused on the social aspects of European integration at the European level. Clearly, major shifts in mental models, ideas on European social policies, strategic objectives, and policy processes have occurred over these years.

Signs of this new political reality abound: first, virtually all recent European Union (EU) presidencies have organised at least one high-level event dealing with the different dimensions of a social Europe, indicating the importance of the new political reality. Second, the regular use of the concept of the European social model (ESM) in different contexts underlines a common ground of policy making towards uniting different welfare regimes. Third, the Social Protection Committee (SPC), based on Article 144 of the Nice Treaty, has been established, to share information among Member States on issues of contemporary significance and on defining strategic objectives. Here the cooperation between the Commission and Member States clearly has shown some potential. Finally, the role of the European Parliament is becoming more significant and visible due to the extension of co-decision making and a more articulated position building. Thus the social dimension of the EU can no longer be ignored.

This chapter aims to further clarify some key issues debated in previous chapters, and to draw together some policy conclusions. (Chapter Thirteen has already summarised the comparative results.) We enter the debate on the ESM concept to assess its potential usefulness in European social policy debates, and identify at least 10 of its dimensions. The chapter ends with policy conclusions on the question of whether we need a new balance in social policy between the Member States and the EU.

The European social model

As previous chapters have shown, European integration has never been exclusively motivated by the interests of the Member States or other European and national actors. Values and ideas on Europe have always played important roles, especially during those rare moments of uncertainty that have shaped the structure and the future of the EU (Blyth, 2002). One concept uniting both interests and ideas is the ESM. As several earlier chapters implied, considerable cross-national variation exists in national understandings of the ESM, along with, in this respect, different epistemological communities within scientific communities. Although social policy experts classify Member State welfare regimes into four or five well-known regimes, discussions at the Member State level of both the ESM and the national models often describe these models simplistically, thus tending to overestimate differences. Emphasising the differences often seems connected to more general critiques of the EU. On the one hand, in some circumstances the strong emphasis on Member State differences may have reflected certain kinds of political perspectives or visionary insights. For instance, the liberal and market-oriented approach to the ESM aims at stressing the Member State differences because differences look better from the point of view of internal markets and competition (Verdun, 1996). On the other hand, some commentators promoting protectionist views (or the superiority of certain institutional structures) may underline the differences in welfare regimes because that approach fits quite well with the 'statist' or 'protectionist' approach. Thus to clarify this debate from different angles, we need first to clarify the history and content of the ESM. (For more details see the growing literature on the ESM, for instance: Scharpf, 2002; Offe, 2003; Adnett and Hardy, 2005; Schmögnerová, 2005; Jepsen and Serrano Pascual, 2006; O'Brien, 2006.)

The history of the European social model

The idea of the ESM was included in several early documents in the 1950s, for example, Articles 2 and 3 of the Treaty establishing the European Coal and Steel Community, signed in Paris in 1951. After that, however, the concept did not appear in mainstream publications until the early 1990s. For some years, the ESM competed with other concepts, such as 'social Europe' or the social dimension of the EU/European integration in various commentaries, conclusions and communications (for example, European Commission, 1993b). It was also regularly but not exclusively used in different guidelines and initiatives (European Commission, 1994).

The triumph of the ESM over other competing concepts resulted mainly from the conclusions of the European Council since the mid-1990s. It returned to regular usage at the Turin European Council (March 1996), where its French origins were recognised: 'President Chirac illustrated the proposals contained in the French memorandum on a European social model'. Some months later, the Dublin Summit declared: 'In its deliberations it has also taken account of the proposals in President Chirac's Memorandum on a European social model with a view to giving greater emphasis to the human dimension of the Union'. At that time, the concept had a reasonably broad coverage, from railways to social policy. At the Vienna Summit (December 1998) the ESM was connected more closely with employment and modernisation: 'Employment is the top priority of the European Union. It is the best way of providing real opportunity for people and combating poverty and exclusion effectively, thereby serving as the basis for the European social model'.

At the turn of the millennium, the substance of the ESM was highlighted in numerous paragraphs and several studies. For instance the Nice Summit in December 2000 concluded that:

> The European social model, characterised in particular by systems that offer a high level of social protection, by the importance of the social dialogue and by services of general interest covering activities vital for social cohesion, is today based, beyond the diversity of the Member States' social systems, on a common core of values.

The Social Policy Agenda, annexed to the conclusions of the Nice Summit, further identified the following features:

> At the heart of its communication the Commission placed the need to ensure a *positive and dynamic interaction of economic, employment and social policies and to mobilise all players to attain that strategic objective.*

In this perspective, the dual objective of social policy needs to be emphasised:

> the Agenda must strengthen *the role of social policy as a productive factor*; it must enable it to be at the same time more effective in the pursuit of its specific aims concerning the protection of individuals, the reduction of inequalities, and social cohesion. The European Parliament and the social partners have laid particular stress on this dual objective. *Economic growth and social cohesion are mutually reinforcing.* A society with more social cohesion and less exclusion betokens a more successful economy. (emphasis added)

At the Barcelona Summit (March 2002) the Heads of the Member States reaffirmed their commitment to European values and institutions in the presidency conclusions:

> *The European social model is based on good economic performance, a high level of social protection and education and social dialogue.* An active welfare state should encourage people to work, as employment is the best guarantee against social exclusion. The European Council considers the Social Agenda agreed at Nice to be an important vehicle for reinforcing the European social model. The Spring European Council must be the occasion for an in-depth review of progress in bringing about its objectives. This review should lend further impetus and lead to appropriate initiatives where necessary. The Lisbon goals can only be brought about by balanced efforts on both the economic and social fronts. (emphasis added)

This is probably so far the most extensive and in many ways theoretically and politically most comprehensive statement on the ESM in the presidency conclusions.

Finally, at an informal summit in Hampton Court (October 2005), during the UK presidency, the Heads of the Member States reaffirmed their commitment to European values. Such values (and certain other European characteristics) were also analysed in the Commission's communication (2005i) published before the summit.

However, a discussion of fundamental values, while valuable in many ways, may shift the focus away from institutional similarities or differences and comparative advantages or disadvantages of different welfare regimes (or, more broadly, related European productions systems) (Amable, 2003). Furthermore, such a discussion is often quite soft and open to many conflicting interpretations, given the different use of key concepts such as rights and freedoms.

From a comparative point of view, some scholars have legitimately pointed out that no such thing as the ESM (in the singular) exists. Comparative research efforts have identified a set of models or regimes that reflect group-specific cultural, geographical, institutional and political legacies. In other words, these regimes seem quite path-dependent, locked in with their histories and, on average, a limited ability to make path-breaking reforms and social innovations.[1] This observation, however, does not necessarily imply that the Member States are 'doomed' to follow pre-existing trajectories, as there is some evidence that certain 'rare moments' may allow Member States to change their policies in radical ways.[2] Nonetheless, evidence also indicates that such 'rare moments' are rare indeed, making quite unlikely the possibility of all Member States experiencing such a moment simultaneously. Yet those who focus solely on the ESM do not pay sufficient attention to such regimes and differences, resulting in too homogeneous (and ideological) a picture of the EU. The need for some kind of balance between these two sets of argumentations – and to finish this debate once and for all – is clear (Hemerijck, 2005).

Common features of the European social model

As we have seen, policy conclusions and recent research efforts on the ESM leave something to be desired. Perhaps the most feasible way of analysing this multidimensional concept, to increase its theoretical and socio-political usefulness, is to identify a set of 'European' characteristics or dimensions, that is, ones that are typical for all Member States. We emphasise that this proposal is not exclusive and that it does not indicate that different welfare regimes do not exist or that their role is secondary in a European framework.

Following are 10 such dimensions or fields for systematic analysis and comprehensive policy making:

Values: normatively, and to some extent in practice, Europeans share certain values. These include the idea of the social market economy, solidarity, social cohesion, equal opportunities, universal access to health care and education, and the recognised roles of social partners, corporations and civil society. A comprehensive and authoritative list of such values is listed in the *Charter of Fundamental Rights of the Union.*

Common identity: Europeans share a certain amount of common identity vis-à-vis the US, Japan, China or India. Although this commonality does not indicate that Europeans would prefer a European identity to a national one, European identity clearly exists in a global context. Furthermore, as recent debates over the membership of certain candidate countries imply, European identity seems to have some geopolitical and geographical connotations. Finally, the countries that accept the Copenhagen criteria (1993) of membership also appear to accept these criteria as part of European identity.

Partnership: all Member States have, at least comparatively speaking in a global context, a tradition of social partnerships and social dialogue among labour, capital and the state. Furthermore, the Treaty and European policy processes also recognise the role of European social partners in both designing and implementing certain parts of European law and policy objectives. In this dimension of the ESM, core labour standards play an important role in global policy making. European non-governmental organisations (NGOs) and networks of other NGOs have established their consultative roles in several relevant policy fields, including age, gender, children, housing, unemployment and, more broadly, social exclusion.

Gender equality: since the Treaty of Rome (1957) the European Community/Union has underlined the importance of equality between women and men. In the early years, equality policies were mainly spillovers from competition policies (Member States tried to avoid market distortions based on gendered pay rates) and from European Court of Justice (ECJ) rulings on the concept of 'pay' in Article 119 (now Article 141) to also cover social benefits. More recently, gender equality has emerged as a policy area in its own right, covering not only work life but all other areas. This policy objective is to be mainstreamed into all policy areas. These ideas and policies have been downloaded, thereby also promoting gender equality in those Member States whose policies have been less developed until recently.

Common challenges: the Member States also agree that they face common challenges, such as globalisation and new global power structures, restructuring and post-industrialisation, ageing and new family structures, unemployment and atypical employment, the lack of social cohesion and inclusion, and the long-term instability and deficits of public economies. They also agree that integration may result in some negative or positive externalities with a potentially major impact on the socio-economic dynamics of the EU.

Common policy responses: all or most Member States seem to respond to various challenges in roughly similar ways. When adjusting their social protection systems, the Member States pay systematic attention to poverty among vulnerable groups, the reconciliation of work and family life, better health, activation and longer working lives, incentive structures, and sustainable health care. Furthermore, the Member States seem to invest quite heavily in policy coordination between labour and social policies, and, to a lesser extent, between these fields and health policies.

Common institutions: the Member States also have an increasingly common institutional environment in which their organisations and households operate. EU membership in itself is one such institutional factor. Others include common organisations, European law and the European Economic and Monetary Union (EMU) (which, while part of European law, also has certain distinct characteristics due to the nature of monetary policy and the independence of the European Central Bank).

Common policy processes: the Member States cooperate through various European policy processes, including the European Employment Strategy (EES), Broad Economic Policy Guidelines (BEPGs), the Cardiff Process[3] (now de facto a part of the integrated guidelines), and the Cologne Process,[4] aimed at promoting the idea of (pro)active and socio-economically sustainable welfare policies. The Lisbon Strategy and the strategy for sustainable development provide a framework for common European policies.

Commitment to the welfare state/society: in most (and perhaps all) Member States the public sector, of which the welfare state/society forms a significant part, plays a major role in allocating resources through redistributive mechanisms and designing legal frameworks aimed at promoting the well-being of citizens. Furthermore, the role of services of general interest (SGI), economic or non-economic, appears quite important, and Member States have a clear view on their roles and responsibilities.

European dimensions: self-evidently, an underlying European dimension often strengthens Member State institutions and their ability to operate in an increasingly global environment. In this respect, the terms 'EU paradox' or 'win–win situation' indicate that the competencies and policy processes at the European level are actually strengthening Member State policies by allowing them more 'European space', enabling their policies, complementing and reinforcing different horizontal levels of governance, and protecting them from global pressures.

Most often, when people debate the need to modernise the ESM, they refer to institutions, policy processes, welfare states and the European dimension. Clearly, the ESM also has some potential value for investigating identities, gender equality and policy responses. Unfortunately, a detailed investigation of whether some convergence within the EU in relation to these 10 dimensions has taken place (or is now taking place) is beyond the scope of this chapter. Further research is clearly needed. Furthermore, in more political terms – and with regard to policy relevance – it is quite clear that the further strengthening of the EU's social dimension would require a more commonly shared conception and politically more strongly articulated application of the ESM.

The future of the European social model

As to the future of the ESM, much attention has recently gone to restructuring and adjustment in the context of the twin challenges of demographic transition and globalisation. (While a third challenge exists, that is, increasing social inequality and weakening of social cohesion, its integration into the European agendas is still only partial when compared to the first two.) The future of the ESM is a theme that – under the concept of *flexicurity* – seems to be the next policy initiative to be mainstreamed into several policy fields, including social protection and social exclusion (European Commission, 2005j). In this area, the Commission and the Council have rightly emphasised the important roles of social partners and civil society.

The recent establishment of a Social Summit has strengthened the role of social partners (employees' and employers' organisations and confederations) in implementing the Lisbon Strategy. The Social Summit institutionalised earlier informal gatherings (since 2000) and replaced an outdated Standing Committee on Employment. It consists of the Council Presidency and the two subsequent presidencies, the Commission and the social partners, represented at the highest level (European Commission, 2002c). The Summit has been held annually before the March European Council (it may also have earlier informal meetings) devoted to the Lisbon Strategy, thereby underlining their role in implementing strategic objectives (European Commission, 2004d).

When it comes to civil society, the Social Exclusion Programme has funded European networks of NGOs, aiming at promoting dialogue among the various actors and support for relevant networking at the EU level between organisations active in the fight against poverty and social exclusion. Community programmes for employment and solidarity (PROGRESS, 2007-13) will extend this support for the promotion of dialogue to social protection (European Commission, 2005k). More broadly, the Commission has recently invested in the transparency of the consultations, to promote openness and accountability – vital parts of good governance – and successful restructuring and adjustment policies (European Commission, 2002d, 2006k).

More concretely, the recent new Globalisation Fund also implies a steadily increasing role of adjustment and restructuring policies at the EU level. The aim of this Fund is to compensate for some social costs resulting from lowering transaction costs and economic restructuring (European Commission, 2006l). The Fund has been legitimised because 'since the EU is responsible for external trade policy and hence for decisions that lead to market opening for all Member States, there is a logic in also undertaking part of the responsibility for restructuring caused by international competition' (Tsoukalis, 2006, p 85). This strategic move highlights the benefits of more open trade but also underlines more strongly than earlier the need to help those Member States and industries experiencing the negative consequences of globalisation through job losses and other forms of trade-related restructuring.

As the Commission's strategy for 2005-09 focuses on growth, employment and the internal market, it assesses social protection mainly from these perspectives. The Commission has also paid systematic attention to the long-term consequences of *not* reforming the institutions of the social protection systems in a way that is compatible with long-term economic and employment objectives (European Commission, 2005l). However, it also recalls the conclusions of various European Councils and emphasises the potential positive role of policy coordination and institutional complementarities:

> Equally we should make policy choices that ensure that our various objectives are mutually reinforcing. Actions that promote competitiveness, growth and jobs, as well as economic and social cohesion and a healthy environment reinforce each other. These are all essential components of

> the overarching objective of sustainable development, on which we must deliver. (European Commission, 2005m)

More recently, however, the Commission has recognised the need to further balance its objectives:

> European solidarity policies and programmes must promote a higher quality of life, social cohesion and increase opportunities for the Union's citizens, working with the national, regional and other authorities on the ground as well as with the social partners, promoting social dialogue and engaging with civil society. *This means that our policies to sustain solidarity must be matched by a more effective means of ensuring citizens' existing rights of access to employment, education, social services, health care and other forms of social protection across Europe.* (European Commission, 2006m, p 5; emphasis added)

The tension mentioned towards the end of this quotation strongly motivates the debate over the future direction of the ESM.

Consequently, it is quite understandable that one theme of Plan D (where D stands for democracy, dialogue and debate), a crucial part of the 'period of reflection' following the 2005 negative votes in France and the Netherlands on the European Constitution, is the future of Europe's social and economic development. More precisely, the theme is: 'the capacity of Europe to generate growth and create more jobs, maximising the effects of the strategy agreed in Lisbon; the common values on which the economic and social models in Europe are based; the reforms needed in order to face global competition and the conditions for sustainable development' (European Commission, 2005n). Such a dialogue/debate is certainly needed. Furthermore, there is some evidence that Member States at the same level of economic and social development differ from each other in their abilities to sustainably combine economic growth and equality (social cohesion). These differences indicate that the future of the ESM is strongly connected to common European policies aimed at promoting policy transfers and good practice.

On policy responses: towards a common ground

Despite differences in welfare regimes, the Member States' responses to the Commission's initiatives (as reviewed in previous chapters) have been surprisingly similar, with some common ground and possible convergence. This section summarises some findings from a policy-relevant perspective, with a focus on the Lisbon Strategy (original and revised), the OMC, internal markets, the EMU and enlargement.

First, all Member States greatly favoured the original Lisbon Strategy. Despite France clearly advocating the social dimension of the EU and the UK favouring less EU involvement in social policy, both Member States welcomed the Lisbon Strategy. Indeed, the Lisbon Strategy seems to be a uniting factor at the EU level. Although the Lisbon Strategy gave equal weight to economic policy, employment policy and social cohesion, it provided enough flexibility for Member State acceptance. The acceptance of the Lisbon Strategy also indicated that the Member States aim at balanced economic and social development. Moreover, given a broad consensus that the Lisbon Strategy had both strengths and weaknesses, after the 2005 revisions, the National Reform Programmes began focusing on economic and employment policies. Again, the revision received broad support, although many politicians expressed their worries over the lack of social cohesion aspects. The broad support for the Lisbon Strategy in both indicates that social protection and especially social cohesion issues deserve more attention at the EU level. It also reflects the general understanding of social protection as a productive factor.

The OMC as applied to social protection is simultaneously both the minimum and the maximum way of cooperation at the EU level. In the early years of the OMC, Member States criticised it for its bureaucracy. Now the streamlined OMC enjoys broad support. It is accepted for non-binding targets, the dissemination of information, and information about good practice, common indicators and raising the awareness of reform pressures. However, binding rules or a 'naming and shaming' approach generates fundamentally divergent opinions. The OMC also seems to be simultaneously a legitimate way of sharing information among Member States and an example of the democratic deficit of the EU. In the latter context, the OMC is often criticised due to the poor involvement of politicians, but very few quarters – except the European Parliament – would like to give the OMC a more political role.

The Member States also welcome in principle the completion of the internal market and thus, among others, the basic ideas of the draft Services Directive on the internal market. However, the Member States would like restrictions in the coverage of the Directive, with exceptions for health and social services. Thus the new draft Services Directive (April 2006), which excludes health and social services, seems acceptable to all. Although Spain was a little doubtful about the original Services Directive in general, it welcomes initiatives on the SGI. Poland and the Czech Republic were quite strongly in favour of the ideas of the Services Directive because they saw that it would create new business opportunities (due, among other things, to lower labour costs).

The EMU divides Member State positions. Many Member States want more flexibility in the implementation of the EMU criteria, partially motivated by social policy reasons (although other reasons have usually been given for opting out of the euro). Nonetheless, the EMU has been utilised (for example, in Italy) for justifying the necessity for pension and other reforms. On enlargement, Member State positions are usually more positive than those of the public. In Germany enthusiasm towards enlargement cooled due to the financial consequences of German unification. In all Member States with high unemployment, enlargement created scepticism due to the possible immigration of cheap labour from the new Member States. In France the fear of increased numbers of foreign workers was one of the reasons for rejecting the Constitutional Treaty, although in this respect many people confused the Treaty with the draft Services Directive.

To summarise and to generalise, we can describe the political attitudes of the Member States towards the EU policy agenda as follows:

Table 14.1: Member States' political attitudes to the EU policy agenda

Ours					Theirs
France	Spain	Greece	Germany	Denmark	UK
Netherlands		Italy	Finland		
		Poland	Czech		

The policy positions of the Member States are placed to approximate their general attitudes towards EU social policy initiatives. This approximation does *not* indicate how strongly the Member States stress the principles of subsidiarity and proportionality. Rather, it assesses the distance between the EU and national social policy agendas.

Two reasons appear for the familiarity and positive acceptance of the EU social policy agenda. Either EU social policy discourses and ideas follow the national agenda (France and the Netherlands) or the Member States expect positive effects from the EU on their social policy model (Spain and Greece). Those who feel otherwise consider European policies from different angles. Overall, although the Member States' variations towards EU social policy initiatives or other initiatives linked to social policy seem very similar, their rhetoric includes many nuances. Despite the emphasis on subsidiarity and proportionality among the 11 Member States, some leanings towards a stronger EU social dimension appear in their positions. For instance, Greece, Italy and to some extent Spain expect a stronger EU impact on their national systems. France is trying to find ways to defend its own social model through EU initiatives, whereas the UK is quite reluctant to have any new social policy initiatives. While Denmark, the Netherlands and Finland would like to strengthen the EU's social dimension, they do not welcome restrictive interference from the EU level, that is, more social policy at the international level but no binding initiatives. Poland and the Czech Republic are quite keen on following the general EU social policy principles but their support is qualified because of their limited financial resources for rapid advancement. Germany's position is a mixture of the French, UK and Dutch positions.

Seeking a new balance

To summarise, European social policy has been at a turning point for some time. Major changes have already been reviewed in Chapter One (this volume). Here, we start by focusing on the discussion around the revised Lisbon Strategy (2005-). As the Lisbon Strategy was refocused on economic growth and jobs (plus internal markets and innovation policies), many social politicians (and many of those who are representing environmental concerns) became more worried about the proper role of social protection in European integration. Several commentators, including several Member States and many European NGOs in the field of social exclusion, reviewed the issue thoroughly. Many promoted the view that social protection and social cohesion should (re-)earn the same status as economic and employment issues within the Lisbon Strategy, or, more precisely, within the integrated guidelines. In other words, compared to the policies of 2000-05, when economic, employment and social policies were understood as separate but mutually reinforcing, now many commentators have promoted a more (or fully) integrated approach. This requirement has been quite popular, despite the simultaneous strong promotion of the principles of subsidiarity and proportionality (that is, the issue of a limited EU competence) in social protection.

The Lisbon Strategy confirmed that economic growth as such is not an objective in itself. Rather, it is an important tool for increasing the welfare of EU citizens and others residing legally within the borders of the EU. The Lisbon Strategy also answered to the demands for more 'human' or 'social' integration. The Commission, the European Parliament and Member States presume that EU citizens regard their common policies as legitimate. From this viewpoint, the EU could probably more easily achieve stronger legitimacy if its social dimension were clearer and more visionary. Changing the social dimension is, however, quite difficult, given the limited competencies in social protection and the different competencies in EU cooperation in various but socio-politically relevant fields of policy making. Political desire for European-wide cooperation is much stronger in economic policy and employment than in social protection.

The OMC is thus a useful measure in social protection, because it is fundamentally about cooperation and learning in the fields of policies where the EU's competence (in a Community method) is quite limited. From this perspective, demanding that social protection should have the same status as economic and employment policies in the Lisbon Strategy is illogical. Yet the majority of Member States recognise that social policy in a Member State cannot be efficiently governed and implemented without fully accounting for the European policy framework. Although the EU is not yet a key player in social protection, it is increasingly designing common institutional structures and strategies for Member State social protection systems.

The interdependence and mutually reinforcing roles of economic and social development is quite obvious, no matter at which level of governance the decisions on these policies are taken. One of the EU's primary objectives is promoting the four freedoms of the internal market. It is therefore understandable that European competencies in markets and competition, and to a lesser extent in economic policies, have partially shifted to the EU level. In the Eurozone monetary policy is already concentrated at the EU level. Consequently, Member State social protection systems have to adapt to the direct and indirect impacts of the internal market. If the influence of EU-level decisions on the four freedoms and competition law on Member State social protection models are not taken into account, the Member States will be forced to redesign their social protection systems in ways that better adjust to the legal framework created by the internal market.

The EU probably does not have the necessary tools for a Europe-wide social policy aimed at (re)balancing such developments. Usually the major tools for supervising and regulating social policy include normative guidance (legislation and other binding forms of guidance), the reallocation of resources and information guidance, and these are at the Member State level. At the EU level normative and information guidance are to some extent available. However, given its limited competencies and resources the EU has minimal opportunities for reallocating resources for social purposes. Even the amount of resources it has allocated to structural funds and other similar policy instruments is quite limited compared to those available to Member States. Furthermore, while valuable for employment and regional policies, the criteria for allocating those resources to different Member States do not fully match conventional socio-political objectives. Finally, in all likelihood the EU's budgetary resources will not increase significantly in relation to GDP (gross domestic product).

However, more important is that despite a perception of divergence among Member States and welfare regimes, several similarities and even perhaps some convergence in Member States' policies exist. All Member States have been committed to a market economy that stresses social cohesion. Member States want to make their social policy decisions at the national level, with some differing nuances in their arguments. Likewise, every Member State seems to accept catchwords like 'work is the best social protection' or 'social policy is a productive factor'. Finally, all Member States will soon face roughly similar challenges: demographic change, new communication technologies and adjustment to the global market mean that the Member State institutional solutions cannot differ too greatly. Achieving common objectives requires European expressions of desired policies.

Only a limited number of Member States want to see the reallocation of competencies from the Member State level to the EU level in key social policy issues (for example, those related to Articles 137 and 152). Despite the interdependence of the various policy sectors and the common challenges, Member States discount social policy decision making at the EU level. This attitude is quite understandable because the differences between the institutional structures and cultural practices of Member States' social protection systems are still manifold, and sufficient institutional convergence is unlikely to occur. Thus common decision making in social policy at the EU level is not very easy to attain, especially when unanimity is required.

EU-level social policy blends subsidiarity (often connected with conservatism), equality (often connected with social democracy) and freedom (often connected with liberalism) (for details, see Chapter Two, this volume). This mix derives from a pragmatic approach and partly explains why only a limited political space is available for a clearly defined and extensive European social policy. However, the European welfare states have been transformed into semi-sovereign welfare states. This trajectory is becoming more visible as the institutional structure of the internal market rapidly evolves to cover those fields that are directly related to social and health policies. Although the Member States still advocate for the subsidiarity and proportionality principles, they are also aware that their citizens wait for some added value from EU cooperation. If the general feeling among the public is that the EU benefits only the creation of the free market, then EU legitimacy is at stake.

Adherence to the subsidiarity (and proportionality) principle has also implied that the Member States have not actively promoted the social dimension of the EU, thereby creating a paradox as the EU influences Member State social policies more through the internal market than expected in the 1990s. If Member States were interested in strengthening EU social policy, the EU's impact on Member State systems would probably be less limited. EU cooperation in social policy should include not only downloading but also uploading. Indeed, the EU's Social Policy Agenda does not appear very strange to the Dutch and French governments precisely because they have been active in the uploading process.

Member State social policy models are challenged not only from above or from the globalised market but also from below. The Treaties of Maastricht (1993), Amsterdam (1999) and Nice (2003) established and extended the idea of a European citizenship. Consequently, for example, the EU regulation on social security coordination (1408/71) covers both third-country nationals and the non-active population. The four freedoms of the internal market cover all EU citizens, and ECJ rulings have increasingly linked the entitlement to transfers and services to the free movement of all, not to citizenship of an individual Member State. While in many ways a positive development, in the long term the four freedoms and related rights may result in some economic and political pressures towards the financing structures of Member State social protection systems.

Member State reforms in the field of social protection mainly result from existing national problems and challenges. The path dependency of reform policies at the national level is a reality. Therefore, demands from outside each Member State (for example, from the EU) semi-automatically face resistance within each Member State. However, when challenges such as demographic change are considered common to all Member States, their policy makers are more willing to take into account the views of European bodies. Furthermore, when the increasing interdependency of the Member States in economic growth is understood, the Member States should be more interested in international cooperation on reform policy. Finally, when and where there are joint commitments, such as the Stability and Growth Pact (SGP), the Member States are forced to some extent to consider EU views in their reform policies.

The EU pressures on the Member States' reforms in social protection are perhaps more indirect than those of economic and employment policies. But because the sustainability and stability of Member States' economies are strongly dependent on, for example, pension and health care expenditure, the EU economic pressures are significant in Member State social policy planning. Thus the Ecofin Council and the Economic Policy Committee (EPC) are dealing with the same topics as the SPC. Those responsible for social protection, however, do not interfere in economic policy issues, although they know the impacts of the economic decisions on social protection.

The need to further discuss the ESM in depth in more political terms is clear. The first step is to accept the existence of very common social policy interests at the EU level. Extensive cooperation instead of confrontation is needed in European social policy. A good starting point for this cooperation is that Member States that have invested in social protection and social cohesion are doing well in economic growth. Social cohesion, economic growth and high employment are mutually reinforcing. We can build on that.

Globalisation has advanced at different paces in various sectors. The real challenge for those responsible for social protection is whether they are willing and able to make a real social policy agenda for the EU. Agreeing with the views presented by the International Labour Organization's World Commission on the Social Dimension of Globalisation should be easy:[5]

> Successful participation in globalisation is bound up with national capabilities and policies. All countries share the goal of better employment. In order to make globalisation a positive force for people, it is important that the rules governing it are fair. We have today a global economy, but not a global society. The governance and rules are clearly lagging behind the economic developments.

Action to achieve fairer rules also needs more coherent and equitable policies at the international level. This is essential to ensure that the benefits of globalisation are more widely distributed and common goals are realised. The key to better international policies lies in the integration of social and economic goals. Besides national governments, also multilateral institutions need to direct their policies towards achieving these common global goals.

At least, we fully agree.

Notes

[1] There seems to be significant variations in the ability of Member States to agree and implement social reforms, which is, in addition to obvious political factors, clearly linked to the interplay between the coordination of interests and the structures of social protection institutions, indicating that some Member States are 'structurally' more able to innovate (see, for instance, Kangas, 2004).

[2] There is a significant debate on this (see Pierson, 2004; Crouch, 2005).

[3] The Cardiff Process (1998) monitors economic reform in Member States in order to improve the functioning of goods, services and capital markets in the EU. From that perspective, the institutions of social protection are sometimes considered as distortive.

[4] The main objective of the Cologne Process (1999) is to encourage dialogue between all the parties involved (representatives of the Council, the Commission, the social partners and the European Central Bank) in macroeconomic policy and to strengthen their confidence, in order to encourage growth and job creation. Due to the nature of dialogue very little is commonly known on its content.

[5] Address by President of the Republic of Finland Tarja Halonen at the International Labour Organization governing body in Geneva, 17 November 2003.

References

Aarts, K. and van der Kolk, H. (eds) (2005) *Nederlanders en Europa*, Amsterdam: Prometheus.

Adnett, N. and Hardy, S. (2005) *The European social model: Modernisation or evolution*, Cheltenham: Edward Elgar.

Aiginger, K. and Guger, A. (2006) 'The European socio-economic model', in P. Diamond, R. Liddle and A. Giddens (eds) *Global Europe, social Europe*, Cambridge: Polity Press, pp 124-50.

Alber, J. (2006) 'The European social model and the United States', *European Union Politics*, vol 7, no 3, pp 393-419.

Alogoskoufis, G. (2005a) 'Speech on the reform of the Lisbon Strategy', Standing Committee on European Affairs, Unpublished Proceedings, 11 March, Athens: Hellenic Parliament.

Alogoskoufis, G. (2005b) 'Speech of the Minister of Economy and Finance to the Committee for the National Program of Reforms in the context of the Lisbon Strategy', Press release, 18 July, Athens: Ministry of Economy and Finance.

Alogoskoufis, G. (2005c) 'Speech on the Directive-Proposal on the services in the internal market', Standing Committee on European Affairs, Unpublished Proceedings, 31 October, Athens: Hellenic Parliament.

Álvarez, S. and Guillén, A.M. (2004) 'The OECD and the reformulation of Spanish social policy: a combined search for expansion and rationalisation', in K. Armingeon and M. Beyeler (eds) *The OECD and European Welfare States*, Cheltenham: Edward Elgar, pp 183-96.

Amable, B. (2003) *The diversity of modern capitalism*, Oxford: Oxford University Press.

APE (2006) *Concerns about social dumping. The positions of the Greek political parties in view of the Bolkenstein Directive*, Athens: APE.

Armstrong, K. (2005) 'Implementing the Lisbon Strategy policy coordination through open methods: how open is the UK to the OMC process on social inclusion', in J. Zeitlin and P. Pochet (eds) *The open method of coordination in action*, Brussels: PIE-Peter Lang, pp 287-310.

Association of the Greek Industries (1991) 'The positions of the Association of the Greek Industries (SEV) on the European Social Charter', *SEV's Bulletin*, issue 523-4/1991, Athens.

Atkinson, A.B., Cantillon, B., Marlier, E. and Nolan, B. (eds) (2002) *Social indicators – The EU and social inclusion*, Oxford: Oxford University Press.

Atkinson, A.B., Cantillon, B., Marlier, E. and Nolan, B. (2005) *Taking forward the EU social inclusion process, The Independent Report commissioned by the Luxemburg Presidency of the Council of the European Union*, (retrieved 19 March 2007 from www.ceps.lu/eu2005_lu/report/final_report.pdf).

Atkinson, A.B., Cantillon, B., Marlier, E. and Nolan, B. (eds) (2006) *Taking forward the EU social inclusion process* (retrieved 1 August 2006 from www.ceps.lu/eu2005_lu/inclusion/report/final_report.pdf).

Balcerzak-Paradowska, B., Chłoń-Domińczak, A., Kotowska, I.E., Olejniczal-Merta, A., Topińska, I. and Wóycicka, I. (2003) 'The gender dimensions of social security reform in Poland', in E. Fultz, M. Ruck and S. Steinhilber (eds) *The gender dimension of social security reform in Central and Eastern Europe: Case studies of Czech Republic, Hungary and Poland*, Budapest: International Labour Office, pp 187-314.

Baldwin, P. (1996) 'Can we define a European welfare state model?', in B. Greve (ed) *Comparative welfare systems. The Scandinavian model in a period of change*, London: Macmillan, pp 29-44.

Baldwin-Edwards, M. and Gough, I. (1991) 'European Community social policy and the UK', *Social Policy Review*, 1990-91, pp 147-68.

Balmaseda, M. and Sebastián, M. (2003) 'Spain in the EU: fifteen years may not be enough', *South European Society and Politics*, vol 8, no 1-2, pp 195-230.

Beskæftigelsesministeriet (2003a) *Danske sociale ydelser i lyset af udvidelsen af EU* (*Danish social security benefits in light of EU enlargement*), Copenhagen: Ministry of Employment.

Beskæftigelsesministeriet (2003b) *Agreement among the Liberals, the Conservatives, the Social Democrats, the Socialist People's Party, the Social Liberals and the Christian Democrats concerning access to the Danish labour market after the enlargement of the European Union on 1 May 2004*, Copenhagen: Ministry of Employment.

Beskæftigelsesministeriet (ed) (2005) *Flexicurity: Udfordringer for den danske model* (*Flexicurity: Challenges to the Danish model*), Copenhagen: Ministry of Employment.

Best, E. (2003) 'Alternative regulations or complementary methods? Evolving options in European governance', *Eipascope*, no 1, pp 2-11.

Blavoukos, S. (2002) 'Socio-economic pressure groups in Greece and enlargement: the case of the Confederation of Greek Industrialists (SEV)', Paper for the 3rd EPIC Workshop, 18-22 September, Florence: European University Institute.

Blunkett, D. (2005) 'Letter to Commissioner Vladimir Spidla, Commissioner for Employment, Social Affairs and Equal Opportunities', 14 October, London: Department for Work and Pensions.

Blunkett, D. and Johnson, A. (2005) *A modern social dimension for Europe: Principles for reform* (retrieved 24 October 2005 from www.dwp.gov.uk/publications/dwp/2005/mod-soc/modern.pdf).

Blyth, M. (2002) *Great transformations – Economic ideas and institutional change in the twentieth century*, Cambridge: Cambridge University Press.

BMA (British Medical Association) (2006) *Doctors' and Dentists' Review Body report 2006*, London: BMA.

Boeri, T. and Brücker, H. (2000) *The impact of Eastern enlargement on employment and labour markets in the EU Member States: A study made for the Directorate General for Employment and Social Affairs*, Berlin and Milan: European Integration Consortium.

Boeri, T. and Brücker, H. (2003) *Potential migration from Central and Eastern Europe: An update*, Brussels: DG Employment and Social Affairs.

Børner, T. (2005) 'Speech by the Secretary of State for Social Affairs, Thomas Børner', Conference on NAPincl, 27 April, Copenhagen.

Börzel, T. (2002) 'Pace-setting, foot-dragging, and fence-sitting: Member State responses to Europeanization', *Journal of Common Market Studies*, vol 40, no 2, pp 193-214.

Börzel, T. (2005) 'Europeanization: how the European Union interacts with its Member States', in S. Bulmer and C. Lequesne (eds) *The Member States of the European Union*, Oxford: Oxford University Press, pp 45-75.

Börzel, T. and Risse, T. (2000) 'When Europe hits home: Europeanization and domestic change', *European Integration online Papers*, vol 4, no 15 (retrieved 20 March 2007 from http://eiop.or.at/eiop/pdf/2000-015.pdf).

Brunetta, R. and Cazzola, G. (2003) 'Nota per una "Maastricht delle pensioni"', Unpublished paper (retrieved 20 March 2007 from www.renatobrunetta.it/documenti/0/700/750/758/maastricht-pensioni.pdf).

Brye, A. (1993) *Trade unions and employers in the Single Market*, London: Policy Studies Institute.

Büchs, M. (2004) 'Asymmetries of policy learning? The EES and its role in labour market policy reform in Germany and the UK', Paper for the ESPAnet Conference, 9-11 September, University of Oxford.

Bundesministerium für Arbeit und Soziales (2006) *Vorhaben Arbeit und Soziales. Materialien zur Information*, Berlin: Bundesministerium für Arbeit und Soziales.

Bundesministerium für Arbeit und Soziales (2007) Messages from the Conference 'Joining Forces for a Social Europe' held in Nuremberg on 8 and 9 February 2007 to the EPSCO Council meeting of 22 February and the Spring Summit of the European Council of 8 March 2007, Berlin: Bundesministerium für Arbeit und Soziales.

Bundesministerium für Gesundheit und Soziale Sicherung (2005) *Sozialbericht 2005*, Bonn: Bundesministerium für Gesundheit und Soziale Sicherung.

Bundesrat (2001) 'Unterrichtung durch die Bundesregierung: Deutsches Positionspapier für den Europäischen Rat in Stockholm am 23/24 März 2001: Für ein innovatives Europa: Wachstumspotenzial und sozialen Zusammenhalt stärken', *Drucksache*, 86/01, 1 February, Berlin.

Bundesrat (2002) 'Unterrichtung durch die Bundesregierung: Entwurf eines deutschen Positionspapiers für den Europäischen Rat in Barcelona am 15/16 März 2002: Europas Wachstumspotenzial steigern, den sozialen Zusammenhalt stärken und die natürlichen Lebensgrundlagen wahren', *Drucksache*, 57/02, 24 January, Berlin.

Bundesrat (2003a) 'Unterrichtung durch die Bundesregierung: Entwurf eines deutschen Positionspapiers für den Europäischen Rat in Brüssel am 21/22 März 2003', *Drucksache*, 35/03, 21 January, Berlin.

Bundesrat (2003b) 'Unterrichtung durch die Bundesregierung: Entwurf eines deutschen Positionspapiers für den Europäischen Rat in Brüssel am 25/26 März 2004', *Drucksache*, 928/03, 2 December, Berlin.

Bundesrat (2004) 'Unterrichtung durch die Bundesregierung: Position der Bundesregierung zur Halbzeitbilanz der Lissabonstrategie (Oktober 2004): Wachstum und Beschäftigung für die Jahre bis 2010', *Drucksache*, 917/04, 18 November, Berlin.

Bundesrat (2005) 'Beschluss des Bundesrates zur Position der Bundesregierung zur Halbzeitbilanz der Lissabonstrategie (Oktober 2004): Wachstum und Beschäftigung für die Jahre bis 2010', *Drucksache*, 917/04 (Beschluss), 18 February, Berlin.

Bundesregierung (2003) *Stellungnahme der Bundesrepublik Deutschland zum Grünbuch zu Dienstleistungen von allgemeinem Interesse der Europäischen Kommission, KOM (2003) 270*, Berlin. Retrieved 18 March 2006 from http://ec.europa.eu/services_general_interest/docs/public_authorities/deutschl.pdf.

Bundesregierung (2005a) 'Die Lissabon Strategie', Press release, 21 November, Berlin.

Bundesregierung (2005b) *Stellungnahme der Bundesregierung zur Mitteilung der Kommission vom 9 Februar 2005, KOM (2005) 33,* Berlin (retrieved 18 March 2006 from www.bmwi.de/).

Bundesregierung (2005c) 'Antwort zum Fragebogen für die Bewertung der Offenen Methode der Koordinierung (OMK) zur Vorbereitung des 'Straffungsprozesses' im Bereich Sozialschutz in Abstimmung mit den Bundesländern und unter Berücksichtigung der Stellungnahmen gesellschaftlich relevanter Gruppen and die Europäische Kommission', Unpublished document, 30 June, Berlin.

Bundesregierung (2005d) *Mitteilung der Regierung der Bundesrepublik Deutschland an die Kommission der Europäischen Gemeinschaften vom 14. September 2005: Stellungnahme zum Grünbuch 'Angesichts des demografischen Wandels – eine neue Solidarität zwischen den Generationen',* Berlin (retrieved 18 March 2006 from www.erfahrung-ist-zukunft. de/).

Bundesregierung (2005e) *Nationales Reformprogramm Deutschland,* Berlin (retrieved 6 June 2006 from www.bundesregierung.de/).

Bundesregierung (2006a) 'Was bedeutet europaweite Freizügigkeit für Arbeitnehmer?', Press release, 9 February, Berlin (retrieved 20 March 2006 from www.bundesregierung.de/).

Bundesregierung (2006b) *Verhandlungsposition der Bundesregierung zur EU-Dienstleistungsrichtlinie – Eckpunkte,* 6 March, Berlin.

Cabrero, R. (2004) 'La protección social a las personas en situación de dependencia en España', in V. Navarro (ed) *El Estado del Bienestar en España,* Madrid: Tecnos, pp 313-29.

Canoy, M., Smith, P.M. and Belessiotis, T. (2005) 'What kind of European social model?', Paper, 28 September, Brussels: Bureau of European Policy Advisers of the European Commission.

Castles, F. and Mitchell, D. (1999) 'Worlds of welfare and families of nations', in F. Castles (ed) *Families of nations: Patterns of public policy in western democracies,* Aldershot: Dartmouth Publishing Group, pp 93-128.

CDU (2001) 'Neue Soziale Marktwirtschaft', *Diskussionspapier,* 27 August, Berlin.

CDU, CSU and SPD (2005) *Gemeinsam für Deutschland. Mit Mut und Menschlichkeit,* Coalition agreement between CDU, CSU and SPD, 11 November, Berlin.

CGP (2001) *Réduction du temps de travail: les enseignements de l'observation,* Paris: La documentation Française.

CNAMTS (Caisse nationale d'assurance maladie), CCMSA (Caisse centrale de la Mutualité Sociale Agricole) and CANAM (Caisse nationale d'assurance maladie des professions indépendantes) (2003) *Contribution to the debate of the French national funds in charge of the mandatory sickness insurance*, Green Paper on services of general interest (retrieved 20 January 2006 from http://ec.europa.eu/services_general_interest/docs/undertakings_partners/caisses_en.pdf).

Comparecencia del Ministro de Industria, Turismo y Comercio (2005) 'Sr Montilla Aguilera, ante la Comisión de Industria, Turismo y Comercio', *Diario de Sesiones del Congreso de los Diputados*, no 461, 27 December, Madrid: Ministro de Industria, Turismo y Comercio.

Comparecencia del Ministro de Trabajo y Asuntos Sociales (2003) 'Sr Zaplana Hernández-Soro ante la Comisión Mixta para la Unión Europea', *Diario de Sesiones de las Cortes Generales*, no 128, 4 March, Madrid: Ministro de Trabajo y Asuntos Sociales.

Consejo Económico y Social (2000) *España 1999. Memoria sobre la situación socioeconómica y laboral*, Madrid: Consejo Económico y Social.

Consejo Económico y Social (2004) 'Efectos de la próxima ampliación de la Unión Europea sobre la economía española', *Informe*, 1/2004, Madrid: Consejo Económico y Social.

Consiglio informale dei Ministri del Lavoro e degli Affari Sociali (2003) *Documento della Presidenza: Domande per orientare il dibattito* (retrieved 20 March 2007 from www.lex.unict.it/eurolabor/documentazione/comunicati/presidenza.pdf).

Coron, G. and Palier, B. (2002) 'Changes in the means of financing social expenditure in France since 1945', in C. De la Porte and P. Pochet (eds) *Building social Europe through the open method of coordination*, Brussels: PIE-Peter Lang, pp 97-136.

Council of the European Union (2004) *Joint Employment Report 2003/2004*, Council document 7069/04, Brussels.

Council of Ministers (2002) *Report on results of negotiations for membership of the Republic of Poland in the European Union has been adopted by the Council of Ministers*, 17 December, Warsaw: UKIE.

Council of Ministers (2003) *The programme of streamlining and reducing of public expenditures*, Warsaw: Council of Ministers.

Council of Ministers (2005a) *Poland's position for the mid-term review of the Lisbon Strategy*, adopted by the Council of Ministers, 15 March, Warsaw: Monitor Europejski (retrieved 15 March 2006 from www1.ukie.gov.pl/HLP/moint.nsf/0/9A74321E67C71E80C125700A00338271/$file/ME_11(84)04.pdf).

Council of Ministers (2005b) *National Reform Programme for 2005-2008*, Adopted by the Council of Ministers on 27 December, Warsaw: Ministry of Economy.

Council of Ministers (2005c) *Position of Council of Ministers European Committee of 17 September 2004*, supplemented on 7 January 2005, Warsaw: Council of Ministers.

Culpepper, P.D., Hall, P. and Palier, B. (eds) (2006) *Changing France: The politics that markets make*, London: Palgrave.

Crouch, C. (2005) *Capitalist diversity and change*, Oxford: Oxford University Press.

Daguerre, A. and Taylor-Gooby, P. (2003) 'Adaptation to labour market change in France and the UK: convergent or parallel tracks?', *Social Policy Administration*, vol 37, no 6, pp 625-38.

Danish Government (2004) 'Danish reflections on the Report from the high level group chaired by Wim Kok', Non-paper, Copenhagen: Prime Minister's Office.

Danish Government (2005a) *Denmark's National Reform Programme, Contribution to EU's growth and employment strategy (the Lisbon Strategy)*, Copenhagen: Ministry of Finance.

Danish Government (2005b) *Questionnaire on the Green Paper 'Confronting demographic change: A new solidarity between generations' – Reply of the Danish Government*, Copenhagen: Danish Government.

DARES – DGEFPP (2005) *Stratégie Européenne pour l'emploi – Rapport d'évaluation des politiques d'emploi et du marché du travail en France (2000-2004)*, Administrative document, Paris.

Davaki, C. and Mossialos, E. (2006) 'Financing and delivering health care', in M. Petmesidou and E. Mossialos (eds) *Social policy developments in Greece*, London: Ashgate, pp 286-318.

De Búrca, G. (ed) (2005) *EU law and the welfare state*, Oxford: Oxford University Press.

De la Porte, C. and Pochet, P. (eds) (2002) *Building social Europe through the open method of coordination*, Brussels: PIE-Peter Lang.

Deutscher Bundestag (2000a) 'Regierungserklärung zu den Ergebnissen der Sondertagung des Europäischen Rates vom 23./24. März 2000 in Lissabon', *Plenarprotokoll*, 14/98, 6 April, Berlin.

Deutscher Bundestag (2000b) 'Entschließungsantrag der Fraktionen SPD und Bündnis 90/Die Grünen zu der Abgabe einer Erklärung der Bundesregierung zu den Ergebnissen der Sondertagung des Europäischen Rates vom 23/24 März 2000 in Lissabon', *Drucksache*, 14/3099, 4 April, Berlin.

Deutscher Bundestag (2003a) *Plenarprotokoll*, 15/32, 14 March, Berlin.

Deutscher Bundestag (2003b) 'Regierungserklärung zur internationalen Lage und zu den Ergebnissen des Europäischen Rates in Brüssel am 20/21 März 2003', *Bulletin der Bundesregierung*, 30-1, 3 April, Berlin.

Deutscher Bundestag (2003c) 'Gesetzentwurf der Fraktionen SPD und BÜNDNIS 90/DIE GRÜNEN. Entwurf eines Vierten Gesetzes für moderne Dienstleistungen am Arbeitsmarkt', *Drucksache*, 5/1516, 5 September, Berlin.

Deutscher Bundestag (2004a) 'Regierungserklärung zu den Ergebnissen des Europäischen Rates in Brüssel am 4/5 November 2004', *Plenarprotokoll*, 15/138, 11 November, Berlin.

Deutscher Bundestag (2004b) 'Antrag der Fraktionen SPD und Bündnis 90/Die Grünen: Stabilitäts- und Wachstumspolitik fortsetzen – Den Europäischen Stabilitäts- und Wachstumspakt stärken', *Drucksache*, 15/3957, 20 October, Berlin.

Deutscher Bundestag (2004c) 'Regierungserklärung durch den Bundeskanzler: Erweiterung der Europäischen Union', *Plenarprotokoll*, 15/106, 30 April, Berlin.

Deutscher Bundestag (2005a) 'Antrag der Fraktion der SPD und der Fraktion Bündnis 90/Die Grünen et al., Für eine zukunftsgerichtete Weiterführung der Lissabon-Strategie – Neue Impulse zur wirtschaftlichen, sozialen und ökologischen Erneuerung', *Drucksache*, 15/5116, 16 March, Berlin.

Deutscher Bundestag (2005b) 'Regierungserklärung durch den Bundeskanzler: Aus Verantwortung für unser Land – Deutschlands Kräfte stärken', *Plenarprotokoll*, 15/166, 17 March, Berlin.

Deutscher Bundestag (2005c) 'Antrag der Fraktion der SPD und der Fraktion Bündnis 90/Die Grünen: Arbeit schaffen – Sozialen Zusammenhalt und wirtschaftliche Dynamik im europäischen Binnenmarkt für Dienstleistungen verbessern', *Drucksache*, 15/5832, 29 June, Berlin.

Deutscher Bundestag (2005d) 'Aktuelle Stunde auf Verlangen der Fraktion der CDU/CSU: Vorstoß des Bundeskanzlers zur Lockerung der Kriterien des europäischen Stabilitäts- und Wachstumspaktes, um mehr Flexibilität bei der Neuverschuldung zu erhalten', *Plenarprotokoll*, 15/151, 20 January, Berlin.

Deutscher Bundestag (2005e) 'Große Anfrage der Fraktion der CDU/CSU et al: Sozialdumping durch osteuropäische Billigarbeiter', *Drucksache*, 15/5168, 15 March, Berlin.

Deutscher Bundestag (2005f) 'Antwort der Bundesregierung auf die Kleine Anfrage der Abgeordneten Albert Rupprecht und der Fraktion der CDU/CSU: Dienstleistungsfreiheit nach der EU-Osterweiterung', *Drucksache*, 15/5546, 27 May, Berlin.

Deutscher Bundestag (2006a) *Plenarprotokoll*, 16/35, 11 May, Berlin.

Deutscher Bundestag (2006b) 'Beschlussempfehlung und Bericht des Ausschusses für Arbeit und Soziales', *Drucksache*, 16/989, 16 March, Berlin.

Deutscher Bundestag (2006c) 'Unterrichtung durch die Bundesregierung. Präsidentschaftsprogramm 1. Januar bis 30 Juni 2007 – Europa gelingt gemeinsam', *Drucksache*, 16/3680, 30 November, Berlin.

DfES (Department for Education and Skills) (1998) *Meeting the childcare challenge: A framework and consultation document*, London: The Stationery Office.

Diamond, P., Ferrera, M., Giddens, A., Liddle, R., Palme, J., Rodrigues, M.J., Soete, L., Tsoukalis, L. and Weil, P. (2006) *The Hampton Court Agenda: A social model for Europe* (retrieved 20 March 2007 from www.policy-network.net).

Dimoulas, K. (2005) 'Occupational training as public policy. The case of Greece (1980-2000)', in M. Karamesini (ed) *Employment policy*, Athens: Ellinika Grammata, pp 241-63.

Dipartimento per le Politiche Comunitarie (2005) *Plan for innovation, growth and employment*, Rome: Presidenza del Consiglio dei Ministri.

Dipartimento per le Politiche Comunitarie (2006a) *Programma nazionale di riforma 2006-2008. Primo rapporto sullo stato di attuazione* (retrieved 20 March 2007 from http://ec.europa.eu/growthandjobs/index_en.htm).

Dipartimento per le Politiche Comunitarie (2006b) *Il Consiglio dei Ministri dell'UE trova l'accordo* (retrieved 20 March 2007 from www.politichecomunitarie.it).

Doménech, R. and Taguas, D. (2003) 'El impacto a largo plazo de la Unión Económica y Monetaria sobre la economía española', in Fundación BBV (ed) *El euro y sus repercusiones sobre la economía española*, Bilbao: Fundación BBV, pp 91-149.

Dupont-Aignan, N. (2005) *J'aime l'Europe je vote Non*, Paris: François-Xavier de Guibert.

DWP (Department for Work and Pensions) (2003) *UK National Action Plan for social inclusion*, London: DWP.

DWP (2005a) *Opportunity for All: 7th annual report*, London: DWP.

DWP (2005b) *The response of the United Kingdom to the European Commission's Green Paper, Confronting demographic change: A new solidarity between generations*, London: DWP.

DWP (2006a) *Helping older workers: A New Deal for Welfare: Empowering people to work*, Cm 6730, London: The Stationery Office.

DWP (2006b) *A New Deal for Welfare: Empowering people to work*, London: DWP.

Economou, C. (2004) *Health policies in Greece and the European Union*, Athens: Dionicos.

Erhel, C. and Zajdela, H. (2004) 'The dynamics of social and labour market policies in France and the United Kingdom: between path dependence and convergence', *Journal of European Social Policy*, vol 14, no 2, pp 125-42.

Erhel, C., Mandin, L. and Palier, B. (2005) 'The leverage effect: the open method of coordination in France', in J. Zeitlin and P. Pochet (eds) *The open method of coordination in action: The European Employment Strategy and social inclusion strategies*, Brussels: PIE-Peter Lang, pp 217-48.

ESEE (2004) 'The positions of the Greek Confederation of Commerce (ESEE) on the Wim Kok report', *Communication*, 23 December, Athens.

Esping-Andersen, G. (1990) *The three worlds of welfare capitalism*, Cambridge: Polity Press.

Esping-Andersen, G. (1999) *Social foundations of postindustrial economies*, Oxford: Oxford University Press.

Esping-Andersen, G. (ed) (2002) *Why we need a new welfare state*, Oxford: Oxford University Press.

Esping-Andersen, G. (2005) 'Why we need a social investment strategy', WRR-Lecture, 8 December, The Hague (retrieved 25 March 2007 from www.wrr.nl/content.jsp?objectid=3750).

Eurobarometer (2004) *Public opinion in the European Union*, Spring, no 61, National Report Greece (retrieved 31 March 2007 from http://ec.europa.eu/public_opinion/archives/eb/eb61/nat_greece.pdf).

Eurobarometer (2005) *Public opinion in the European Union*, Spring, no 63 (retrieved 31 March 2007 from http://ec.europa.eu/public_opinion/archives/eb/eb63/eb63_en.htm).

Eurobarometer (varies issues) *Public opinion in the European Union* (retrieved 31 March 2007 from http://ec.europa.eu/public_opinion/index_en.htm).

European Commission (1993a) *Growth, competitiveness, employment: The challenges and ways forward into the 21st century*, White Paper, COM (1993) 700, final.

European Commission (1993b) *Options for the Union*, Green Paper on European social policy, COM (1993) 551, final.

European Commission (1994) *European social policy: A way forward for the Union*, White Paper, COM (1994) 333, final.

European Commission (1995) *The future of social protection: A framework for a European debate*, COM (1995) 466, final.

European Commission (1997) *Modernising and improving social protection in the European Union*, COM (1997) 102, final.

European Commission (1998) *From guidelines to action: The national action plans for employment*, COM (1998) 316, final.

European Commission (1999a) *A concerted strategy for modernising social protection*, COM (1999) 347, final.

European Commission (1999b) *Towards a Europe for all ages: Promoting prosperity and intergenerational solidarity*, COM (1999) 221, final.

European Commission (2000a) *Social Policy Agenda*, COM (2000) 379, final.

European Commission (2000b) *Strategic objectives 2000-05: 'Shaping the new Europe'*, COM (2000) 154, final.

European Commission (2000c) *The future evolution of social protection from a long-term point of view: Safe and sustainable pensions*, COM (2000) 622, final.

European Commission (2000d) *The contribution of public finances to growth and employment: Improving quality and sustainability*, COM (2000) 846, final.

European Commission (2000e) *Services of general interest in Europe*, COM (2000) 580, final.

European Commission (2000f) *Employment and social affairs*, Luxembourg: Office for Official Publications of the European Communities.

European Commission (2001a) *Employment and social policies: A framework for investing in quality*, COM (2001) 313, final.

European Commission (2001b) *Supporting national strategies for safe and sustainable pensions through an integrated approach*, COM (2001) 362, final.

European Commission (2001c) *The future of health care and care for the elderly: Guaranteeing accessibility, quality and financial viability*, COM (2001) 723, final.

European Commission (2002a) *On streamlining the annual economic and employment policy co-ordination cycles*, COM (2002) 487, final.

European Commission (2002b) *Report requested by Stockholm European Council: 'Increasing labour force participation and promoting active ageing'*, COM (2002) 9, final.

European Commission (2002c) *The European social dialogue: A force for innovation and change*, COM (2002) 341, final.

European Commission (2002d) *Towards a reinforced culture of consultation and dialogue: General principles and minimum standards for consultation of interested parties by the Commission*, COM (2002) 704, final.

European Commission (2003a) *The future of the European Employment Strategy: A strategy for full employment and better jobs for all*, COM (2003) 6, final.

European Commission (2003b) *Scoreboard on implementing the Social Policy Agenda*, COM (2003) 57, final.

European Commission (2003c) *Mid-term review of the Social Policy Agenda*, COM (2003) 312, final.

European Commission (2003d) *Joint report on social inclusion summarising the results of the examination of the National Action Plans for Social Inclusion (2003-2005)*, COM (2003) 773, final.

European Commission (2003e) *Strengthening the social dimension of the Lisbon Strategy: Streamlining open coordination in the field of social protection*, COM (2003) 261, final.

European Commission (2003f) *Green Paper on services of general interest*, COM (2003) 270, final.

European Commission (2004a) *Strengthening the implementation of the European Employment Strategy*, COM (2004) 239, final.

European Commission (2004b) *Proposal for a directive of the European Parliament and of the Council on services in the internal market*, COM (2004) 2, final.

European Commission (2004c) *White Paper on services of general interest*, COM (2004) 374, final.

European Commission (2004d) *Partnership for change in an enlarged Europe: Enhancing the contribution of European social dialogue*, COM (2004) 557, final.

European Commission (2005a) *On the social agenda*, COM (2005) 33, final.

European Commission (2005b) *Working together, working better: A new framework for the open coordination of social protection and inclusion policies in the European Union*, COM (2005) 706, final.

European Commission (2005c) *Confronting demographic change: A new solidarity between the generations*, Green Paper, COM (2005) 94, final.

European Commission (2005d) *Second report on the practical preparations for the future enlargement of the euro area*, COM (2005) 545, final.

European Commission (2005e) *Common actions for growth and employment: The Community Lisbon Programme*, COM (2005) 330, final.

European Commission (2005f) *Evaluation of the open method of coordination on social protection and social inclusion. A synthesis of replies of Member States and other actors to the evaluation questionnaire on the open method of coordination in the fields of social inclusion and adequate and sustainable pensions*, Commission Staff Working Paper, SEC (2005), Brussels.

European Commission (2005g) *Working together for growth and jobs: A new start for the Lisbon Strategy*, Communication to the Spring European Council, COM (2005) 24, final.

European Commission (2005h) *Joint report on social protection and social inclusion*, COM (2005) 14, final.

European Commission (2005i) *European values in the globalised world: Contribution of the Commission to the October Meeting of Heads of State and Government*, COM (2005) 525, final.

European Commission (2005j) *Restructuring and employment: Anticipating and accompanying restructuring in order to develop employment: The role of the European Union*, COM (2005) 120, final.

European Commission (2005k) *Amended proposal for a decision of the European Parliament and of the Council establishing a Community programme for employment and social solidarity – PROGRESS*, COM (2005) 536, 21 October.

European Commission (2005l) *Sustainable financing of social policies in the European Union*, SEC (2005) 1774, final.

European Commission (2005m) *Strategic objectives 2005-2009. Europe 2010: A partnership for European renewal: Prosperity, solidarity and security*, COM (2005) 12, final.

European Commission (2005n) *The Commission's contribution to the period of reflection and beyond: Plan-D or democracy, dialogue and debate*, COM (2005) 494, final.

European Commission (2006a) *Joint report on social protection and social inclusion 2006*, COM (2006) 62, final.

European Commission (2006b) *The demographic future of Europe: From challenge to opportunity*, COM (2006) 571, final.

European Commission (2006c) *Towards an EU strategy on the rights of the child*, COM (2006) 367, final.

European Commission (2006d) *Amended proposal for a directive of the European Parliament and of the Council on services in the internal market*, COM (2006) 160, final.

European Commission (2006e) *Communication from the Commission to the European Parliament pursuant to the second subparagraph of Article 251 (2) of the EC Treaty concerning the common position of the Council on the adoption of a Directive of the European Parliament and of the Council on Services in the Internal Market*, COM (2006) 424, final.

European Commission (2006f) *Implementing the Community Lisbon programme: Social services of general interest in the European Union*, COM (2006) 177, final.

European Commission (2006g) *Report on the functioning of the transitional arrangements set out in the 2003 Accession Treaty (period 1 May 2004–30 April 2006)*, COM (2006) 48, final.

European Commission (2006h) *Evaluation of the open method of coordination for social protection and social inclusion. A synthesis of replies by Member States and other actors to an evaluation questionnaire on the open method of coordination in the fields of social inclusion and adequate and sustainable pensions*, Commission Staff Working Document, SEC (2006) 345, 8 March, Brussels.

European Commission (2006i) *The Commission's assessments of National Reform Programmes for growth and jobs. Poland* (retrieved 10 January 2007 from http://ec.europa.eu/growthandjobs/pdf/2006_annual_report_poland_en.pdf).

European Commission (2006j) *Time to move up a gear: The new partnership for growth and jobs*, COM (2006) 30, final.

European Commission (2006k) *European transparency initiative*, Green Paper, COM (2006) 194, final.

European Commission (2006l) *Proposal for a regulation of the European Parliament and of the Council establishing the European Globalisation Adjustment Fund*, 2006/0033 (COD), COM (2006) 91, 1 March.

European Commission (2006m) *A citizens' agenda: Delivering results for Europe*, COM (2006) 211, final.

European Parliament, Greek Office (2003) *The European Constitution*, Athens.

European Task Force Employment (2003) *Jobs, jobs, jobs: Creating more employment in Europe* (retrieved 16 March 2007 http://ec.europa.eu/employment_social/employment_strategy/pdf/etf_en.pdf).

Eurostat (2007) *European social statistics. Social protection, expenditure and receipts, Data 1996-2004*, Luxembourg: Office of Official Publications of the European Communities.

Evandrou, M. and Falkingham, J. (2005) 'A secure retirement for all? Older people and New Labour', in J. Hills and K. Stewart (eds) *A more equal society? New Labour, poverty, inequality and inclusion*, Bristol: The Policy Press, pp 167-88.

Evans, M. (1998) 'Social security: dismantling the pyramids?', in H. Glennerster and J. Hills (eds) *The state of welfare*, Oxford: Oxford University Press, pp 257-307.

Fabbrini, S. and Piattoni, S. (eds) (2007) *Italy in the European Union*, Lanham, MD: Rowman & Littlefield.

Falkner, G., Treib, O., Hartlapp, M. and Leiber, S. (2005) *Complying with Europe: EU harmonisation and soft law in the member states*, Cambridge: Cambridge University Press.

Featherstone, K. (2005) '"Soft" coordination meets "hard" politics: the European Union and pension reform in Greece', *Journal of European Social Policy*, vol 12, no 4, pp 733-50.

Featherstone, K., Kazamias, G. and Papadimitriou, D. (2001) 'The limits of external empowerment: EMU, technocracy and reform of the Greek pension system', *Political Studies*, vol 49, no1, pp 462-80.

Federal Ministry of Labour and Social Affairs (nd) *Sozialpolitik in Europa* (retrieved 17 March 2006 from www.bmas.bund.de/BMAS/Navigation/Soziale-Sicherung/sozialpolitik-in-europa.html).

Ferge, Z. (2001) 'Welfare and "ill-fare" systems in Central-Eastern Europe', in R. Sykes, B. Palier and P. Prior (eds) *Globalization and European welfare states*, Basingstoke: Palgrave Macmillan, pp 127-52.

Ferrera, M. (1996) 'The "southern model" of welfare in social Europe', *Journal of European Social Policy,* vol 25, no 1, pp 17-37.

Ferrera, M. (2002) 'The European social model and the open method of coordination', *Revue Belge de Sécurité Sociale*, vol 3, pp 469-72.

Ferrera, M. (2005) *The boundaries of welfare: European integration and the new spatial politics of social protection*, Oxford: Oxford University Press.

Ferrera, M. and Gualmini, E. (2004) *Rescued by Europe: Social and labour market reforms in Italy from Maastricht to Berlusconi*, Amsterdam: Amsterdam University Press.

Ferrera, M. and Sacchi, S. (2005) 'The open method of coordination and national institutional capabilities: the Italian experience', in J. Zeitlin and P. Pochet (eds) *The open method of coordination in action*, Brussels: PIE-Peter Lang, pp 137-72.

Finnish Government (1995) *Hallituksen selonteko Eduskunnalle* (*Government's explanation to the Parliament*), 14 February, Helsinki: Finnish Parliament.

Finnish Government (1997) *Hallituksen selonteko Eduskunnalle* (*Government's explanation on EMU to the Parliament*), 20 May, Helsinki: Finnish Parliament.

Finnish Government (1998) *Hallituksen selonteko Eduskunnalle* (*Government's explanation to the Parliament*), 24 February, Helsinki: Finnish Parliament.

Finnish Government (2004) *Hallituksen selonteko Eduskunnalle* (*Government's explanation to the Parliament*), E 134, Helsinki: Finnish Parliament.

Finnish Government (2005a) *Governmental Bill (HE) 33/2005*, Helsinki: Finnish Parliament.

Finnish Government (2005b) *Governmental Bill (HE) 172/2003*, Helsinki: Finnish Parliament.

Flash Eurobarometer (2002) November, no 139 (retrieved 31 March 2007 from http://ec.europa.eu/public_opinion/flash/fl139_en.pdf).

Flash Eurobarometer (2005) November, no 175 (retrieved 31 March 2007 from http://ec.europa.eu/public_opinion/flash/fl175_en.pdf).

Flight, H. (2005) 'Chancellor's efforts have ruined his credibility', *The Times*, 5 September.

Fouarge, D. (2003) *Costs of non-social policy*, Report for DG Employment and Social Affairs, 3 January, Brussels.

Frederiksen, C.H. (2003) 'Bred aftale om adgang til det danske arbejdsmarked for arbejdstagere fra de nye EU-lande' ('Broad agreement on access to the Danish labour market for workers from the new EU countries'), Press release, 2 December, Copenhagen: Ministry of Employment.

Giannitsis, T. (2004) 'The political economy of Greece's course to EMU', in G. Papantoniou, T. Giannitsis, P. Solbes, G. Stournaras, S. Tarvlos and G. Zalm (eds) *Greece: The accession to EMU and the future challenges*, Athens: Kastaniotis, pp 44-5.

Giddens, A. (1999) *The third way: The renewal of social democracy*, Cambridge: Polity Press.

Giuliani, M. (2006a) *Dov'è il problema? L'Italia e il recepimento della normativa comunitaria*, URGE Working Paper No 1/2006.

Giuliani, M. (2006b) *La politica europea*, Bologna: il Mulino.

Giuliani, M. and Piattoni, S. (2006) 'Italy: back to the future or steps toward normality?', in E. Zeff and E. Pirro (eds) *The European Union and the Member States* (2nd edn), Boulder, CO: Lynne Rienner, pp 85-106.

Golinowska, S. (2005) 'Ubóstwo i wykluczenie społeczne w polskiej polityce społecznej okresu transformacji' ('Poverty and social exclusion in Polish social policy'), in S. Golinowska, E. Tarkowska and I. Topińska (eds) *Ubóstwo i wykluczenie społeczne. Badania. Metody. Wyniki* (*Poverty and social exclusion. Research, methodology, results*), Warsaw: Instytut Pracy i Spraw Socjalnych.

Goodin, R. et al (1999) *The real worlds of welfare capitalism*, Cambridge: Cambridge University Press.

Governmental EU-Secretary (2004) 13 February, Helsinki: Finnish Parliament.

Grand Committee (2000) Reports (SuVL) 19/2000, Helsinki: Finnish Parliament.

Grand Committee (2002) Reports (SuVL) 1/2002, Helsinki: Finnish Parliament.

Grand Committee (2003) Reports (SuVL) 2/2003, Helsinki: Finnish Parliament.

Grand Committee (2004) Reports (SuVL) 2/2004, Helsinki: Finnish Parliament.

Grand Committee (2005a) Reports (SuVL) 1/2005, Helsinki: Finnish Parliament.

Grand Committee (2005b) Reports (SuVL) 5/2005, Helsinki: Finnish Parliament.

Grand Committee (2005c) *Confronting Democratic Change*, Green Paper, E 33, Helsinki: Finnish Parliament.

Greek Government (1982) *Memorandum to the President of the European Council, The positions of the Greek government on the relations between Greece and the European Communities*, 19 March, Athens.

GSEE (2000) 'The positions of GSEE for the implementation of the Lisbon European Council Resolutions, 23-24 March', *Enimerosi*, no 64/2000.

GSEE (2005) *The National Reform Program 2005-2008: A program for a knowledge economy and full employment or a program for the deregulation of the economy and the labor market?*, Athens: GSEE.

Guillén, A. and Álvarez, S. (2001) 'Globalization and the Southern Welfare States', in R. Sykes, B. Palier and P. Prior (eds) *Globalization and European Welfare States: Challenges and Change*, London: Macmillan.

Guillén, A.M. and Álvarez, S. (2004) 'The EU's impact on the Spanish welfare state: the role of cognitive Europeanisation', *Journal of European Social Policy*, vol 14, no 3, pp 285–300.

Guillén, A. and Matsaganis, M. (2000) 'Testing the social dumping hypothesis in Southern Europe: welfare policies in Greece and Spain during the last 20 years', *Journal of European Social Policy*, vol 10, no 2, pp 120-45.

Haas, E.B. (1958) *The Uniting of Europe: Political, Social, and Economic Forces 1950-1957*, Stanford: Stanford University Press.

Hainsworth, P. (2006) 'Contemporary issues: France says no: the 29 May 2005 Referendum on the European Constitution', *Parliamentary Affairs*, vol 59, no 1, pp 98–117.

Hansen, H. (2002) *Elements of social security*, Copenhagen: Danish National Institute of Social Research.

Heikkilä, M. and Kautto, M. (eds) (2004) *Welfare in Finland*, Helsinki: Stakes.

Hemerijck, A. (1998) *Social policy and economic performance*, The Hague: Ministry of Social Affairs and Employment.

Hemerijck, A. (2005) 'Recasting Europe's semi-sovereign welfare states and the role of the EU', in E. Palola and A. Savio (eds) *Redefining the social dimension in an enlarged EU*, Helsinki: Stakes and Ministry of Social Affairs and Health, pp 26-61.

Hemerijck, A. and Berghman, J. (2004) 'The European social patrimony: deepening social Europe through legitimate diversity', in T. Sakellaropoulos and J. Berghman (eds) *Connecting welfare diversity within the European social model*, Oxford: Intersentia, pp 9-54.

High Level Group (2004a) *Report by the High Level Group on the future of social policy in an enlarged European Union*, Brussels: EC DG Employment and Social Affairs.

High Level Group (2004b) *Report from the High Level Group on the Lisbon Strategy*, chaired by Wim Kok, November, Brussels.

Hiilamo, H. (2002) *The rise and fall of Nordic family policy. Historical development and changes during the 1990s in Sweden and Finland*, Helsinki: Stakes.

HM Treasury (2001a) *Delivering savings and assets for all*, London: HM Treasury.

HM Treasury (2001b) *Savings and assets for all*, London: HM Treasury.

HM Treasury (2005) *Growth and opportunity: Prioritising economic reform in Europe*, London: HM Treasury.

HM Treasury (2006) *Paper for the Treasury Committee on the Treasury's approach to the preliminary and technical work: The euro*, London: HM Treasury.

IGC 96 Task Force-European Commission (1996) *Greece's contribution to the 1996 IGC for a democratic European Union with political and social content* (Summary), 22 March, Brussels.

Impact evaluation of the European Employment Strategy. Italian employment policy in recent years: Impact evaluation, Final report (retrieved 20 March 2007 from www.europa.eu.int/comm/employment_social/ employment_strategy/eval/eval_it.pdf).

Jabůrková, M. and Mátl, O. (2006) *Evropská strategie zaměstnanosti a dobrá veřejná správa v kontextu víceúrovňového vládnutí* (*European Employment Strategy and good public administration in the context of multi-level governance*), Research Paper, Centre for Social and Economic Strategies, Prague.

Jäntti, M., Saari, J. and Vartiainen, J. (2006) *Equity and growth: Social risk management in Finland*, WIDER/World Bank, World Development Report (retrieved 16 December 2006 from http://siteresources. worldbank.org/INTWDR2006/).

Jepsen, M. and Serrano Pascual, A. (2005) 'The European social model: an exercise in deconstruction', *Journal of European Social Policy*, vol 15, no 3, pp 231-45.

Jepsen, M. and Serrano Pascual, A. (eds) (2006) *Unwrapping the European social model*, Bristol: The Policy Press.

Jessoula, M. and Alti, T. (2007) 'Italy: an uncompleted departure from Bismarck?', Paper for the workshop on 'The politics of reform in Bismarckian welfare systems', 8-10 March, Paris.

Kaelble, H. (2000) 'Wie kam es zum Europäischen Sozialmodell?', *Jahrbuch für Europa- und Nordamerika-Studien*, vol 4, pp 39-53.

Kangas, O. (2004) 'Development of sickness cash–benefit programmes in OECD countries', *Social Policy and Administration*, vol 38, no 2, pp 190-203.

Kangas, O. (2006) *Pensions and the pension funds in the making of a nation-state and national economy. The case of Finland*, Social Policy and Development Paper, No 25, Geneva: United Nations Research Institute for Social Development.

Kangas, O. (2007) 'Finland: labor markets against politics in the development of pension systems', in K. Anderson, E. Immergut and I. Schultze (eds) *Handbook of West European pension politics*, Oxford: Oxford University Press, pp 248-396.

Kangas, O. and Palme, J. (eds) (2005) *Social policy and economic development in the Nordic countries*, London: Palgrave Macmillan.

Karamanlis, C. (2005a) Speech at the Hellenic Parliament on the ratification of the European Constitution, 18 April, Athens.

Karamanlis, C. (2005b) 'The vision of a stronger Europe through its leaders', Speech at the Economist Conference, 19 April, Athens.

Katrougalos, G. and Lazaridis, G. (2003) *Southern European welfare states*, New York, NY: Palgrave.

Kattelus, M. and Saari, J. (2006) 'Terveyspolitiikan eurooppalaistuminen – Reflektioprosessi sisämarkkinoiden tasapainottajana' ('The Europeanisation of health policy'), *Yhteiskuntapolitiikka*, vol 71, no 1, pp 73-88.

Kautto, M., Fritzell, J., Hvinden, B., Kvist, J. and Uusitalo, H. (eds) (2001) *Nordic welfare states in the European context*, London: Routledge.

Klaus, V. (2003) 'The future of the euro: a view of a concerned outsider', Lecture, 20 November, Washington, DC: CATO Institute.

Klaus, V. (2005) 'Principy zdravé sociální politiky' ('The principles of healthy social policy'), *Sondy*, vol 31, no 31.

Klaus, V. (2006) *Klausova kritéria pro přijetí (či nepřijetí) společné evropské měny (Klaus' criteria for acceptance (or refusal) of the common European currency)*, Prague, 20 January (retrieved 12 December 2006 from http://hrad.cz/cms/cz/prezident_cr/klaus_projevy/3175.shtml).

Koen, V. (2000) *Public expenditure reform: The health care sector in the United Kingdom*, OECD Economics Department Working Papers, No 256.

Kok, W. (2004) *Facing the challenge: The Lisbon Strategy for growth and employment*, Luxembourg: European Communities.

Kosonen, P. (1987) *Hyvinvointivaltion haasteet ja pohjoismaiset mallit (The challenges of the welfare state and Nordic model)*, Tampere: Vastapaino.

Kvist, J. (1997) 'Retrenchment or restructuring: the emergence of a multitiered welfare state in Denmark', in C. Jochen (ed) *Social insurance in Europe*, Bristol: The Policy Press, pp 14-39.

Kvist, J. (2002) 'Activating welfare states. How social policies can promote employment', in J. Clasen (ed) *What future for social security?*, Bristol: The Policy Press, pp 197-210.

Kvist, J. (2004) 'Does EU enlargement lead to a race to the bottom? Strategic interaction among EU member states', *Journal of European Social Policy*, vol 14, no 3, pp 301-18.

Lane, J.E. and Ersson, S. (2002) 'The Nordic countries', in J. Colomer (ed) *Political institutions in Europe* (2nd edn), London: Routledge, pp 245-77.

Lange, P. (1992) 'The politics of the social dimension', in A.M. Sbragia (ed) *Euro-politics: Institutions and policymaking in the 'new' European Community*, Washington, DC: The Brookings Institution, pp 225-56.

Le Grand, J. (2002) 'The Labour government and the National Health Service', *Oxford Review of Economic Policy*, vol 18, no 2, pp 137-53.

Le Grand, J. (2003) *Motivation, agency and public policy: of Knights and knaves, pawns and queens*, Oxford: Oxford University Press.

Le Grand, J. and Vizard, P. (1998) 'The National Health Service: crisis, change or continuity?', in H. Glennerster and J. Hills (eds) *The state of welfare*, Oxford: Oxford University Press, pp 75-121.

Lehmann, H., Ludwig, U. and Ragnitz, J. (2005) 'Originäre Wirtschaftskraft der neuen Länder noch schwächer als bislang angenommen', *Wirtschaft im Wandel*, vol 11, no 5, pp 134-45.

Leibfried, S. (1992) 'Towards a European welfare state: on integrating poverty regimes in the European Community', in Z. Ferge and J.E. Kolberg (eds) *Social policy in a changing Europe*, Frankfurt: Campus Verlag.

Leibfried, S. and Pierson, P. (eds) (1995) *European social policy: Between fragmentation and integration*, Washington, DC: The Brookings Institution.

Leibfried, S. and Pierson, P. (2000) 'Social policy – left to courts and markets?', in H. Wallace and W. Wallace (eds) *Policy-making in the European Union*, Oxford: Oxford University Press, pp 267-92.

Louri, E. (2005) 'A new course for the Lisbon Strategy', *Kathimerini*, 2 December.

Luxembourg Income Study (2007) *Relative poverty rates for the total population, children and the elderly*, Luxembourg (retrieved 5 February 2007 from www.lisproject.org/keyfigures/povertytable.htm).

McKnight, A. (2005) 'Employment: tackling poverty through "work for those who can"', in H. Glennerster and J. Hills (eds) *The state of welfare*, Oxford: Oxford University Press, pp 23-46.

Madama, I. and Maino, F. (2005) 'Italy: the reforms of the welfare state in the 1990s and 2000s', Paper for the conference on 'The State of the Welfare State Anno 1992 in the EU: Ten Years Later and with Ten New Member States', 16-18 October, Leuven.

Madsen, P.K. (1999) *Flexibility, security and labour market success*, Employment and Training Papers, No 53, Geneva: ILO.

Majone, G. (1993) 'The European Community between social policy and social regulation', *Journal of Common Market Studies*, vol 31, no 2, pp 153-70.

Mangen, S. (1996) 'The "Europeanisation" of Spanish social policy', *Social Policy and Administration*, vol 30, no 4, pp 305-23.

Martinsen, D.S. (2004) 'European institutionalisation of social security rights: a two-layered process of integration', PhD thesis, Firenze: European University Institute.

Martinsen, D.S. (2005a) 'The Europeanisation of welfare – the domestic impact of intra-European social security', *Journal of Common Market Studies*, vol 43, no 5, pp 1003-30.

Martinsen, D.S. (2005b) 'With the European Court towards an internal health market', *West European Politics*, vol 28, no 5, pp 1035-56.

Matsaganis, M. (2002) 'Yet another piece of pension reform in Greece', *South European Society and Politics*, vol 7, no 3, pp 109-22.

Ministère de l'emploi, de la cohesion sociale et du logement (2006a) *Evaluation de la méthode de coordination dans le domaine de l'inclusion sociale et des retraites 2000-2005: Projet de contribution de la France*, Paris: Ministère de l'emploi, de la cohesion sociale et du logement.

Ministère de l'emploi, de la cohésion sociale et du logement (2006b) *Circulaire N° DPM/DMI2/2006/200 du 29 avril 2006 relative aux autorisations de travail délivrées aux ressortissants des nouveaux Etats membres de l'Union européenne pendant la période transitoire*, Paris (retrieved 15 January 2007 from www.travail.gouv.fr/IMG/pdf/Circulaire_No_DPM-DMI2-2006-200_du_29_avril_2006.pdf).

Ministère de l'emploi et de la solidarité (2001) *National Action Plan for employment, France, Mai 2001*, Paris: Ministry of Social Affairs.

Ministerie van Sociale Zaken en Werkgelegenheid (1997) *Social policy and economic performance*, The Hague: The Dutch EU presidency.

Ministerio de la Presidencia (2005) *Programa Nacional de Reformas de España. Convergencia y Empleo. October*, Madrid: Ministerio de la Presidencia, Secretaría General Técnica.

Ministerio de Trabajo y Asuntos Sociales (2004) *Cuestionario servicios sociales de interés general*, Madrid (retrieved 2 April 2007 from http://ec.europa.eu/employment_social/social_protection/docs/replies/es_es.pdf).

Ministerio de Trabajo y Asuntos Sociales (2005a) *Propuestas de medidas de reforma de la Seguridad Social*, November, Madrid: Ministerio de Trabajo y Asuntos Sociales.

Ministerio de Trabajo y Asuntos Sociales (2005b) *Informe de la estrategia de España en relación con el futuro del sistema de pensiones al Comité de Protección Social de la UE*, July, Madrid: Ministerio de Trabajo y Asuntos Sociales.

Ministero della Solidarietà Sociale (2006) *Circolare no 21/2006, 31 July*, Rome: Ministero della Solidarietà Sociale.

Ministero dell'Interno and Ministero della Solidarietà Sociale (2006), *Circolare no 2/2006, 28 December*, Rome: Ministero dell'Interno and Ministero della Solidarietà Sociale.

Ministero del Lavoro (2001) *Libro bianco sul mercato del lavoro. Proposte per una società attiva e un lavoro di qualità 2001*, Rome: Ministero del lavoro.

Ministero del Lavoro (2005) *Aggiornamento del quadro informativo sulle politiche del lavoro*, Rome: Ministero del lavoro.

Ministries of Finance and Industry and Trade, and the Czech National Bank (2005) *Vyhodnocení plnění maastrichtských kritérií a stupně ekonomické sladěnosti ČR s eurozónou* (*The evaluation of the Maastricht convergence criteria fulfilment and the level of economic harmonisation of the Czech Republic with the Eurozone*), Joint paper of the Ministry of Finance, Ministry of Industry and Trade and the Czech National Bank approved by the Czech government on 23 November, Prague.

Ministry of Economic Affairs (2004) *Official reaction of the Dutch government to the green book services of general interest*, Green Paper, The Hague: Ministry of Economic Affairs.

Ministry of Economic Affairs (2005a) *Nationaal Hervormingsprogramma Nederland 2005-2008*, The Hague: Ministry of Economic Affairs.

Ministry of Economic Affairs (2005b) *Kabinetsreactie op het ontwerpadvies SER*, The Hague: Ministry of Economic Affairs.

Ministry of Economy and Finance (2005a) *National Reform Programme for growth and jobs 2005-8*, Athens: Ministry of Economy and Finance.

Ministry of Economy and Finance (2005b) Press release, 17 October, Athens.

Ministry of Economy and Finance (2005c) Press release, 15 December, Athens.

Ministry of Economy and Finance (2005d) *The Hellenic reply on social and health 'SGIs' questionnaire*, Internal Paper, 3 February, Athens.

Ministry of Economy and Finance (2005e) *To the Greek Parliament, Question No 8968/21-03-2005*, Internal Paper, 28 April, Athens.

Ministry of Economy and Finance (2006a) 'Greece's positions on the Directive of Internal Services', Press release, 8 February, Athens.

Ministry of Economy and Finance (2006b) Press release, 14 February, Athens.

Ministry of Employment and Social Protection (2004) *National Action Plan for employment 2004*, Athens: Ministry of Employment and Social Protection.

Ministry of Employment and Social Protection (2005) *Greek response to the questionnaire for the evaluation of the open method of coordination (OMC) in order to prepare the streamlining in the field of social protection*, Internal Paper, Athens.

Ministry of Finance (2005) *Budget*, The Hague: Ministry of Finance.

Ministry of Foreign Affairs (1988) *Memorandum to the European Commission priorities and goals of the Greek presidency for the establishment of the single social space*, 21 March, Athens: Ministry of Foreign Affairs.

Ministry of Foreign Affairs (2004), *Kabinetsreactie op het rapport van de High Level group olv de heer Kok 'Facing the challenge'* (retrieved 16 March 2007 from http://europapoort.eerstekamer.nl).

Ministry of Foreign Affairs (2005), *Poland's policy position to the informal meeting of the European Council on 27 October 2005 at Hampton Court*, Warsaw: Ministry of Foreign Affairs.

Ministry of Industry and Trade (2006) *Pozice ČR k výsledkům prvního čtení návrhu směrnice o službách v Evropském parlamentu (The bargaining position of the Czech Republic toward the first reading of the Directive on Services in the European Parliament)*, Internal document, Prague: Ministry of Industry and Trade.

Ministry of Labour and Social Affairs (2004a) *National Action Plan for employment 2004-2006*, Prague: Ministry of Labour and Social Affairs.

Ministry of Labour and Social Affairs (2004b) *Joint Inclusion Memorandum*, Prague: Ministry of Labour and Social Affairs (retrieved 19 March 2007 from www.mpsv.cz/files/clanky/2059/memo.pdf).

Ministry of Labour and Social Affairs (2004c) *Stanovisko MPSV. Bílá kniha o službách v obecném zájmu (The MLSA position. White Paper on services of general interest)*, Prague: Ministry of Labour and Social Affairs.

Ministry of Labour and Social Affairs (2005a) *National Action Plan on social inclusion 2004-2006*, Prague: Ministry of Labour and Social Affairs (retrieved 12 December 2006 from www.mpsv.cz/files/clanky/1103/NAPSI_eng.pdf).

Ministry of Labour and Social Affairs (2005b) *Koncepce rodinné politiky* (*The Family Policy Conception*), Prague: Ministry of Labour and Social Affairs.

Ministry of Labour and Social Affairs (2005c) *Questionnaire for the evaluation of the open method of coordination in the area of social protection for the preparation of the streamlined process*, Internal document, Prague: Ministry of Labour and Social Affairs.

Ministry of Labour and Social Affairs (nd) *Sociální služby v obecném zájmu – dotazník* (*Social services of general interest – questionnaire*), Internal document, Prague: Ministry of Labour and Social Affairs.

Ministry of Labour and Social Security (2003) *National Action Plan for employment 2003*, Athens: Ministry of Labour and Social Security.

Ministry of Social Affairs and Employment (2004) *Evaluatie Sluitende Aanpak 1999-2003*, The Hague: Ministry of Social Affairs and Employment.

Ministry of Social Affairs and Employment (2005) 'Official reaction to the Green Paper on demographic change', Letter, 11 October, The Hague: Ministry of Social Affairs.

Ministry of Social Affairs and Health (2006a) *Pension reform 2005* (retrieved 25 November 2006 from www.stm.fi/Resource.phx/eng/subjt/socin/pensi/reform05.htx).

Ministry of Social Affairs and Health (2006b) *Strategies for social protection 2015 – Towards a socially and economically sustainable society* (retrieved 22 November 2006 from www.stm.fi/Resource.phx/publishing/documents/7634/index.htx).

Ministry of Social Policy (2003) *The strategy of the social policy*, Warsaw: Ministry of Social Policy.

Ministry of Social Policy (2005) *Answer of Polish government to the questionnaire for the evaluation of the open method of coordination (OMC) in order to prepare the streamlining in the field of social protection*, Warsaw: Ministry of Social Policy.

Ministry of Social Policy (2006) *Answers to the 'Questionnaire for the evaluation of the open method of coordination (OMC) in order to prepare the streamlining in the field of social protection'*, Warsaw: Ministry of Social Policy.

Mossialos, E. and McKee, M. (2002a) *EU law and the social character of health care*, Brussels: PIE-Peter Lang.

Mossialos, E. and McKee, M. (2002b) *The influence of EU law on the social character of health care systems*, Brussels: PIE–Peter Lang.

Natali, D. (2006) *Le pensioni nell'Europa a 25. Il coordinamento delle strategie di riforma*, URGE Working Paper, No 2/2006.

Niemelä, H. and Salminen, K. (2006) *Social security in Finland* (retrieved 28 March 2007 from www.kela.fi/in/internet/liite.nsf/NET/280606095303EK/$File/socialsecurity.PDF?OpenElement).

O'Brien, N. (ed) (2006) *Beyond the European social model*, Brussels: Open Europe.

OECD (Organisation for Economic Co-operation and Development) (2004) *OECD Economic Survey of the United Kingdom 2004*, Paris: OECD.

Offe, C. (2003) 'The European model of "social capitalism" – can it survive European integration', *The Journal of Political Philosophy*, vol 11, no 4, pp 437-67.

Office of the Government (2004) *Strategy of sustainable development*, Prague: Office of the Government (retrieved 19 March 2007 from www.ochranaprirody.cz/res/data/068/010027.pdf).

Office of the Government (2005a) *Strategy of economic growth*, Prague: Office of the Government.

Office of the Government (2005b) *National Reform Programme 2005-2008*, Prague: Office of the Government (retrieved 19 March 2007 from www.vlada.cz/assets/cs/eu/oeu/lisabon1/ls_a_cr/npr_cr/national_reform_programme_en.pdf).

OKE (2005) 'Priority areas in view of the mid-term evaluation of the Lisbon Strategy in 2005', *Own-initiative Opinion*, 23 March, Athens.

Orenstein, M.A. and Haas, M.R. (2003) *Globalization and the development of welfare states in postcommunist Europe*, Harvard University, MA: J.F. Kennedy School of Government.

Öström, N. (2003) *Swedish-Polish co-operation in the field of pension reforms 1996-2002*, SIDA Evaluation 03/20 (retrieved 15 March 2006 from www.oecd.org/dataoecd/44/26/35208758.pdf).

Pagalos, T. (1998) 'Hellenic Parliament', *Parliament Proceedings*, Session 3-11-1998, Athens: Hellenic Parliament, pp 561-3.

Pérez Díaz, V. and Torreblanca, I. (1999) *Implicaciones políticas del Euro*, ASP Research Papers, 30(a).

Permanent Representation of Greece in the EU (2005) *To the Ministry of Employment and Social Protection on the results of the European Council of Employment, Social Affairs, Health and Consumers 2-6-2005*, Internal Paper (Fax), 7 June, Brussels.

Perrineau, P. (2005) 'Le référendum français du 29 mai 2005: l'irrésistible nationalisation d'un vote européen', in P. Perrineau (ed) *Le vote européen 2004–2005: De l'élargissement au référendum français*, Paris: Presses de Sciences Po, pp 3-19.

Petersen, J.H. (1985) *Den danske alderdomsforsørgelseslovgivnings udvikling I. Oprindelsen*, Odense: Odense Universitetsforlag.

Pierson, P. (2004) *Politics in time*, Princeton, NJ: Princeton University Press.

Pochet, P. and Vanhercke, B. (eds) (1998) *Social challenges of Economic and Monetary Union*, Brussels: European Interuniversity Press.

Polish Government (2006) *Position of the Polish government on guidelines for action at EU level to promote the active inclusion of the people furthest from the labour market*, Warsaw (retrieved on 15 March 2007 from http://ec.europa.eu/employment_social/social_inclusion/docs/2006/active_inclusion/poland_en.pdf).

Polyzogopoulos, C. (2002) 'The social aspects of the enlargement of the EU', *Enimerosi*, no 85/2002.

Polyzogopoulos, C. (2005) 'The Lisbon Strategy and the need for another developmental model', *Enimerosi*, 119/2005, July/August.

Potůček, M. (1999) *Křižovatky české sociální reformy (Czech social reform at the crossroads)*, Prague: Sociological Publishing House.

Potůček, M. (2004) 'Accession and social policy: the case of the Czech Republic', *Journal of European Social Policy*, vol 14, no 3, pp 253-66.

Potůček, M. (2007) 'Czech National Action Plan on social inclusion 2004-2006: did it matter?', Paper for the conference 'Changing European Employment and Welfare Regimes. The Impact of the Open Method of Coordination on National Labour Market and Welfare Reforms', 23-24 February, University of Bamberg (retrieved 19 March from www.martinpotucek.cz).

Prime Minister's Office (2004) *Finland for people of all ages*, Helsinki (retrieved 22 May 2006 from www.vnk.fi/julkaisukansio/2004/j27-28-34-hyvae-yhteiskunta-kaikenikaeisille/pdf/en.pdf).

Prosser, T. (2005) 'Competition law and public services: from single markets to citizenship rights', *European Public Law*, vol 11, no 4, pp 543-63.

Rasmussen, A.F. (2002) 'The European Council: one Europe', Speech by the Danish Prime Minister, Meeting of the European Council, 12-13 December, Copenhagen.

Rawnsley, A. (2000) *Servants of the people: The inside story of New Labour*, London: Hamish Hamilton.

REIF (2005) *Debate on the Green Paper of the European Commission: Confronting demographic change: A new solidarity between generations – Contributions from CCMSA, CNAF, CNAMTS, CNAV, EN3S and ORGANIC*, Paris.

Représentation permanente de la France (2003) *Memorandum of the French authorities – Answers to the Green Paper on services of general interest presented by the European Commission* (retrieved 21 January 2006 from europa.eu.int/comm/secretariat_general/services_general_interest/docs/public_authorities/pic_en.pdf).

Représentation permanente de la France auprès de l'Union Européenne (2005) *Contribution française au débat lancé par le livre vert de la Commission « face aux changements une nouvelle solidarité entre des générations »* (retrieved 15 January 2006 from http://ec.europa.eu/comm/employment_social/social_situation/responses/a25851_fr.pdf).

Rodriguez Zapatero, J.L. (2005a) 'A more dynamic welfare state for a more dynamic Europe', *Progressive Politics*, vol 4, no 3, pp 2-7 (retrieved 31 March 2007 from www.progressive-governance.net/uploadedFiles/Publications/Publications/Zapatero.2.pdf).

Rodríguez Zapatero, J.L. (2005b) 'Discurso del Presidente del Gobierno en el Pleno del Congreso de los Diputados', 21 December (retrieved 20 March 2007 from www.la-moncloa.es/presidente/intervenciones/sesionesparlamento/).

Rollén, B. (2003) 'EU:s utvidgning och arbetskraftens rörlighet', *SOU*, 2002: 116, Stockholm: Foreign Ministry.

Saari, J. (2001) *Reforming social policy: A study on institutional change in Finland during the 1990s*, Helsinki: Social Policy Association, and Turku: Department of Social Policy.

Saari, J. (ed) (2002) *Euroopan sosiaalinen malli* (*European social model*), Helsinki: Finnish Federation for Social Welfare and Health.

Saari, J. (2003) *Uusi aikakausi – Yhdentyvä Eurooppa ja sosiaalipolitiikka* (*The new era – European integration and social protection*), Helsinki: Finnish Federation for Social Welfare and Health.

Saari, J. (2005a) 'Hyvinvointivaltio ja sosiaalipolitiikka' ('Welfare state and social policy', in J. Saari (ed) *Hyvinvointivaltio* (*The welfare state*), Helsinki: Helsinki University Press.

Saari, J. (ed) (2005b) *Köyhyyspolitiikka* (*Poverty politics*), Helsinki: Finnish Federation for Social Welfare and Health.

Saari, J. (2006) 'Sosiaalipolitiikka', in J. Saari (ed) *Suomen malli – Murroksesta menestykseen* (*The Finnish model – From restructuring to success*), Helsinki: Helsinki University Press, pp 227-61.

Saari, J. and Kari, M. (2006) 'Sosiaali- ja terveyspolitiikka – nopeasti muuttunut politiikkalohko' ('Social and health policy – rapidly evolving field of policy making'), in T. Raunio and J. Saari (eds) *Eurooppalaistuminen – Suomen sopeutuminen Euroopan integraatioon (Europeanisation – Finland's adjustment to European integration)*, Helsinki: Gaudeamus, pp 140-80.

Sacchi, S. and Bastagli, F. (2005) 'Striving uphill, but stopping halfway: the troubled journey of the experimental minimum insertion income', in M. Ferrera (ed) *Welfare state reform in Southern Europe*, London: Routledge, pp 84-140.

Sakellaropoulos, T. (2004) 'The open method of coordination: a sound instrument for the modernization of the European social model', in T. Sakellaropoulos and J. Berghman (eds) *Connecting welfare diversity within the European social model*, Antwerp: Intersentia, pp 55-92.

Sakellaropoulos, T. and Angelaki, M. (2007) 'The politics of pension reform in South European welfare states', in J. Van Langedock (ed) *The right to social security*, Antwerp: Intersentia, pp 121-41.

Salminen, K. (1993) *Pension schemes in the making: A comparative study of the Scandinavian countries*, Helsinki: Central Pension Security Institution.

Scharpf, F.W. (1999) *Governing in Europe: Effective and democratic?*, Oxford: Oxford University Press.

Scharpf, F.W. (2002) 'The European social model: coping with the challenges of diversity', *Journal of Common Market Studies*, vol 40, no 4, pp 645-70.

Schmögnerová, B. (2005) *The European social model – A view from a newcomer*, Bonn: Friedrich Ebert Stiftung.

Secretary of State for Foreign and Commonwealth Affairs (2004) *Prospects for the European Union in 2004*, London: Foreign and Commonwealth Office.

Secretary of State for Foreign and Commonwealth Affairs (2005) *Prospects for the European Union in 2005*, London: Foreign and Commonwealth Office.

Secretary of State for Foreign and Commonwealth Affairs (2006) *Prospects for the European Union in 2006*, London: Foreign and Commonwealth Office.

Secretary of State for Work and Pensions (2006) *Security in retirement: Towards a new pension system*, Cm 6841, London: The Stationery Office.

Select Committee on European Scrutiny (2006) *Streamlining the open method of coordination for social protection policies, 18th report*, London: UK Parliament.

SEV (Association of Greek Industries) (2004) 'Remarks and positions by SEV on the Wim Kok report on the intermediate reform of the Lisbon goals', *Communication*, December, Athens.

Sherrington, P. (2006) 'Confronting Europe: UK political parties and the EU 2000-2005', *British Journal of Politics and International Relations*, vol 8, no 4, pp 69-78.

Siegel, N. (2004) 'The political economy of labour market reforms', Paper presented at ESPAnet 2004 Conference, University of Oxford.

Simitis, K. (2000a) 'Greece's positions for the Lisbon European Council', Letter from Prime Minister K. Simitis to the Portuguese Prime Minister A. Gutierres, *To Bima*, 27 February.

Simitis, K. (2000b) 'Reply to the question on the preparation of the Lisbon Summit', *Parliament Proceedings*, Session 1-3-2000, Athens: Hellenic Parliament.

Simitis, K. (2000c) 'Interview: what I am intending to do after the elections', *To Bima*, 12 March.

Simitis, K. (2001a) 'Opening address in the discussion about Greece's course in the EU', *Parliament Proceedings*, Session 23-1-2001, Athens: Hellenic Parliament.

Simitis, K. (2001b) 'The future of Europe and Greece', Speech to the EKEM conference, 11 July, Athens.

Sleegers, P.J. (2005) *Changing welfare states, An institutional explanation for the susceptibility to policy learning by means of the OMC social inclusion* (retrieved 1 August 2006 from http://eucenter.wisc.edu/OMC/Papers/Enlargement/sleegers.pdf).

Social Affairs and Health Committee (2004a) Reports (StVL) 2/2004, Helsinki: Finnish Parliament.

Social Affairs and Health Committee (2004b) Reports (StVL) 14/2004, Helsinki: Finnish Parliament.

Social Affairs and Health Committee (2005) Reports (StVL) 5/2005, Helsinki: Finnish Parliament.

Social and Economic Council (2005) *Advies over de Dienstenrichtlijn*, The Hague: Social and Economic Council.

'Social services of general interest: UK response to Commission questionnaire' (retrieved 20 March 2007 from http://ec.europa.eu/employment_social/social_protection/docs/replies/uk_en.pdf).

'Sociální doktrína České republiky' ('Social doctrine of the Czech Republic') (2002) *Sociální politika*, vol 28, no 1, pp 7-11 (retrieved in English 12 December 2006 from www.uni-konstanz.de/potucek/).

Socialministeriet and Beskæftigelsesministeriet (2006) *Rådsmøde for beskæftigelse og sociale anliggender den 1 juni, Samlenotat*, 17 May, Copenhagen: Ministries of Social Affairs and Employment.

Sotiropoulos, D. (2004) 'The EU's impact on the Greek welfare state: Europeanization on paper?', *Journal of European Social Policy*, vol 14, no 3, pp 267-84.

Stewart, K. (2005) 'Towards an equal start? Addressing childhood poverty and deprivation', in H. Glennerster and J. Hills (eds) *The state of welfare*, Oxford: Oxford University Press, pp 143-66.

Streeck, W. (1995) 'From market making to state building? Reflections on the political economy of European social policy', in S. Leibfried and P. Pierson (eds) *European social policy: Between fragmentation and integration*, Washington, DC: The Brookings Institution, pp 389-431.

Tinios, P. (2005) 'Pension reform in Greece: "reform by installments" – a blocked process', *West European Society and Politics*, vol 28, no 2, pp 402-19.

Traser, J. (2006) *Who's still afraid of EU enlargement?*, Report for the European Citizen Action Service (retrieved 20 March 2007 from www.ecas.org).

Tsoukalis, L. (2006) 'Why we need a globalisation adjustment fund?', *The Hampton Court Agenda – A social model for Europe*, London: Policy Network, pp 81-9.

Turner, A. (2005) *A new pension settlement for the twenty-first century: The second report of the Pensions Commission*, London: Pensions Commission.

Udenrigsministeriet (2006) *Lissabon-strategien og Kommissionens Fremskridtsrapport. Grundnotat (The Lisbon Strategy and the Commission Progress Report)*, Working document, Copenhagen: Ministry of Foreign Affairs.

Valiente, C. (2003) 'Pushing for equality reforms: the European Union and gender discourse in post-authoritarian Spain', in U. Liebert (ed) *Gendering Europeanisation*, Brussels: PIE-Peter Lang, pp 187-222.

Van de Brink, T. (2005) 'De Nationale Verzorgingsstaat en het Recht van de Europese Unie', Unpublished manuscript, The Hague: WRR.

Vaughan-Whitehead, D. (2003) *EU enlargement versus social Europe: The uncertain future of the European social model*, Cheltenham: Edward Elgar.

Verband Deutscher Rentenversicherungsträger (2002) *Offene Koordinierung der Alterssicherung in der Europäischen Union*, DRV-Schriften Bd 34.

Verdun A. (1996) 'An asymmetrical Economic and Monetary Union in the EU: perceptions of monetary authorities and social partners', *Journal of European Integration*, vol 20, no 1, pp 60-81.

Visser, J. and Hemerijck, A. (1997) *A Dutch miracle: Job growth, welfare reform and corporatism in the Netherlands*, Amsterdam: Amsterdam University Press.

Welfare Ministry (2006) *Circolare no 15/2006*, 3 May, Rome: Welfare Ministry.

Wilthagen, T. (1998) *Flexicurity: A new paradigm for labour market policy reform?*, Wissenschaftszentrum Berlin für Sozialforschung Discussion Paper, No 202, FS I 98-202.

World Bank (1994) *Averting the old-age crisis: Policies to protect the old and promote growth*, Washington, DC: World Bank.

Wóycicka, I. (2003) *Wydatki społeczne w Polsce w latach 2000-2020. Prognoza oparta na Budżecie Polityki Społecznej (Social spending in Poland, 2000-2020. Projection based on social policy budget)*, Warszawa: IBnGR.

WRR (Wetenschappelijke Raad voor het Regeringsbeleid) (1990) *Een werkend perspectief, arbeidsparticipatie in de jaren '90,* Rapporten aan de Regering 38, The Hague: SDU Uitgevers.

WRR (2000) *Doorgroei van Arbeidsparticipatie*, Rapporten aan de Regering 57, The Hague: SDU Uitgevers.

Zeitlin, J. and Pochet, P. (eds) (2005) *The open method of coordination in action: The European Employment Strategy and social inclusion strategies*, Brussels: PIE-Peter Lang.

Index

Note: Page numbers followed by *tab* refer to information in a table. For expansion of abbreviations, please refer to List of Abbreviations on page ix.